A Burmese Heart

by Tinsa Maw-Naing & Y.M.V. Han

Copyright © 2015 by Yin Mon Vanessa Han

All rights reserved. No part of this publication may be reproduced, stored in a retrieval system, or transmitted, in any form or by any means, electronic, mechanical, photocopying, recording or otherwise, without the prior permission of the copyright owner.
All rights reserved.

ISBN: 0996225404
ISBN-13: 978-0-9962254-0-3

Disclaimer: The authors have tried to recreate events, locales and conversations from Tinsa Maw-Naing's personal memories.

CONTENTS

Part I: Of Things Past

May 1966	Pg 1
Chapter One	Pg 3
Chapter Two	Pg 20
Chapter Three	Pg 35
Chapter Four	Pg 49
Chapter Five	Pg 73
Chapter Six	Pg 92
Chapter Seven	Pg 120
Chapter Eight	Pg 135
Chapter Nine	Pg 149

Part II: The Invisible War

Chapter Ten	Pg 169
Chapter Eleven	Pg 184
Chapter Twelve	Pg 193
Chapter Thirteen	Pg 202
Chapter Fourteen	Pg 212
Chapter Fifteen	Pg 219

Chapter Sixteen	Pg 230
Chapter Seventeen	Pg 239
Chapter Eighteen	Pg 253
Chapter Nineteen	Pg 263
Chapter Twenty	Pg 270
Chapter Twenty-One	Pg 277
Chapter Twenty-Two	Pg 286
Chapter Twenty-Three	Pg 290
Chapter Twenty-Four	Pg 300
Glossary	Pg 305
About the Authors	Pg 311

Part I

Of Things Past

MAY 1966

One by one, the people whom I loved the most slowly disappeared, chased in the night by shadowy figures in army greens. It began almost a year ago when my husband ignited a war, vanishing to the Thai-Burma border. The men of Rangoon trailed behind him, leaving their mothers, fathers, wives and children in their wake. It was only a matter of time before they came for me, too.

The regime dispatched its best men to retrieve me as the sun was rising over the city's cracked wooden rooftops, the grass drenched in dawn rain. Soldiers in jade uniforms, armed with colonial-era rifles with the barrels sawed off, hid behind thick brush in the back of my home on University Avenue. A grand display of terror and intimidation for anyone thinking to follow in my husband's footsteps. I cradled my four-month-old son, Zarni, in my arms as my escorts tied a dark towel around my head, the executioner's mark. My son intuited the fear in my veins, warm tears streaming down his cheeks, little fingers grasping at my breast to be comforted. He was a final parting gift from my husband, conceived mere weeks before his departure, the only reason that they had waited so long to come for me.

I was placed in the back of a black sedan, windows darkened and insulated from prying eyes and curious lips. I did not need to ask where I was going. In the previous months, anti-government protesters and the wives of exiled men had gone missing, their names reduced to nothing but gossip and whispers. No one had made it back to tell their tales, a thunderous silence closing in on the Burmese.

The car jolted along hot asphalt until it gave way to a dirt path and jagged rocks. They removed the towel from my head, my eyes straining to discern a cavernous, barn-like structure, the entrance for many but exit for few. I was at Ye Kyi Aing Detention Center just outside of Rangoon, to be remembered in history as one of the most brutal detention centers in the world. Holding my son closer to my chest, I took a deep breath and stepped inside the corrugated iron gates, now officially an enemy of the state.

CHAPTER ONE

In the tradition of Burmese spiritualism, a series of events, people and cosmic factors aligned to script my fate long before I entered this world on March 16, 1927. I was named Tinsa based on the day and time that I was born, my name and an ancient prayer inscribed on a cured palm leaf in an offering to the universe as my ancestors had done before me. Born on a Wednesday afternoon, my natal astrological chart presaged that I would be at the mercy of the planet Rahu. Burmese spiritualists consider Rahu, the Vedic deity who tried to swallow the sun, to be one of the most powerful planets. When placed negatively in one's astrology, Rahu threads chaos, evil and darkness through one's roots. At his best, he gives his wards great opportunities of wealth, power and the ability to make friends out of enemies. To be a Rahu-born is to play with fire, life always a balancing act between boundless harmony and unfettered bedlam, never destined to settle for the middle path.

Chaos was not a concept new to my family. I was born with it in my blood. My ancestors' histories weave tales of bravery, adventure, heartbreak, loneliness, ambition and conquest in the midst of Burma's wild days, not unlike many of the tribulations that I would endure. The earliest ancestor that I can trace is my great-great-grandmother from the port city of Tavoy, a central trade route on the Asian seaboard. The city beckoned roughshod traders, diamond merchants, spice kings, explorers, ruthless mercenaries, pirates and anyone brave enough to see for themselves what this distant, golden land could offer. Perhaps it was the essence of adventure in the Tavoy air that caught a hold of my great-great-grandmother, for she was fearless. Of Mon blood, she was a legendary beauty: tall and lithe with skin as pure as jasmine petals and hair as fine as Inle silk, masking steel beneath a porcelain exterior. One drizzling night, a burglar tried to break into her home while the family slept. As a city of vagabond traders and transient mercenaries, home invasions in Tavoy generally resulted in the loss of limbs or death for unlucky homeowners. Hearing rustling in the front yard, the Mon beauty stalked her home until she found the culprit: a would-be robber hanging from the crooked fence beams, his fingertips grasping the edges of the wooden slabs and the rest of him hidden in shadows.

There was no choice between fight or flight. She crept to the kitchen, her hands finding the handle of a large butcher knife normally used to decapitate chickens. I'm sure the burglar had his regrets, because the next thing he knew, she had sliced off the ends of his fingers that had been gripping the edge of the fence. The thief ran away screaming into the haze of night, leaving a trail of blood and finger stubs that mysteriously ended at the wharf.

The Mon beauty's knife-wielding reputation scared off any potential well-to-do suitors, but she found love with a man named Theodore. I don't know much about my great-great-grandfather, only that he was either an engineer or a ship captain. It is impossible to know whether he was a local man who adopted a Christian name or if he was one of many young men looking for wealth and exotic lands and ended up staying in Burma. His skin, the hue of refined palm sugar, was indistinguishable from the fairer Mon or the darker Portuguese or Armenian traders, his almond eyes and high cheekbones not giving away a thing.

She and Theodore had a son named U Maung Maung, an administrator for the Maubin jail system who married another fearless woman in the family line, Daw[1] Khin. Maubin was a growing city on the banks of the Ayeyarwaddy River in southwest Burma, known for its ultra-orthodox monastic teachings and also for producing the most pungent *nga-pi* (fermented fish paste) in the south. It was the final days of the monarchy, the great King Mindon's legacy overshadowed by his son Thibaw's weak governance and cowering personality. Daw Khin did not have patience for what she viewed as the games of an isolated monarchy in an increasingly anarchic and lawless society. She took matters into her own hands, assembling local officials and appointing herself the town's ombudswoman without the explicit consent of the authorities, who were intimidated by her domineering personality but in awe of her leadership. No one dared to challenge her, her stern visage enough to quell naysayers, a one-woman government policing Maubin's muddy streets.

U Maung Maung and Daw Khin had eight children including my grandmother, Daw Thein Tin, a shrewd and notoriously stubborn woman. Among all of the adventurers and heroes in my bloodline, my grandmother's story upended our family's trajectory and altered the path of Burma's modern history. Maubin could hardly contain Daw Thein Tin, who grew to be just as strong-willed as her mother. She met her future husband, U Shwe Kye, under scandalous circumstances involving her running off to a local political rally against her parents' wishes and falling in love with a handsome, full-blooded Mon man from Moulmein in the crowd. Tall, fair and erudite, U Shwe Kye was an engaging speaker whose intellect had caught the attention of King Mindon. Family lore has it that Daw Khin wept when her beautiful daughter married such an unapologetic monarchist, an insipid minion of a deteriorating court, in her eyes.

U Shwe Kye was born into modest means, the bright and ambitious young man earning himself a scholarship to study at Dr. Mark's School in Moulmein. Gifted with English and

---

[1] *Daw* is an honorific term for an elder woman or aunt.

modern languages, he became a courtier at the royal palace in Mandalay when Prime Minister Kinwun Mingyi asked him to accompany the court as a diplomatic attaché to London and Paris in 1872. An account of the trip, the *Kinwun Mingyi Diary*, is considered to be one of the most important documents in our modern history, chronicling the last great foreign mission of the Burmese monarchy before it fell to the British. Many believe that U Shwe Kye wrote the account on behalf of the Prime Minister, who spoke English conversationally but was not known to have mastered prose on the level displayed in the diaries.

When King Mindon died in 1878, the kingdom went into deep mourning, his successor Thibaw throwing the country into chaos. The British had already captured Lower Burma and marched north to the capital, preparing to annex the third and most important piece of the country: Mandalay. King Thibaw, consumed with family and court politics and with no formal military training, lost Mandalay to the British in 1885. British troops entered the palace gates with little resistance, minimal bloodshed and wanton destruction only occurring when drunken soldiers set fire to the palace in celebration of their victory. My grandfather, U Shwe Kye, watched as flames swallowed hundreds of years of artifacts, the hand-carved teak ceiling caving in and entombing the memories of a dying but proud kingdom. He and the other courtiers watched as the library, containing handwritten palm leaf scrolls chronicling over one thousand years of our history, turned to dust. Harboring a profound loathing for the foreign invaders, he refused to take an oath of service under the colonial government and disappeared from Mandalay.

My grandfather resurfaced in Maubin where he lived with Daw Thein Tin and their two sons. What happened to him next remains shrouded in mystery. Many believed that he, a fervent nationalist and staunch royalist, left Maubin to form an underground anti-British movement from his hometown of Amherst (now called Kyaikkami). Days before his departure, U Shwe Kye donated a small pagoda made of silvery coastal stone to a local monastery, perhaps as penance for leaving behind his young wife and two little boys, Ba Han and Ba Maw.

My grandmother, Daw Thein Tin, witnessed King Thibaw's royal barge en route to his exile in India, never to step foot in his homeland again. Like so many Burmese at the time, she felt that although the monarchy was by no means perfect, an independent Burma was better than a country controlled by foreign hands. This instilled in her, and in the rest of the Burmese, a nationalist sentiment that was passed on to her sons, Ba Han and Ba Maw. "Be proud of who you are and fight for what you think is right. However, your duty is not only to this country but also to your family," she taught them in the aftermath of their father's disappearance.

My father, Ba Maw, and his older brother, Ba Han, had no clear recollections of the early parts of their childhood. They did not remember their father but their faces would light up when speaking of their mother. Left penniless and without any means of support after U Shwe Kye's disappearance, Daw Thein Tin was essentially widowed in an era in which the presence of an abandoned woman raised eyebrows. Nevertheless, she gave up all luxuries and her own needs in order to raise her sons as best as she could. Disregarding social norms and cold shoulders, Daw Thein Tin invested her scant savings in a single pony cart that grew to a fleet of gharries (hackney carriages). She sometimes drove the cart by herself, men groping her from the back seat, knives drawn to her throat in silenced back alleys. She and her two sons lived hand-to-mouth, impoverished, but they managed to survive. To my father, his mother was akin to a mythic being, his source of light through the darkness of his early years. Whatever humiliations she endured at the hands of poverty in order to provide for her two sons were not lost on Ba Maw and Ba Han.

I never knew my paternal grandmother, Daw Thein Tin, the very mention of her name enough to send my father and uncle into a misty-eyed state. "You would have loved and feared her at the same time," they boasted of their mother. Phay Phay, as I affectionately called my father, later chose my mother, Kinmama, a force of nature in politics and history and expected his daughters and granddaughters to live up to their illustrious predecessors. To him, women were the beacon, the dark, rich earth from which all life grew.

The greatest gift that Daw Thein Tin would bestow on her young sons was their education. She knew that Maubin's schools, primarily monastic academies led by saffron-robed monks with little experience of the world beyond the city's confines, could not prepare her sons for a future under British rule. If her sons were to grow in the harsh light of colonial society, they needed an education to survive in the increasingly cutthroat and multicultural lion's pit. In short, they needed a western education. With her natural shrewdness, tenacity and the help of generous relatives, she enrolled Ba Han and Ba Maw at St. Paul's School in Rangoon.

St. Paul's was the best boarding school in Rangoon, admitting the sons of British-Indian officers, Anglo-Burmese, Indian merchants and wealthy Burmese. It also took in financially disadvantaged boys and Daw Thein Tin seized this opportunity for her children. These "boys of charity" were third-class students, entitled to the same education but without the comforts of first and second-class students such as private tuition before exams, personal ties to the headmaster, or cricket lessons to prepare them as gentlemen of leisure. My father's time at boarding school was a humbling experience. To be considered little more than a student of charity was yet another struggle, a thousand small cuts dealt to his pride, but it had an unusual advantage for him and his brother. They studied diligently, drawing on the pain of being separated from their beloved mother to forge ahead with unyielding determination. When older boys would corner them in the schoolyard, they fought back, living the school motto of *Labor Omnia Vincit* through bruised knuckles and calloused writing hands.

My father often recounted one of the most bitter and

enlightening moments of his bleak adolescence. One sunny day, he wandered the streets near his childhood home in Maubin, a single-room shack with dirt floors and a tin roof continually battered by a patch of low-hanging coconut trees. An adventurous and inquisitive boy, he entertained himself by zigzagging through tree-lined streets, peering inside the iron gates of wealthier residents. Gardeners meticulously clipped flower bushes, the landscape never uneven with wild poppies or pesky weeds. Chauffeured lorries gleamed as their drivers slept under the shade of mango trees, rubbing their eyes awake when the families needed to go to market.

He stopped, mesmerized by what lay in a serpentine driveway. Blood-red metal glistening and summoning him. The owner, a flaxen-haired, blue-eyed boy whose crisp cottons had never touched the dirt of the world outside of his wrought iron gates, sat beneath a stone portico and was lost in a world of toy trucks and tin soldiers. Phay Phay yearned to yell at him, to open the gates and play with him on the dusty streets, the realities of their divergent existences disappearing for a fleeting moment. He had never had a *bo* friend before, a Caucasian or European playmate, especially not one with such a beautiful tricycle. Perhaps the boy would even let him ride it, two new friends exploring the world together on three wheels.

Phay Phay could no longer contain his excitement, inching nearer to the gate to have a look at the red beauty. He thought about all of the places that he could go and how jealous his brother would be. While he was wading in his thoughts, a shadow appeared on the other side of the gate, blocking his view of the boy and the tricycle. "What are you doing here, boy?" barked the opaque figure. A woman's face, caked in *thanaka*[2] like the street vendors from his neighborhood, confronted him as if he were a sewer rat that had crawled over her shoes. He stood frozen as the blonde boy turned to stare at the scene, not knowing whether to run or to endure the

---

[2] *Thanaka* is a paste made from the bark of the Thanaka tree. It is a natural skin remedy and a traditional form of makeup.

humiliation of the nanny's shouts. "Go back to where you came from! You don't belong here!" she continued to bark.

Cheeks burning, his dusky eyes singed with tears, Phay Phay took off, unable to contain the hot flushes of embarrassment and indignity that boiled in his gut. He ran until the manicured, oak-lined avenues gave way to the familiarity of dirt paths covered in rubbish and feral dogs nipping at his blistered heels. He now knew his place in society, that he and the blonde boy were seen differently: one would enjoy the niceties in life while he wasn't even good enough for a look at a mere toy. A child's humiliation, ingrained, seared for a lifetime.

My father often said that his only regret of his early years was not the pressing poverty, treatment as a second-class citizen, or the superficial humiliations he endured as a child. His greatest regret was that he could not provide the kind of life that his mother so greatly deserved before she passed away. She did not witness the fabled heights to which her sons rose, Ba Han becoming a famed legal scholar and academic and my father becoming the first Burmese to lead the country in the colonial era.

* * * * *

When my parents met in 1926, my mother Kinmama and her sister Kinmimi were two of the most eligible young women in Rangoon given their beauty and even more beautiful dowries, the kind of girls who instinctively knew when to bow their heads and dared not to eat or drink first in the presence of elders. My father had returned from his studies at Cambridge, Gray's Inn and completed his doctorate at the University of Bordeaux by way of generous bursaries and careful savings, to become the first Burmese appointed to the English department at Rangoon College in 1917. Having not only mastered academia, Ba Maw had perfected the art of European conversation, socialization, and dress. What must my mother, outwardly a daisy of a woman in her silk *longyis*[3], have thought of Ba Maw, a gregarious young man who preferred cocktail parties over traditional tea houses?

Back row: Daw Sein (grandmother), Dr. Ba Maw (father), Daw Kinmama Maw (mother) and baby Binnya, Kinmimi (aunt)
Front row: Mala, Tinsa, Onma, Theda, Zali

Kinmama saw past his tuxedoes and silk jackets, his armor against the prejudices of colonial Burma. Despite her wealth, she and Kinmimi were born to modest means like Ba Maw and Ba Han, also raised by a single mother whose dogged determination ensured that her two daughters would have a better chance at life. Born on December 13, 1905, she was the eldest of three daughters born to U Htwa Nyo and Daw Sein. Kinmama lost her father at a young age, U Htwa Nyo retiring to bed one night and suddenly dying of heart failure. Her

---

[3] *Longyi* is a traditional sarong skirt.

mother, Daw Sein, became a widow at twenty-five years old, another tragedy occurring when one of the daughters passed away not long afterwards.

Daw Sein refused to capitulate to hardship, becoming a teacher at the American Baptist Mission School (ABM) in Rangoon. Her students stood shoulder-to-shoulder with her, twice the size of street children of the same age. Daw Sein remained undaunted by their size and status, caning them with rigid bamboo stalks when her brawny students were out of line. "I had to do it," she recounted. "If I were to flinch just once when handling the cane, those children would have never respected me again."

A schoolroom could hardly contain her ambitions. Like all Burmese women then and now, there was always a private home business going on behind closed doors to supplement incomes, as well as to provide a rare social opportunity for women of the middle class. Befitting her name (Madame Diamond in Burmese), my grandmother began to buy and sell small pieces of jewelry to her circle during afternoon tea breaks. Since she did not have enough capital for a large enterprise, she built her credibility through introductions to reputable Indian jewelers who controlled the diamond trade from across the border. Their patrons commissioned diamond lattice chokers, amethyst chandelier earrings, spinel beads the size of quails' eggs, but these jewelers sought a broader commercial base. Daw Sein became their intermediary and brokered sales for middle-class housewives with an insatiable appetite for gems. Through hard work, integrity and a spotless reputation, my grandmother expanded her clientele and handled larger pieces of bespoke jewelry with specific orders for diamonds.

Daw Sein finally lived up to her name and opened her own brokerage in downtown Rangoon, the only Bamar[4] who dared to set up shop in the middle of the Indian quarter. Pigeon's

---

[4] *Bamar* is the dominant ethnic group, comprising nearly two-thirds of the population.

blood rubies from Mogok. Cornflower blue sapphires from the north. Turmeric yellow diamonds from India. Daw Sein was rumored to be so rich that she would frequently leave bowls of jewelry outside of her front gate, alerting con artists, social climbers and others who wished to use her for nefarious means to take what they wanted and to leave her alone. She bought large tracts of land including a house on 50th Street where Kinmama and Kinmimi lived as daughters of the upper middle class. My mother, Kinmama, learned her numbers by sitting with her mother nightly at their teak dining table and helping her settle accounts from the brokerage. She became an astute businesswoman and learned to appreciate money at a young age, that wealth was earned and not an entitlement.

Kinmama and Kinmimi enrolled at St. John's Convent, run by an army of Catholic nuns imported from Europe. It was the finest education for young women in Rangoon, learning social graces alongside arithmetic and literature. My aunt, Kinmimi, resisted the idea of school altogether, refusing to go until the age of seven when their mother bribed a police officer to escort her to the front gates. My mother, Kinmama, on the other hand, thrived in an academic environment. She retained an excellent grasp of English, something that would be invaluable to her as a barrister's wife and the future First Lady. She excelled in mathematics as a result of handling her mother's accounts, her school marks surpassing that of her peers, male and female. Perhaps in a different era, my mother would have gone on to become a scientist or groundbreaking mathematician, but those were unthinkable professions for a respectable girl at the time. Her academic prowess was celebrated throughout the colonial school system, a young woman lauded for her achievements within convent walls as long as it was understood that she would take her place inside the home after her schooling.

She eschewed moss-covered university dorms to focus on marriage like her peers. In those days, it was fashionable to employ a matchmaker who shuffled through various social circles, purse overflowing with miniature portrait photos of potential suitors. Kinmama did not have to wait long before setting her sights on Ba Maw, a young barrister who had recently returned from Europe. The jolly, corpulent matchmaker delighted in handing Kinmama a small photo of Ba Maw. "He just finished his doctorate in Bordeaux," the matchmaker auntie cooed. "He is sophisticated, worldly, staying true to his roots in Rangoon."

"He may be a man of the world, but I'm a Burmese girl," quipped Kinmama. "Well then, let's meet this world traveler."

My parents were engaged immediately, the details of their first meeting taken to their graves. I tried my best to convince my mother to divulge the lurid details in later years, only for her to blush and tell me to mind my own business. Dr. Ba Maw and Daw Kinmama were married in April 1926, by all means a happy marriage resulting in seven children. I was born in 1927, my brother Zali in 1928, sister Mala in 1929, followed by Theda, Onma, Binnya and Neta in 1931, 1934, 1937 and 1947.

One of the earliest and most vivid memories that I have of my childhood is of my mother's silk *longyis*. Every morning, she would come to my bed and rouse me, an apple-cheeked child rolling awake at the warmth of May May's (as I called my mother) tone dripping like honey, the aria of my childhood. As the eldest, I was allowed to sit in her dressing room, enraptured as she opened her wardrobe doors to release a sharp burst of aged wood and the unmistakable scent of tightly woven silk, the smell of mountain air and earth. In that instant, the room would explode in a firework display of mauve, lavender, fuchsia, turquoise, emerald and china white, every imaginable hue set alight by the morning sun and shouting at my mother for her attention. *Pick me! Pick me!* they clamored.

"Tinsa, which one should I wear today?" she would ask me, her smile revealing teeth like ivory piano keys.

I traced each pile with both hands, the silk as cool as deep water, the stiff fabric rustling at my fingertips like leaves. Every design was unique, each thread and weave telling the story of their origins. Her Inle *longyis* were landscapes of Shan State, jagged pastels and tribal blots evoking lily blossoms floating on the great northern lake, hills and valleys etched on the horizon. The Kachin and Arakan pieces boasted arrow-shaped embroidery, remnants of thousands of years of warrior tradition. Or, I could have chosen the Burmese-Indian paisley prints blooming with millions of teardrops. Yet how could I possibly settle on one when all of Burma was sitting in my mother's wardrobe?

I never did choose, worried that if I were to deem one more beautiful than the rest, that the other proud fabrics would hate me. "Tinsa!" May May's breathy laugh would pull me from the deep well of my imagination, while her deft hands plucked the lucky winner from the stack, to be wrapped triumphantly around her tiny waist for the day. Aunt Kinmimi and my grandmother Daw Sein also lived with us, the gentle clacking of stones and heavy gold trailing them as they left for their jewelry brokerage every morning.

My siblings and I were merely planets orbiting around the sun and the moon that were my parents. If my mother was the lens through which I saw Burma, then my father was my key to unlocking the outer world. So much of this book and my early life are about him and the choices that he made. Phay Phay wanted to ensure that my siblings and I saw not only Burmese life but also the world past our gates, the fire-spitting cauldron that was Rangoon and beyond. One of the first things that I remember him saying to me was, "Learn everything there is to know about the world, about people and their ways. Apply the good and learn from the bad." If there was one thing that my father wanted for us, it was to keep an open mind about everything that the universe had to offer while keeping our hearts rooted in Burma, a lesson learned from his own upbringing.

The first time that my father took us to see a Charlie Chaplin film, my brother Zali and the other children in the audience bawled at the sight of the Tramp's ghostly pallor and strange little moustache, the comedian contorting his face and body in a manner to which my little brother was not accustomed to seeing. My sister Mala and I feigned tears in solidarity. Phay Phay was so alarmed by our collective screeching that he collected all three of us in his arms and left the theater in the middle of the film, the first and last time that we would ever see Chaplin in a proper cinema.

Christmas was by far the most eccentric spectacle in our home. To this day, I'm still not sure how my father convinced my devoutly Buddhist mother to cook a proper Christmas dinner and source a miniature palm tree for our living room year after year. She spent hours preparing roasted chicken, potatoes, gravy, ham, cauliflower au gratin and fruitcake, but she drew the line at giving Christmas presents, balking at the idea of gifting on occasions other than weddings and the birth of a child. My father treasured these dinners just as he had in Europe. As a student, he had looked forward to snow on Christmas Eve, blanketing the concrete avenues of Great Britain and France in a thick powder, something that he would never see in Burma. Families and friends would sit together for a warm meal, forgiving the ills of the previous year. Even a young Burmese man could be invited to the table, tasting lean Christmas goose and smelling smoky nutmeg in the air for the first time in his life.

I began my schooling at three years old at my mother's alma mater, St. John's Convent, and my sister Mala joined me two years later with the same plump nuns rearing a new generation of our family. My classmates were from the wealthiest families in the country, mostly Burmese but included a fair mix of Indian, Chinese and half-European girls. The school was in the middle of the bustling downtown center north of the Sule Pagoda, the demarcation line for the Chinese and Indian neighborhoods. Women in headscarves hawked piping hot samosas with their robes billowing in the gusts of humid city wind, their Chinese rivals lining their counters with fresh crullers, our school smocks steeped in smoke from their cooking oil.

Though we were Buddhist, we knelt before the image of Christ nailed to the crucifix every morning during chapel service, his skeletal frame and agonized expression giving Mala nightmares for three months straight. I was more perturbed by King George's portrait in the front hallway keeping a watchful eye over his empire, his severe and penetrating stare judging me every time I went to the ladies' room. The nuns used to discipline unruly girls with rulers to the knuckles during morning mass, blunt reminders of their duty to remain well-behaved "Catholic" ladies. Mala and I never frayed far from the edges of propriety, my mother's brand of old-fashioned Burmese justice enough to keep us in line, a bamboo stalk or sugar cane stem always within arm's reach.

There was little time for social or extracurricular activities, not that there were many options for Catholic schoolgirls at the time. As we grew older, the nuns did their best to organize tennis lessons, basketball tournaments and swimming, all away from the eyes of leering male voyeurs, of course. My mother banned Mala and me from partaking in swimming classes; she had never learned to swim and was deathly afraid of something happening to us in the water. "There is simply no need for anyone to go in or near an open body of water!" she proclaimed. My aunt Kinmimi echoed these sentiments, in addition to cursing modern bathing suits that revealed far too much of a woman's modesty. Socialization prospects outside of the convent were grim. There was always a supposed threat of vagabonds lurking in the bushes ready to kidnap children, or perhaps someone waiting to corrupt young minds with indecent thoughts. One could get hit by a car or, worst of all, be mistaken for a "commoner" on the street.

St. John's was a microcosm of the greater society, reflecting class and socioeconomic relations. Mala and I were students of the first school, daughters of elite families paying full fees. There was a second school that existed for students of "charity," like my father had been at St. Paul's. Every day, students from the first and second schools attended the same classes in our navy blue pinafores, starched white shirts, institutional black leather shoes and neat bobs in an assembly line of Catholic schoolgirls. During meals, the first school students had our own dining hall with new sets of china and silverware, and the second school girls would disappear to a room just behind the kitchen, a windowless but clean hall where they would take their meals separately, silently.

The racial divide was quite clear. It was not so much that us local girls clashed with our Anglo-Saxon counterparts; there weren't any British students for us to interact with at all. As with other aspects of life in Rangoon, the British community kept to themselves and their matters separate. The halls of the Strand Hotel, where the likes of Kipling and Maugham escaped the tropical heat in claw-footed bathtubs from France, or the Pegu Club, famous for its namesake cocktail doused in spicy gin and musky lime, were lined with signs reading *No Burmese Allowed*. *Bo* children would have been raised by surly governesses in the home until the age of eight or so, then sent to boarding school in India, England, or Switzerland. Playgrounds, swimming pools and public parks were segregated, boorish policemen and guards patrolling the parameters of "Whites Only" areas, waxed wooden batons ready to reprimand ruffians daring to step outside of their carefully delineated bounds.

It did not occur to me at such a young age that my life was different from anyone else's. It is eerie how my younger years seems so extraordinary to me now. My childhood was an upper middle class reverie, Chaplin films and Christmas dinners shielding me from the realities of the world, the cruelties and hardships of politics and hunger threatening to rip Burma apart at its core. The British Empire was at the apex of its power by the 1930s. Edged between two giants – India and China - Burma remained a postscript, its mineral wealth and natural resources paling in comparison to India's jewels and industry. My country was little more than an afterthought along the trade route between east and west, losing its formal identity when we were annexed to India in the late nineteenth century. We were no better than a province in another man's land. Hundreds of ethnic groups – a patchwork of mountain tribesmen, sea gypsies, desert nomads, city suits – that had been at war for centuries with one another, breathed tenuously under foreign guns knowing that conquest and unity were two very different things.

As fate would have it, the supposed powers had already written my story by the time I turned three years old. Burma was on the edge of collapse, enabled by a part-time soothsayer and rebel king by the name of Sayar San. He would disrupt the course of Burmese history and my life in his wake, whether I was ready or not.

CHAPTER TWO

By 1930, one-sixth of Burma's arable land was in the hands of Indian traders and the rest in the British government's ownership, natives second-class citizens in their own country while the colonists and a small population of Anglo-Burmese and Indian merchants controlled trade, agriculture and government. Rice paddies constituted over two-thirds of the country's arable land, laborers toiling under the red sun for a pittance, shiploads of fragrant jasmine rice reaching every corner of the world. In addition to rice, teak and petroleum were shipped to India to feed the global trade. The average Burmese male struggled to find menial work, the colonial government encouraging immigration from neighboring countries to undercut local wages. Impoverished, disempowered, angry – the country was on the brink of chaos.

Sayar San, a meek bureaucrat and sometime medicine man, had spent six years surveying the countryside for the General Council of Burmese Associations (GCBA) and studying rural living conditions. He saw his destiny in those jungles, the true state of Burma, where people were nothing better than serfs in their own land. People lived in wrenching poverty in the areas of the countryside that time and Rangoon had forgotten. Children ran around in rags and the ones who didn't die of cholera as infants could look forward to chronic malnutrition and illiteracy during adolescence. Adulthood held little promise, a lifetime tending to fields and forests that they would never own. While Rangoon high society boasted of expensive tea at the Strand and the Shwedagon Pagoda bathed the city in a glittering light after nightfall, the rest of the country remained in a dark abyss.

In December 1930, Sayar San organized revolts in the Tharrawaddy division against the proposal of a new poll tax. Tharrawaddy was a backwater locale four hours from Rangoon, an unlikely springboard for a nationalist storm. What began as small sit-ins amongst villagers, farmers and laborers in this rural outpost quickly set the rest of lower Burma aflame. The Crown dispatched ten thousand troops to crush the villagers, who fashioned themselves as an army. Rumors spread of Sayar San's powers, political and mythical, his army adopting the Galon as their symbol, an ancient creature whose powerful wings and intelligence could overpower the dragon-like Nagas[5] (the British). Murmurs crept through rice stalks, bamboo huts, darkened mine shafts.

He's here to save us.
The Galons' swords are blessed with powerful magic.
Only they can stop the Nagas.

By the time Sayar San was captured in August 1931, three thousand of his followers were dead and nine thousand detained, rotting in makeshift jails as they awaited the fate of their Galon King. The court system, determined to keep up with the pretense of a fair trial, allowed for an ambitious young lawyer to take up Sayar San's defense. U Saw (founder of the Myochit Party; Prime Minister; convicted and hanged for Aung San's assassination in 1948) was at the time a lower-level barrister who saw an opportunity to further his personal ambitions in the midst of the greater nationalist outbreak. A member of the General Council of Burmese Associations (GCBA), the largest political party, U Saw sought political laurels but lacked certain educational credentials, barring him from defending Sayar San without a supervisor. The court

---

[5] *Naga* is a mythical dragon-like creature with great powers, natural enemy of the Galons.

required an elite barrister to oversee the defense before a Special Tribunal, preferably a product of the British-style educational system and had attended university in England. Few were willing to take the role, a guaranteed loss. What qualified barrister would tarnish his record with such a high-profile loss? Who would dare to challenge the Crown in an open court?

My father, Dr. Ba Maw, had been following the events acutely since the outbreak of rebellion. Phay Phay and May May, as I called my parents, were members of the educated bourgeoisie, settling in a respectable part of Rangoon by Kandawgyi Lake dotted with hand-carved teak mansions and wild rose gardens, ideal for Rangoon's top-ranked lawyer and his wife. They would have otherwise been destined for a life of ennui as Burmans-about-town had it not been for the unflinching Sayar San. My mother was not the sort to get involved with politics unless it directly affected her affairs, but my father could not and would not avert his eyes from the changes happening around us. He followed the case obsessively, entranced by the villagers' dogged courage, a mirror of his own impoverished upbringing.

I remember hearing my parents uttering the words *galon* and *naga* over and over again, my imagination weaving a rich tale of a sprawling winged beast swooping down to defeat a ferocious serpent in an ultimate battle of good versus evil. In my mind, a child's mind, it was just another chapter from one of our many mythological tales, bedtime stories told so often to me by my elders that I made no distinction between fact and fiction. There was no doubt in my mind that the *galons* would surely conquer the *nagas* like in the story, the natural order of things.

I was hiding behind my mother's *longyi* when U Boon Swan, an acquaintance of my father's, paid a visit to our lakeside home shortly after the Galon rebels' arrest. U Boon Swan would become one of the pioneers of the independence movement as a founder of the Wunthanu Party, but at the time he was a second-tier barrister like U Saw. My father knew him professionally, a cordial but distant relationship. An outspoken and jovial man, he entered my father's study with great trepidation, head bowed, eyes darting back and forth. "What a great pleasure to see you in my home," Phay Phay greeted him, equally apprehensive about the nature of his visit.

The coffee and tea snacks had barely cooled on the table when U Boon Swan confessed the purpose of his visit. He wanted to speak with my father on the matter of the Sayar San trial. My father was prepared to offer legal advice but was taken aback by the extent of his guest's request. "Why don't you become a part of Sayar San's defense team?" U Boon Swan asked bluntly, wincing.

A thick tension settled over the room, my father choking on his coffee and my mother suppressing a gasp from behind the door from which she was eavesdropping. "We, his supporters, need someone like you to defend his case." U Boon Swan mustered the courage to straighten his posture, a mischievous smile escaping his lips. "The peasants don't have money so you'll only be paid a pittance, whatever the government is willing to give for a regular criminal's trial. Sayar San will lose, no doubt, so you'll have to deal with that on your record and the wrath of the Governor. Sayar San is also one of the most stubborn defendants I have ever met in my life, so you'll get little help from him."

"With all due respect, you're making an awfully weak case for yourself," my father joked.

U Boon Swan laughed boisterously. He sipped his coffee with a steadied grip, indefatigable with his plea. "You are the only barrister in this country who can do this case justice. I've heard you in court, I've read your writings. You're brilliant and you know that. I also know that you are a nationalist and you must do what is right for our country. The point is not to win the trial, but to expose the greater ills of the colonial government." The two men looked at each other, U Boon Swan's conviction staring my father in the eye, my father absorbing the gravity of the proposal.

"Dr. Ba Maw, are you brave enough to do this?"

Phay Phay went to see his newest client at the decrepit

Tharrawaddy Jail, mildew coating the stone pillars, the stench of stale urine and rotting garbage lingering in the air. He was surprised to find not a rebel leader sprouting great Galon wings, but an ordinary and quiet man swathed in filth and fear. Sayar San mirrored the farmers who supported him: his hair matted with dirt and sweat, a dense film of grime and destitution casing his body. If he hadn't known better, Phay Phay could have mistaken him for another petty criminal, a bicycle thief or common robber.

Sayar San backed into a corner as my father approached the cell, crossing his arms across his skeletal frame, bony elbows pointed like knives. He dared not utter a word, not even to the man who would be defending him at trial. My father trod softly, careful footsteps and words to mollify the Galon leader. *How are your conditions in this jail? Are your other comrades here? Are you getting enough to eat? How about your family?*

Sayar San's eyes flickered. He confided that he had a wife and children whom he worried for every day. He missed his village, the sight of monks and their alms bowls glinting in the sunlight. "Are my children safe? Will you make sure that my family will be safe?" He searched my father's face for an answer, a challenge enfolded in a simple request.

Phay Phay was conflicted with deep empathy and mounting impatience for his defendant. Whereas Sayar San was quick to cede to government pressure, my father saw an opportunity for him to speak out against the ills of the colonial government in the most public platform in Burma. The Galon King had not heard of the Indian National Congress and the Vietnamese fighting parallel battles across the borders. Gandhi had concluded his Salt March, the lessons of civil disobedience yet to reach Burmese ears and minds. In Vietnam, the Yên Bái mutiny bared nationalists' simmering discontent, mirroring the Galon Army's sentiments. My father asked Sayar San if he was willing to air his grievances in court once and for all.

No. Still timid. Still afraid.

My father reasoned carefully, expecting the initial refusal. "The government will see to it that you get the death penalty no matter what, so you might as well use your trial to speak your mind about the injustices inflicted on our country. That way you'll become a hero to our people, won't you?" Sayar San processed his counsel's words slowly, cautiously.

"They have already decided to hang me."

"You will lose this battle and your life, Sayar San."

Silence. The light was gone from the elder man's eyes.

"Sayar San, I will ask you again. Will you do this for your country?"

At his trial, the Galon King remained hunched in the far left corner of the tribunal room, making himself as small as possible. Not a word from his parched lips. Dr. Ba Maw and U Saw filled the vast void with tales of anguished laborers in the countryside who struggled to feed their families, children dying of curable diseases because they could not afford medicine, women sewing by candlelight for extra income. They portrayed Sayar San not as a mythical war hero, but as an ordinary citizen who felt the crushing weight of economic and political oppression. His silence was a boon for the defense, an ultimate act of dignity in the eyes of a public clamoring for more details.

A scraggy middle-aged woman and her children stood outside of the jail every day, perhaps a member of the public so entranced by the morbid details of the trial that she had to see it in person. They looked like beggars with their threadbare clothes, world-weary composures and unmistakable hunger in their sunken eyes. The mother panted under the burning autumn sun hoping that an official or jailer would notice them. The British counsel happened to pass them on his way to the chamber, discreetly slipping a ten-rupee note into the mother's hand, the fresh bill sitting precariously on her dirty palm. Ten rupees meant a hundred meals, new clothes, school fees for an entire village.

The woman threw the note back at the counsel, her anger visceral, searing him and a crowd of bystanders. She spat venomously, "Aren't you the man trying to kill my husband, their father?" pointing her long, gaunt fingers at Sayar San's children. The counsel flushed strawberry red, wanting to run, but the women's glare fixed him on the spot. "I want justice for my husband. So tell me, sir, what is the price for that?"

There would be no justice for her husband or for seventy-seven of his followers. The Galon King was hanged at the public jail on November 28, 1931, his remains left unclaimed as his wife and children disappeared altogether after the verdict. Burma pulsated with pride for this meek man who stood eye to eye with an empire, an unlikely first hero of the independence era.

The trial also created two heroes to be remembered in the chronicles of our history. My father and U Saw would be fêted for their overly dramatic but fearless defense of Sayar San, paving the way for each of them to become Prime Minister during the last days of the colonial regime, their paths splintering in the haze of war and independence. One would lead the independence movement, while the other would orchestrate a murder so abhorrent that it still echoes in my mind.

* * * * *

The Galon King awakened a series of events ensuring that I was to stay true to my chaotic Rahu roots, an early initiation of the turmoil that would dog me for the remainder of my life. By the time that I was old enough to feel, if not understand, the complexities of my life, a cyclone had already swept me into its spiral.

The protests and anger did not die with Sayar San. His death only exacerbated the political climate. In response to the peasant rebellions and widening public discontent, the Crown relented in replacing absolute rule with preliminary self-government. Phay Phay, who joined the General Council of Burmese Associations (GCBA) Party following his Sayar San fame, accepted the post of Minister of Education and Health in 1934. My father did not consider the motives behind his appointment, whether it was intended to mollify his increasingly nationalist tendencies or a genuine overture on the part of the colonial government. Whatever the case was, Phay Phay took his post seriously, creating overseas scholarships for promising university scholars inspired by King Mindon's initiatives to infuse Burma with knowledge from global academic hubs. He also slashed auxiliary university fees that prevented poorer students from reaching higher education, such as a relocation tax that penalized rural residents wanting to study in Mandalay or Rangoon.

My father's tenure as minister was not without criticism. Ko Daw Hmaing, the most famous Burmese poet and philosopher of the twentieth century, openly questioned the motives of British-educated elites like Dr. Ba Maw, our families living in gated estates in contrast to the majority of Burmese living in bamboo huts. Ko Daw Hmaing tested my father's wits when they encountered each other in front of the Secretariat one day. "And what do you hope that your scholars will bring back from the colonists' lands? Do we not have enough British minds and hearts in Rangoon?"

My father, never one to back away from a debate, retorted, "Your generation used pitchforks and spells against an empire, U Ko Daw Hmaing, and were crushed. The new generation will fight with the most powerful weapon of all – a modern mind." The elder man laughed uproariously at the young minister's artful jab, my father laughing and entering a parliamentary session.

The public only saw my father's steely exterior but I witnessed him struggle with the very issues that Ko Daw Hmaing echoed. His anxieties intensified when a more radical party emerged in the political patchwork. Ko Daw Hmaing and his cohort founded the Thakin movement amidst the anti-Indian riots of the early 1930s, caused by British shipping firms hiring temporary Burmese workers to replace Indian dockworkers who were on strike. When the strike ended, the Burmese slaughtered their Indian rivals and their families, blaming them for conspiring with the British to economically oppress the locals. The Thakins, influenced by this episode, Sayar San's rebellion and the lessons of the Russian

Revolution, sanctioned the use of violence in their quest for an independent Burma. These revolutionaries called themselves Thakins, or masters, inspired by the practice of calling a European person "sir," a racially charged custom.

One day, when I was about seven or eight years old, my family fell ill from the first flu of the cold season. My mother, aunt, grandmother and siblings rested underneath thick cotton sheets drenched in fever, a cloud of eucalyptus and chamomile hanging above them. My father and I were lucky to have escaped its clutches, but my mother rasped from her bedside that I was not to go to school in case I were to transfer the flu to my classmates. Phay Phay chuckled at the absurdity of my mother's delirium-induced order but he knew better than to argue with her. He took me by the hand, my palm shaking with joy at the thought of spending the whole day with my beloved father.

I gazed down from a balustrade overlooking the government hall while rows of men filed into the Parliament chamber. A gavel dropped to announce the start of the session and I glanced Phay Phay on the left side of the room, crane-like among a legion of ebony jackets and silk caps. Ko Daw Hmaing sat on the opposite side of the great hall, his winding charcoal beard and knotted hair his only distinguishable features in an identical sea of black and silk. I recognized the faces in the crowd as neighbors, family friends and parents of my classmates. Suddenly, the muted chamber combusted with voices disagreeing with one other, signaling the start of the debate. What struck me was not what was being said, but that these men who spoke in similar lilting university-educated tones, whose perfect English accents indicated years of monk-like study in higher education, could have so much in common yet have so much to argue about. They waved their hands theatrically, clean white fingertips and fleshy palms sparring to the tune of an invisible orchestra.

Phay Phay and I snuck out during the lunch break to a nearby café run by a local entrepreneur who thought to serve British fare alongside Burmese dishes. I could taste the thick aroma of cottage pie pouring in from the kitchen. The patron sitting next to me devoured a plate of chicken curry so spicy that his face began to turn an alarming shade of red. My father and I tried our best to hide our giggling at the poor man's plight, burying our faces in our mounds of fish and chips. "Phay Phay, why do you and the other men fight so much at work? Aren't they our friends?" I asked him in between mouthfuls of buttery fish melting atop my tongue.

I expected some sort of glib response to be followed by laughter, the kind that my parents usually gave my siblings and me whenever we asked about things that were not meant for our young ears. Phay Phay did not answer me immediately, chewing the last few morsels of his meal and dabbing the sharp tips of his mouth with his cloth napkin. His eyes slowly lifted to meet mine, the seriousness of his gaze pinning me to my chair. I sat paralyzed because it the first time in my life that my father looked at me not as his daughter, his child, but as a grown being capable of understanding what he was about to say.

"Tinsa, we are not fighting because we hate each other." He took a small sip of his ice water, its cold sweat trickling down his right hand and seeping into his sleeve.

"People don't fight if they like each other. That doesn't make sense," I interjected, my hands propped defensively on my waist.

My interrogative tactics drew a wide smile from him. "The other parliamentarians and I argue with each other because we love Burma very much. And right now...let's just say Burma is sick, and we are trying to figure out the best medicine for it, just like what the doctor did for May May today. We just can't agree on what medicine will make our country heal, because there are so many different kinds and not all of them will work."

"You're a lawyer, not a doctor, Phay Phay."

"No, Tinsa, I'm not," he laughed, "but I want to try to help. Do you remember your mother and I telling you about how we grew up? How poor we were? Well, a lot of strong people helped to look after me when I was weak and now I feel that it is my turn to do the same. And the same goes for you, too, because you are among the strong."

I absorbed my father's words, surprised to discover their weight, heavy as marble sinking in my chest. *You are among the strong.* Those words had anchored themselves in the pit of my stomach just below my lungs where I believed my soul to be. They did not sit right and I felt the urge to expel them from that sacred place. I felt as if he weren't speaking to me, at least not the little girl sitting before him. They were meant for the person that I was to become, the premonitory advances of an adulthood that I was not sure that I was ready for yet.

Power and politics, especially in Burma, do not wait for little girls to grow into their strength, as I came to learn. In 1935, when I was eight years old, the Crown enacted the Government of Burma Act in which the bicameral legislature and all ministerial positions would be designated solely for the Burmese. Men over 18 and females over 21 were to vote for their regional representatives and for Prime Minister. What's more, Burma would also stand as a separate country from India. The Crown granted the Burmese the superficial concessions that any colonized subjects would want, but the Governor-General still wielded absolute power and veto rights. He would choose the ministers, could impose taxes to prevent local goods from competing fairly with British and Indian goods, and could remove elected officials at whim. He could also dismantle legislative chambers should they be deemed unfit for the interests of the Crown.

My father broke away from the GCBA Party to form the Sinyetha (Poor Man's) Party in 1936, dissatisfied with the bickering of the various parties and their inability to unite against the root causes of landlessness and poverty in Burma. Their motto, *Three acres and a cow*, targeted the colonial financial system in which farmers and the working poor were forever indebted to Chettiars[6] and British trade interests. It echoed the sentiment that the Burmese did not need much initially but wanted their fair share of assets, enough for a simple and content life. When Burma formally separated from India on April 1, 1937, my father declared his candidacy for the Prime Minister's seat.

The doors of our Kandawgyi home flung open to house a myriad of hard-nosed parliamentarians, determined student leaders, politicized monks and union leaders ranging from dust-covered farmers to petrol-soaked factory workers. My house now resembled a hospital waiting room flooding with patients who were waiting to see if the good doctor could provide the cure for their political ailments. Phay Phay spoke to the hundreds of people who walked through our door, flocks of vultures and doves shrieking at all hours of the day. I cannot recall him sleeping a full night during that period, spending the twilight hours pacing his study, reciting texts from his favorite writers, lost inside of his own mind. His face remained smooth and uncreased as sprouts of gray hair began to pepper his temples, which had the distinct advantage of masking his fatigue with an aura of refinement.

My mother spent countless hours making tea and snacks for the parade of politicos pouring in. May May never complained once, though the tart scent of her perspiration became stronger by the day beneath her layers of perfume and soap. I couldn't stand to look at the beads of sweat defiling her otherwise flawless forehead, so I decided that I would do my part for the campaign by fanning my mother and wiping her face with a cotton handkerchief. She smiled at me with her head pressed against my palm, exhaling lightly into the crook of my wrist. "Are you done with your homework?" she asked.

"Yes."

"All of it?" she sighed with one eyebrow cocked.

---

[6] Chettiars represented the South Asian mercantile and banking class in Burma. They served as moneylenders to poor Burmese, often with high interest rates.

"Alllll of it," I sang.

May May reached up to cup my hand in hers, her eyes fraught with concern. "Tinsa, I worry that you are too young to be a part of this, even if you are trying to help. You don't have to do this if you don't want to. You can play upstairs with your siblings, if you'd like." She removed both of our hands from her cheek, the sweat-stained handkerchief falling on the ground between us.

My mother's concern felt strange to me because there had been no doubt in my mind that I wanted to help her and Phay Phay, to be strong for them. I knew little about politics and was just a passenger in my life at that point, but what I did sense was the urgency in her sweat, my father's restless nights and the way in which the tranquility of our house seemed to escape breeze by breeze with each opening of the door. I did not know what I was helping, only that I felt capable of contributing in some small way.

"No, May May, I want to stay," I said without hesitation, and I meant it. I picked up the fallen handkerchief, still wet to the touch from my mother's perspiration.

There is an old proverb about Burmese politics that warns, "King Cobras do not feed on weaker animals. They eat their own kind." True to form, Burma's first election resembled a back alley brawl, shocking the sensibilities of the colonial government. The GCBA-led Nga Bwint Saing[7] faction won 43 seats while my father's Sinyetha Party collected a paltry 16 seats. Ko Daw Hmaing and the Thakins won 3 seats despite registering in only 28 voting constituencies. The GCBA had expected to serve as the ruling party and to install a candidate of their choice, but their coalition splintered immediately after the results were released, scattering loose votes and allegiances across the floors of the Secretariat.

In the midst of infighting between the various GCBA representatives, Phay Phay surreptitiously courted the

---

[7] *Five Flowers in One*; a coalition named after the five heads of the United GCBA.

remaining 12 independent seats, who agreed to ally with him. He then recruited the defected GCBA seats from right under the party's nose, seizing the necessary number of seats to win a majority. It was now in the hands of the British government to decide if they wanted to keep a maverick at their front gates in light of my father's unorthodox victory. They could either denounce the rogue coalition or simply go with the majority. Thus, my father, Dr. Ba Maw, became the first Burmese Prime Minister in 1937.

As the new Head of State, my parents' first official visit was to England for King George VI's coronation at Westminster Abbey in May 1937. The well-heeled residents of Rangoon awaited gossip about royal intrigues and society happenings thousands of miles away, especially news about Edward's abdication and his pending marriage to Wallis Simpson. My siblings and I remained in Rangoon under the care of Aunt Kinmimi and our grandmother, Daw Sein. My parents wrote to us daily via telegram and I ran from my school to the telegraph office on Phayre's Road every day to retrieve their messages, panting as the office clerk handed me the freshly printed sheet, its cornflower blue ink bleeding in my palms. I missed my parents but I was happy for them, hoping that Phay Phay and May May would find some respite on the other side of the world, that they would dance their nights away (my mother begrudgingly, of course), brush elbows with world leaders in their black lapels and military pennants, and toast champagne flutes in the shade of laughter. I imagined that all eyes would be on the new Burmese Prime Minister and his beautiful wife gliding about London, their silk jackets reflecting in the waters of the Thames.

The veneer of pomp and circumstance would soon be stripped away by the blinding glare of Burma's struggles. The new administration had inherited a broken, determined country, too far removed from its monarchial roots but not yet destined for life outside of the imperial cage. I would be thrown into the center of the ring as the Prime Minister's eldest daughter, a little girl's mettle to be tried against fate.

Dr. Ba Maw and Daw Kinmama Maw, London, May 27 1937

CHAPTER THREE

One June morning, shortly after my parents returned from their trip abroad, I jolted awake to the sound of three women screaming at the top of their lungs. I kicked the blanket off my body and ran down the winding staircase to find my mother, aunt and grandmother standing on our porch, shrieking like angry spirits in the night. The three caryatids of our Kandawgyi home were dressed in matching white cotton nightgowns that glowed in the light of the morning sun, and they were hugging one another so tightly that my eyes could not detect the source of their madness. Aunt Kinmimi broke rank to seize a nearby broomstick and I managed to spy two faces smiling sheepishly at me through the space between my mother and grandmother. The man and woman could have been a couple, or siblings. Their skin was the same shade of rich toffee and their rounded bellies and ironed shirts indicated that they were not here to beg. My immediate thought was to fear these strangers, assuming that those who had snuck onto our property were there for nefarious reasons. I searched their eyes for any trace of ill will, of that glint of menace that would give them away, but I found none. The man and woman stared at me too, their eyes filled with pure curiosity.

"Gatekeeper! Gatekeeper!" my aunt screamed for our night watchman, who was nowhere to be found. She advanced and pointed the broom at the man and woman, who backed away with their hands held up as if it were a gun. "Who are you?

Have you come to rob us?" Aunt Kinmimi screamed.

My father had quietly entered the fracas, disoriented and scanning the scene twice before his eyes settled on our uninvited guests. "Well, you heard my sister-in-law. What brings you to our home?" Phay Phay asked.

The woman gasped and covered her mouth with her right hand while her comrade crept forward to have a closer look at my father. "It really is him, the Prime Minister!" he shouted to the woman, while pointing his stubby index finger at my father's face.

"Do you have any pressing issues that you must bring to my attention...at this early hour?" My father's tone shifted from sheer confusion to amusement.

"Oh no, not at all, Dr. Ba Maw. You see, we just wanted to see you in person. You're very famous now." There was not a trickle of artifice in the man's voice or expression. The man and woman stood smiling at my father while ignoring the rest of us, including my aunt who continued to hold the broom like a weapon.

"I'm dreaming, aren't I, Phay Phay?" I asked my father in jest, but I was also hoping that this bizarre episode was a product of my imagination, that it was anything but the surreal trappings of my life from that point forward. I went upstairs to my bedroom, pulling the sheets over my head and humming to myself, until finally my eyes closed shut.

Aunt Kinmimi continued to stand guard on our porch at dawn every morning, sometimes chasing gawkers from our driveway with her trusty broom, busybodies curious to peek inside the home of a state leader. We were no longer a private family, my father now the most lauded and scrutinized man in the country. The headlines read: *Dr. Ba Maw: First Burman to Serve as Prime Minister. A Nation Takes Pride in One of Our Own.* My parents strived to keep life as normal as possible, especially my mother who refused to alter her daily routine. "I go to the same market, eat the same food, drive the same roads, breathe the same air. Nothing else has changed, so why should I?" she would snap at anyone trying to put on airs around her.

Thankfully, the gawking and pointing seemed to be limited to the area surrounding my home. Once I stepped out of the parameters of Kandawgyi Lake and into the dirt and steam of the downtown area, I could go about my life as I always had. I went to school without any of my friends blinking an eye. If anything, it seemed like the nuns gave my classmates and me even more work to do as we entered middle school. While my friends complained of their homework, I imbibed my assignments, finding comfort and routine in the company of algebra equations and biology experiments.

I was not yet privy to the real spectacle, which was taking place inside the halls of Parliament. My father went about his days as he normally would, saving the pageantry and grandeur for office. His first act in office was to release all remaining prisoners from the Sayar San rebellion. The Sinyetha Party pushed for compensation for the families of the imprisoned or executed Galon rebels, but the Crown quashed the motion, the upstart Prime Minister teetering too close to the edges of the government's coin purse. *You are to be seen and not heard*, warned the royalists. Phay Phay marched forward anyway, officiating National Day as an annual holiday in commemoration of the 1920 Student Boycott, the first large-scale rebellion that protested the cog mentality of the colonial educational system.

Naturally there was opposition to his election, particularly from Ko Daw Hmaing whose Thakin Party maintained a tenuous alliance with the Sinyetha Party. The poet wrote of my father, "I cannot dare to think of entrusting the golden throne to a water-sprinkled Anglican." It was not only Ko Daw Hmaing who doubted Dr. Ba Maw but a sizeable faction of citizens that questioned the loyalties of an English and French-educated leader. They suspected my father of being in cahoots with Archibald Cochrane, a stiff and overly formal man who served as the Governor-General from 1936 to 1941. He was not one to toy with his seat and more importantly, his duty. Should the new Prime Minister and his coalition cross the Governor in any way, the latter made it clear that he would not hesitate to dissolve Congress in the best interests of the

Crown.

Therefore, it was a big shock when my father refused to bow to Cochrane during their first state meeting and all subsequent meetings thereafter. All Burmese were required by protocol to bow before the Governor. Cochrane, apparently stunned by the new leader's break with tradition, called the meeting to order, his voice muffled with confusion. My father came home that night and announced to us bewildered children, "You are the sons and daughters of this beautiful nation. Never kowtow to anyone who doesn't earn your respect first!" This refusal to bow would be my father's trademark, later to be adopted by the Thakins and other nationalists. He would not bow to the British, he did not bow to the Japanese during the war, nor to anyone he felt did not earn the true respect of a Burman.

I idolized my father, his showmanship second to none in the circus that was the Secretariat. Phay Phay had captured power, a strange and feral animal that had eluded the other politicians for six decades. Power was never acquiescent, forcing my father to chase after her in the ring, to dance with her when she felt playful. I watched, mesmerized, as my father used words and not force to mollify that wild beast.

Power also bared her teeth when she felt like it, showing that no man can truly tame her, that she is the master and not the other way around. In the fall of 1937, I accompanied my mother and father to the Pansodan Jetty to give a farewell to a batch of scholars embarking on a passenger ship to Europe. The banks of the Ayeyarwaddy River contained a floating city governed by uniformed ship captains, cheroot-smoking dockworkers, and merchants who waved bricks of rupees in the air as they came to collect their treasures from around the world. U Nyo Mya, a prolific writer, nationalist, intellectual and himself a product of my father's scholarship initiative, greeted us at the dock and placed a small rectangular object covered in wax paper in my palm. I pried the package open to reveal a rose-pink treasure, coated in powdered sugar and with bits of pistachio trapped in its gummy center. "The finest Turkish

Delight to grace Burma's shores," U Nyo Mya said to me proudly. "A well-deserved prize for your high marks."

"I told him about you earning second place in your fifth grade class, Tinsa," Phay Phay smiled at me. "Indeed a well-earned prize for your hard work."

"Careful now, Dr. Ba Maw, I think we've got a future politician in front of us. She might even unseat you!" I blushed as the adults laughed, embarrassed at the sudden spotlight.

I bit the Turkish Delight piece by piece as we walked to the jetty gate, letting its gummy texture dissolve in my mouth and crawl over my teeth. As it was not an official visit, my parents had not alerted the jetty officials in advance and did not want to divert attention from the scholars whose special day it was. Before we could go any further on the walkway, I felt the barricade swing and push against me, its force kicking the wind out of my chest. "Keep back, passengers only!" barked the gruff gatekeeper. He appraised us up and down, smirking as his eyes caught Phay Phay's black silk *gaungbaung* and *paso*[8] glistening under the sun.

"We've come to say our congratulations to the scholars," my father said politely, pointing to the group of scholars who had noticed the Prime Minister at the front of a growing crowd, the young men nervous and curious as to what he would do. Would he announce himself? Yell at the gatekeeper? Imprison him for his oversight? I knew that Phay Phay was far too well mannered to publicly reprimand the ornery gatekeeper but a certain rage began to boil within me. It was not because I felt that the gatekeeper should have recognized my father, but rather his sneering at Phay Phay's traditional attire and the disparaging look that he gave to us as a group.

"Burmese, eh?" the gatekeeper grinned through his yellowed, cigar-stained teeth, his pockmarked cheeks puffing with amusement. "Master," he mocked, "please enter." Finally, the doors swung open and we slipped in unnoticed, blending

---

[8] *Gaungbaung* (men's hat) and *paso* (men's sarong or longyi) are traditional attire.

in with the crowd of passersby and acquaintances gathering at the gate.

"Why didn't you reprimand the gatekeeper? He's nothing but a colonial lackey!" cried an incensed U Nyo Mya.

My father sighed at him, explaining unconvincingly, "Young man, if you can avoid hurting a man's pride, then do so. People never forget the feeling of humiliation."

But what about your pride? What about the gatekeeper humiliating you? I wanted to scream at him, his vague explanation only fueling my rage. I then realized that the source of my rage was not the gatekeeper or my father. It was that I had seen the world for what it was, a world in which my presumptions were turned upside down and I did not like it. The sneering remarks, the judgment and the bullying were a part of a stronger power, one that granted men the right to feel superior over another just by sheer virtue of skin color and race. My father was not the lion tamer, after all. On the contrary, perhaps he was the one who was being tamed.

I was right about my father's fallibility, unfortunately. Rangoon began to burn barely a year into my father's term and his position was powerless to stop it. In December 1938, oil workers from the Burmah Oil Company staged a strike in the Magway division where they had been working for pennies at one of Southeast Asia's most profitable oil fields. The men - hair sticky with crude oil, calloused hands and feet - marched from Chauk through the dry zone towards Rangoon after months of indecision by the colonial government. Their faces were etched with a lifetime of grueling labor, eyes bright with hope and fear, staring in awe at the Secretariat building. They had never seen anything as beautiful as perfectly laid brick. At the same time, university students were staging their yearly sit-in protesting the colonial government, joining forces in the largest political demonstration since the Sayar San rebellion.

My father and his cabinet sought to negotiate with the protesters in a rare showing of cooperation among the parties. The students and oil workers followed non-violent tactics and it was difficult not to sympathize with them when they preached change through peaceful means, borrowing Gandhi's methods from across the border in India. These doves of men and women infused Rangoon with a sense of hope, that real and true change could and should happen without resorting to more drastic means. Everything was happening just as my father had said to Thakin Ko Daw Hmaing years earlier, that the Burmese needed to fight not with pitchforks and machetes, but modern minds.

Before the administration could reach out to the protesters, a poisonous rumor spread that an Indian merchant had written a disparaging and racist article about the oil workers' strike, catalyzing bloodlust. There was already tension between the Burmese and the Indian and Chinese migrants who had flourished under the colonial system, finding entrepreneurial niches that excluded locals such as gold trading, currency exchange, property development and textiles. They had become wealthy and lived a strained existence amongst the locals, decades of ethnic tension and "otherization" combusting in an instant. Thousands of ethnic Burmese who were not involved with the original protests stormed the streets, ransacking Indian and Chinese-owned businesses in the heart of the city, blazes bursting and encircling the two-thousand-year-old Sule Pagoda. Nationalist gangs, or so they deemed themselves, scoured the alleyways for anyone looking remotely Indian or Chinese and beat them to a pulp. They tossed victims onto the streets with nothing except for the clothes on their backs, made to watch as generations of their hard work and savings turned to ashes. These bad elements of society, young men seeking a thrill through looting and killing in the name of faux nationalism, clashed with the students and oil workers on the lawn of the Secretariat.

Of course, the article could not be found and the supposed author did not exist when the student leaders tried to trace its origins in an attempt to mitigate the damage. The students' investigation only angered the looters, who believed them to be siding with the Indians, Chinese and colonists. It was a classic case of misdirection, a very old trick used by colonial governments to divide and conquer. I need not say more than that, because the Crown did what it needed to do next in order to distract and seize power from the students and oil workers.

In December 1938, the Governor crushed the protests with a flick of his pen, making no distinction between political protesters and looters. He dispatched hundreds of policemen, sweeping through every back alley in downtown Rangoon, a stampede reverberating through the entire city. On December 20, 1938, the police beat remaining protesters with metal batons and those who fell were handcuffed and taken to the nearest prison. The first victim, Aung Kyaw, was a student without any known displays of rebellion. He and his friends had decided to join the movement hoping to support nationalism in whatever way they could. Witnesses reported that Aung Kyaw did not see the glint of the baton before it hit him on the side of his head, his friends believing that he would wake up momentarily. He became the first hero of the pre-war nationalist movement, martyred and posthumously given the title of Bo (*Bogyoke* meaning General).

My father was devastated and furious. I could tell by the slow pacing of his footsteps in his study and the way that his bloodshot eyes were perpetually downcast, sullen. Though his pride would never let him admit it, I knew that he felt guilty that these riots had broken out under his guard, not because it was a blemish on his record but because innocent people were made to pay for the games of an empire. While he was furious that the looters had taken the bait, he could not bring himself to judge those who took to the streets, the powerless who found unity and a collective identity in xenophobia. He would never condone violence, but was aware that diplomacy was a luxury for the educated elites, those protected from hunger and the banal injustices of the streets. These young men were left with nothing but resentment to fill their empty bellies, who found cheap empowerment by terrorizing those weaker than them.

I did a very foolish thing on the day of the crackdown. All of the schools and universities had been closed for several days and I was growing restless without homework or the company of my school friends. My mother had gone to my father's office to support him and my aunt and grandmother were at their jewelry brokerage in the Indian neighborhood, preoccupied with contingency planning in case things were to worsen. My siblings and I were left at home with our nannies, who did not know what to do with us after we grew bored with the tower of board games on our dining room table. I had been in my room all day and desperately wanted to go for a walk, to stretch my legs and breathe fresh air even for a few minutes. "Tinsa," my younger sister Mala called to me from her room. "I'm bored. I want some ice cream."

The thought of freshly churned milk ice cream made my mouth water, salivating not just at the idea of a sweet treat but also at the prospect of brief freedom. I knew precisely where the ice cream man and his bicycle were, always stationed two blocks away on the main road facing the lake. The walk was no more than five minutes through a residential neighborhood and I knew all of my neighbors. Surely, nothing would happen on the way there, I convinced myself. I tiptoed to Mala's room and made her promise not to tell a soul. "This is our secret. You can't tell Phay Phay or May May or else they're going to be so mad at us." Mala smiled in agreement and we slipped through the back door of the house under the sleeping eyes of our gatekeeper.

I really did not think anything could happen to us. It's not that I was unaware of how dangerous the riots were. I was eleven years old, old enough to read newspapers and understand the warnings that my parents repeated to me day after day. I just thought that adult matters wouldn't affect me at all because I was just a child. I wore this naïve cloak of invincibility as Mala and I skipped down the avenue, stopping in our tracks when we heard screaming from the street next to ours.

Fear held me captive. My heart was a hammer against my chest and cold sweat ran from the base of my hairline down my back. *Run*, my common sense told me, but I could not bring myself to move. Mala's hand was no longer in mine and I turned my head to see her running towards the direction of our home. Another scream tore through the air, a young girl's cries. *Turn back*, yelled my inner voice, until I felt an invisible hand pull me towards the direction of the screams, my legs snapping and propelling me to the girl's voice.

Tinsa, Mala and Theda

There were four houses on the street, each separated by several isolated acres of land. I had never noticed how lonely this street was in comparison to my own, where the houses were close enough that we could yell over the fence and ask to borrow a bottle of milk. I kept walking past the houses until the clipped bushes and trees gave way to the source of the screaming. Three Burmese men, no older than twenty-five years old with their low-slung *pasos* and short-sleeved shirts, were holding cheap paring knives in their filthy hands. Their blades were pointed at two young girls whom I immediately recognized as Nilar and Divya, sisters and two of my friends from my convent school. Their father was a successful spice merchant who had emigrated from Bombay as a boy and their mother was a great beauty from a prominent Burmese-Indian family. I knew them well as Nilar was in my class and Divya was the same age as Mala, and they lived two streets over from where we were standing.

I still don't know to this day why they were on that particular street, if they had ventured out like my sister and me and found themselves in a difficult situation, or if they had been forced there. The contents of their matching lilac purses were scattered in front of them. A rupee here and there. Crushed bits of peppermint candy. Small family photos. Nilar and Divya did not seem to be physically hurt, but Nilar burst into tears when she saw me. The three men turned to look at me, amused when they saw a skinny girl no taller than their chests.

"Are you all right?" I addressed Nilar and Divya, surprised by the confidence in my tone. I was not trying to be brave. Actually, I was not thinking at all and my actions were completely impulsive, which had the unique effect of immobilizing my thought processes, leaving me with nothing but my instincts to rely on. My first and only instinct was to help my friends.

"This is none of your business, little sister," interrupted the one standing closest to me. His mouth bled a deep orange-red liquid that oozed through his teeth, the product of betel nut chewing. He spat as he waited for me to turn around, leaving an ugly blood-red stain on the grass.

"Leave them alone!" My fierce battle cry came out as a whimper.

He approached me and I could smell his revolting body odor mixed with alcohol and cigarettes. "You sympathize with their kind? These thieves who steal from our country? These people who work with the colonists to starve us?" the man hissed at me.

I did what any little girl does when she feels that she is in danger. Mustering all of the courage I had in me, I invoked that holy phrase that turns the sky black and rains daggers from the clouds, the only powerful hand that I could deal. "If you don't leave, I'm...I'm...I'm going to tell my father!"

The men started laughing at my declaration instead of my intended effect of instilling terror in their hearts. Divya, the more gregarious of the two sisters, helped me as I stood speechless. "Her father is Dr. Ba Maw," she said with quiet conviction.

Her statement was enough to send two of the men running, but the betel-chewing instigator remained, gazing at the knife in his right hand. He did not look up when he spoke to me. "Your father's name won't mean much soon. Just remember that," the thug warned me. It sent a chill through me because I wasn't sure if he was preparing to kill me at that moment, or foreshadowing bleak events to come. I held my breath in case he were to lunge at me, closing my eyes so that I would not have to see the knife coming.

I heard the familiar sound of a car engine behind me and opened my eyes to find the man gone, having run from the scene through the woods and leaving no trace of himself except for his betel nut spit.

My mother had returned home moments earlier and came immediately after Mala confessed everything. There was blackened fury in her eyes, the intensity of her glare and stony demeanor scaring me more than the men did. "Girls, get in the car. Nilar and Divya, I'll drive you home," May May ordered, and we did as we were told. The car ride was silent except for my friends' sobbing and polite thank you to my mother when we dropped them off.

I burst into tears as soon as we arrived home, a slow concoction of fear and anger permeating my body. My mind spun backwards to the gatekeeper incident, reopening a recent wound of being made to feel inferior because of my race. Yet, it was the very thing that had separated me from Nilar and Divya, the perceived superiority of my Burmese blood and class protecting me briefly. The thug's final words to me had left a rotten aftertaste in my mouth, a haunting admonition. Confusion wracked my very being and I didn't know what to think or believe anymore.

I followed my mother to the kitchen, where she placed a cold glass of water in my hand. "Drink," she ordered, her minced words and curt tone cutting my senses. "That was a very stupid thing that you did, Tinsa. You could have been hurt. You could have been…" May May's voice broke as she said this. It was one of the few times I would ever see my mother look vulnerable. I did not regret my actions but I felt responsible for causing her to feel this way, to be a source of pain for someone who did nothing but care for me.

"I know that I shouldn't have gone out, but what was I supposed to do when I saw my friends? They were in trouble," I reasoned.

She grabbed me by my shoulders, pulling me so close that the coolness of her silk clothing made my hot skin shiver. "I'm not going to tell your father, he has enough to worry about. But I am concerned for this Burmese heart of yours, Tinsa. Do you know that saying?" I shook my head no and she released her grip, leaving a dull ache where her hands had been.

"There is a fable going back before the time of the Buddha, when the first kings ruled this country. We were a poor people then and there were other kings desiring to fight us for our land, so the Burmese prayed to the gods for a favor. They answered our prayers and granted us not swords, but the hearts of gods to conquer our enemies. The young king who ruled during that time decided to use his power in his first battle, his heart beating so loudly and fiercely that the earth split and mountains shattered, trapping the invading armies. He continued to conquer his wars but he also grew weaker each time, his young man's body no match for the strength of a god's heart. The king collapsed on the eve of his most important battle, not dying from an enemy's blade but from exhaustion and misunderstanding his own power. Now what do you think this phrase means, a Burmese heart?"

"That the hearts of gods are not meant for mortals," I whispered.

"Right. It also means that we as a people, and especially you, are blessed and cursed with great strength. You must be sure to use it wisely and sparingly, " May May cautioned. She left me alone with this knowledge, the room silent except for my jumping pulse.

The thug had been right about my father. The riots were cause to remove my father from office, his rivals waiting patiently for the cracks to widen. The Thakins and independents flocked to join the GCBA Party, who promised equal representation in the new administration. The GCBA filed a formal petition lobbying for Dr. Ba Maw's resignation, citing a failure to control the peace, and U Chit Hlaing and U Pu emerged as the frontrunners for the soon-to-be vacant Prime Minister's seat. Phay Phay fought the charges though he had lost faith in the system and his seat by then, proven to be a ceremonial post all along. Only the Governor had the power to ameliorate the riots because he controlled the city's police force. Burma had no standing army of her own, thus the Prime Minister was useless in times of emergency without an independent armed force. It was also no coincidence that at the time, my father and the Sinyetha Party had plans to reform the tax structures of oil, teak and rubber companies, ruffling the feathers of foreign companies and providing an opportune moment for the Governor to rid himself of an increasingly radical administration.

Whatever his anxieties were, Phay Phay did not show an ounce of worry, going to his office every day and wearing the same mien of calm and continuity. I admired the way that he stood tall, his hands never trembling with sadness or fear, and how he wore a smile to his resignation in February 1939.

CHAPTER FOUR

I was elated when the schools reopened in February 1939 after an extended break period, having spent the greater part of my holiday grounded as a result of the ice cream incident. Mala and I rushed through the doors of St. John's with our school bags bouncing against our hips and our braids flying in the air, not caring if the nuns would give us a demerit for our bold hairstyle choice that day. We gathered in the assembly hall for the headmistress's welcome together with hundreds of schoolgirls collectively shrieking and hugging one another. I looked for Nilar and Divya's heads in the crowd, hoping that their amber eyes would be searching for mine too. I scanned the hall once, twice, five times, with no luck. "Marie," I nudged my friend, "where are Nilar and Divya?" Marie was one of my closest friends and neighbors, her family living three houses down from mine. She was a tiny wisp of a thing, almost a head shorter than me, and her poor vision required her to wear thick tortoiseshell glasses that magnified her onyx eyes to twice their original size. In spite of her bookish appearance, Marie had the ears of an owl and a mouth like a machine gun, so I knew that she could tell me where our friends were.

"Don't you know?" She seemed surprised by my question. "They're gone. Shipped off to Darjeeling for boarding school. Their whole family's gone," Marie said a matter-of-factly.

Before I could press her for more information, the doors in the back of the hall flung open, our cue to take our seats. Us schoolgirls scrambled to organize ourselves as the nuns walked to the stage in a neat line, their black habits flowing in rhythm. I was shocked by what I saw, or rather didn't see, when we were seated. The assembly hall, in which we used to tussle with each other for a place on the benches, was one quarter empty. "Students! Students!" our headmistress shouted over our loud whispers. "Please fill the seats in the front." The room was at a standstill as her hands flicked to several empty rows in front of the stage. My classmates and I scanned the room in unison, searching the pews for missing faces and smiles in vain.

I lost contact with Divya and Nilar, not knowing if they and the other girls from St. John's left because of what happened during the riots, or if their families sensed what was coming and escaped Rangoon before it was too late. On March 31, 1939, Great Britain announced that it would use military means to defend Poland's independence, the announcement that all of the nationalist activists were waiting for. The Crown had repeatedly denied self-determination for India and Burma, but was willing to go to war to preserve a European neighbor's sovereignty. U Pu from the GCBA had succeeded my father following his resignation, and the Governor wanted the new administration to declare war on behalf of the country following Great Britain's formal declaration of war on Germany on September 3. The new Prime Minister did not agree with involving Burma in a war thousands of miles away without the promise of independence. When the Governor and the Crown refused to discuss independence at all, U Pu ultimately refused to issue a war declaration and resigned as Prime Minister shortly thereafter. Galon U Saw, my father's partner during the Sayar San trial and the founder of the Myochit Party, seized the poisoned throne, becoming the third and last Prime Minister under British rule.

I began to notice a steady trickle of Japanese expatriates in Rangoon. There was already a small population of doctors and professionals who had emigrated during the previous two decades, fleeing their own wars and revolutions. One of the original Japanese émigrés, our family physician Dr. Suzuki, quietly maintained a general practice near my father's law office. The doctor was a placid, bespectacled man whose gentle touch and good bedside manner made him a trusted part of Rangoon's elite. I often saw him walking along the banks of the lake with his charcoal gray fedora and leather physician's bag, making house calls to lakefront villas. While many of us dreaded the unmerciful Rangoon heat, he did not seem to mind at all, smiling as he sauntered along the dusty roads without a drop of sweat in sight.

The new crop of Japanese transplants consisted of young men of university age, inconspicuously placed in Japanese companies and the embassy. Others found themselves awkwardly thrust into administrative roles at doctors' offices and clinics, ill at ease when patients sought help for their maladies. They did not seem want to blend in with the rest of Rangoon, never stopping to smile at a passerby or tipping their hats to a lady, content in their bubbled existence and hiding behind the safety of their desks.

I was too young to know that many of them were spies and too young to understand that war had already reached Burma. Two of these young men approached my father at his practice one day under the guise of seeking legal advice, dressed in smart, wool suits and their heavy leather shoes clacking on the freshly waxed floors. "How can I help you, gentlemen?" He assumed that they were businessmen looking to export food and rice back to Japan.

They told him brusquely that they were there on behalf of the Japanese government and that they were willing to offer a substantial amount of money for him to disrupt the Burma to Yunnan Road, the infamous Burma Road. The idea was so jarring and ludicrous that my father thought it a practical joke. Did the GCBA send them? Was it U Saw? At worst, the Governor or rival political factions had planted them to test his resolve. Even if he wanted to join the war at that point and was forced to choose between the Allied and Axis Powers, he did not have an army and Burma lacked a functioning government from which to launch such an enormous campaign. My father dismissed the young men, putting such thoughts out of his head. They did not seem perturbed by his refusal. The taller one tipped his hat, that small gesture suggesting that he would be seeing my father again.

All of the scattered pieces fell together shortly after when the Thakins came running back into the arms of the Sinyetha Party, the same young men who had all but abandoned Phay Phay during his resignation. A scandal had erupted in the Secretariat several days prior when U Saw and his Myochit Party had beaten the Thakins with bamboo sticks and palm leaves like some sort of teahouse fracas, fighting over the issue of separation from the British when war loomed. One by one, Aung San[9], Ba Hein[10], Thakin Than Tun[11] and U Nu[12] from the Thakins trickled into our foyer. My mother placed a pot of coffee and biscuits in front of them, the young men gorging on the fresh food as if they had not eaten in days. The nascent revolutionaries had come to my father for a simple reason: they needed him to start a rebellion.

These men are now historical giants – revolutionaries, ministers, presidents, martyrs – but they were young, inexperienced and utterly lost at the time. They were like unruly students approaching the headmaster for a second chance at a failed exam, repentant of their shortcomings and vowing to try harder. Aung San was undoubtedly the most charismatic and stubborn of the lot. He walked with a determined gait, his eyes always focused intently on the object or person of his interest. He had a habit of fixating on certain

---

[9] Thakin Party member, War Minister under Dr. Ba Maw, co-founded the Anti-Fascist People's Freedom League (AFPFL), assassinated with his cabinet on July 19 1947 (Martyrs' Day).

[10] Student leader; member of Thakin Party.

[11] Founding member of the Communist Party, formed in 1939. Minister of Land and Agriculture in Ba Maw government. Went underground in 1946 and assassinated on September 24 1968.

[12] Foreign Minister under Ba Maw government, first Prime Minister of the Union of Burma from January 1948 to June 1956, again from February 1957 to October 1958 and April 1960 to March 1962.

things with his entire being and would not relent until he had conquered an argument or obtained the object of his mania. Anything else was not worth his time, the young man unable to feign interest in things that did not draw his honest passion. Aung San was the shortest of the lot, perhaps an inch or two taller than my mother, but he possessed the power to command an entire room's attention with a glimpse of an eye, a divine propensity for charming the masses.

Thakin Than Tun, U Nu and Bo Let Ya[13] (who later joined the nightly meetings) were my parents' favorites from that rambunctious crowd. Phay Phay took an immediate liking to U Nu who was a cantankerous and erudite activist. U Nu's lopsided smile and rounded, traditional Bamar features belied a fierce intellect and formidable oratory skills, a man not accustomed to losing arguments. Whereas the others showed a polite deference to the elder (as most Burmese are culturally bound to do), he showed no fear in the presence of the former Prime Minister. U Nu found immense amusement in walking up to my father and baiting him into a heated debate. "The boy wastes no time," Phay Phay would boast of Thakin Nu. "In the sometimes duplicitous nature of our people, one face to show in public and another in private, that young man does not partition himself. He has, most importantly, gumption."

My mother found an immediate kinship with Than Tun and Bo Let Ya, both sharp-tongued and unforgivingly witty, but never unkind. Than Tun was openly Communist and was not shy about it. He was the author of some of the most brilliant and inflammatory articles against the colonial government, pamphlets as thin as rice paper floating in the mires of Rangoon's underground web. Than Tun made a habit of bringing two fresh copies of his articles to our home – one for

---

[13] A member of the Thirty Comrades, founding member of the Communist Party, Commander in Chief of the Burma Defence Army (BDA) under Gen. Aung San in 1944, Deputy Prime Minister under U Nu until 1952, joined Yan Naing and U Nu in their insurgency in 1969, killed by the Karen National Union (KNU) on November 29 1978.

my father and one for Ma Ma Gyi (Big Sister, as the Thakins came to call my mother) – slipped surreptitiously in between the pages of romance novels.

They were a ragtag bunch of untested revolutionaries who dreamed of a better destiny for their country, needing someone with the expertise and diplomacy to provide legitimacy for their movement. Thus, my father and the Sinyetha Party began talks with the Thakins and student leaders, the same young men who had left his side a year earlier. Nothing had changed about their fundamental beliefs since the early days of the Sinyetha and Thakin Parties. Dr. Ba Maw would always be a pragmatic realist, someone who valued patience and diplomacy, while the Thakins reveled in attacking and dismantling the status quo. Furthermore, there had been increasing arguments between Phay Phay and Aung San. Aung San accused my father of surrounding himself with sycophants and bottom-feeders and my father lashed out at Aung San for having a rose-tinted view of a world that he had not yet fully lived in as a young man in his early twenties. With an average age of twenty-five, these Thakins were barely out of their school greens, yawning like schoolboys when Phay Phay tried to explain to them that building a nation involved more than just blind faith in idealistic dogma.

I listened to and sometimes watched all of this, the birth of a new Burma, from the top of the staircase. Every evening after dinner, when the front door inevitably opened and the Thakins strutted in, my aunt Kinmimi and grandmother Daw Sein would perform a thorough inspection of the ground floor and ask us children to go upstairs to our bedrooms. My brother Zali, Mala and I used to sneak out of our rooms when we heard our aunt and grandmother's doors closing, listening to secret plans and whispers like spies in a novel. Zali and Mala abandoned me days into our mission, so I kept a stack of books on a nearby table to entertain me during the silences, squinting to read the words under a dim hallway sconce. On the third evening, I opened *The Jataka Tales* to find a copy of Thakin Than Tun's Communist pamphlet and a note.

To my youngest comrade, some readings for you to ponder the revolution.
Also, we can see the top of your head from the staircase, so you'd better work on your espionage skills if you are to help us.
TTT

I wanted to help but I didn't know how. My world had become such a dark and confusing place as of late. The gatekeeper incident and Nilar and Divya's suffering revealed a new side of my country to me, echoing my father's belief that Burma was ill and that the maladies of prejudice and injustice needed to be cured. The mass exodus of my friends and neighbors confirmed this diagnosis, that there was something terribly wrong that was scaring people away. I fell asleep at the top of the stairs during my philosophical pondering, stirring awake in my father's warm arms as he carried me to my room.

"Phay Phay, is something bad going to happen? Worse than before?" I asked him through a deep yawn, stretching my arms and legs across my mattress.

"Tinsa, what makes you think that?" he asked, his forehead rippled with concern.

"Because of all of these awful things that have happened. I have this funny feeling that, I don't know, it's building up to something. Your and May May's secret meetings only make this feeling worse, especially when you yell at the other men and they yell back."

"Oh." His face relaxed, giving way to a small but tired smile. "Do you remember all those years back when I told you that I fought with the other politicians not because I hated them, but because we were just trying to figure out how to help our country? Well, this is the exact same thing. All of the bad things that have happened are the things that we are trying to fix. It's not easy, but I do think things will get better."

"How can you be sure?"

"I can't, but I believe in justice. Do you know what that is? It's believing that righteousness and good will always win in the end."

My eyelids sank in the middle of our conversation but I did not let myself fall asleep before making my father promise me something. "Phay Phay, I don't like these secret meetings. I'm not a child anymore and I want to see what all of this means for myself. Will you and May May promise that you'll include me when you can?"

He held out his hand and we shook on it. "You're right, you're not a child anymore, Tinsa. I promise, you'll see for yourself what all of this means soon, though I'm not sure if that's a good or bad thing. Don't expect so much of adulthood, because your childhood and time itself are things that you can never have back. It's not so easy for us on this side of life."

In October 1939, the Sinyetha Party, the Thakins and student leaders formed the *Bama Htwet Yat Gaing* movement[14], forever enshrined as the Freedom Bloc. My father was elected President and Aung San the Secretary, making no secret of their differences. It proved to be more politically savvy to publicize their differing ideals, showing the nation that two men, the older generation and the new, could put aside their differences for the sake of independence. By December, the Freedom Bloc had aligned with every national political party with the exception of U Saw and the Myochit Party.

My father kept his promise. In February 1940, I accompanied my parents to the Secretariat for my father's first formal appearance as the leader of the Freedom Bloc and what would also be his last speech as a parliamentarian before resigning several months later. May May and I watched from the upper balcony as my father walked to the podium, the Freedom Bloc members saluting him along the way. Phay Phay bowed his head to the audience, and I could not tell if it was a hearty farewell or a respectful tribute to the very place that had elevated him to the highest office in the land but had also

---

[14] *Bama Htwet Yat Gaing* translates to "Burmese Association of the Way Out".

knocked him down. This February speech would become his most famous discourse as a politician, my father saying everything that needed to be said about the Crown's two-faced policy on independence, how they would rally to Poland's aid but never to their own colonies. How this deception bled through the hearts of the Burmese, that the colored peoples of the world would never find justice under imperialism. "Freedom and independence cannot be one thing in the west and another in the east. Our Burma deserves better!" he closed to a silenced chamber, my heart stopping when I felt the force of his tone. It was like a dagger viciously splitting every molecule in the room in half. I was not afraid of the finality of his words, a goodbye to the office that held mixed blessings. Instead, I feared that this was not simply an ending, but also the beginning of a cataclysmic shift, my father's speech sparking the light for a hidden fuse.

May May, Phay Phay and I were preparing to return home when we heard footsteps scrambling to catch up with us in the hallway. It was Somerset Butler, brother to the Earl of Carrick, his eyes brimming with admiration. Butler was a bit of an anomaly in Rangoon as a member of the fashionable Anglo set. He was one of few who openly socialized with the Burmese as a member of the House of Representatives. He tried to encourage my father to visit the Pegu Club as one of the privileges of being Prime Minister but Phay Phay would always decline, choosing instead to have tea with Butler in a café near the Secretariat. "I say, Dr. Ba Maw, it was an awfully good speech, one of the best I have ever heard. I wish I could speak like that."[15] To my father, men like Butler personified everything that was good and gracious about the British character, of great refinement, honor and humility. Another such man was Sir Stafford Cripps, who supported Burmese independence but wanted Burma to remain in the Commonwealth. There were many others like Butler and

---

[15] Dr. Ba Maw. *Breakthrough in Burma: Memoirs of a Revolution 1939-1946*. New Haven: Yale University Press, 1968.

Cripps who removed the veneer of prejudice and superiority and preferred to see men eye to eye.

I don't think Phay Phay knew how to reply to Butler's compliment because he remained uncharacteristically silent and solemn. Perhaps he was grappling with the realization that the looming war would inevitably separate them as enemies. Reading Dr. Ba Maw's furrowed eyebrows and faraway stare, Butler gave a graceful and sad smile. "I don't take it personally, Dr. Ba Maw. Politics...indeed a savage business."

My father shook Butler's hand and gave him a small, reassuring pat on the shoulder, a gesture that I had never seen him give to anyone before and certainly not to a Caucasian person. Mr. Butler got down on one knee to address me at eye level and I was transfixed by the clarity and intensity of his eyes. It is strange that I cannot recall the color of his eyes now, yet I can still feel their kindness and warmth, two pools of the clearest and stillest waters that I have ever seen. "Miss Tinsa," he addressed me with a grin, "I hear that you are quite the star student. If that is the case, keep up the good work. This country needs bright young people like you."

I was stricken with melancholy and confusion at Mr. Butler's sincerity. Was I truly looking into the eyes of a future enemy? Was war so savage that it turned a good and decent man into a foe, purely on the basis of differing politics? These are questions that continue to haunt me in my elder years. I have not yet found an answer.

At school, the nuns asked us to pray for the souls of those in Europe lost in war. They did not teach us about the ongoing atrocities but I listened to the news on the radio every evening. Patchy radio waves depicted blitzed villages and mass executions, unmarked graves piled high with crooked limbs. Hitler was bombing Europe bit by bit and his message of Aryan supremacy grew louder by the day, a sounding alarm that Asia would not be free under the Axis Powers. Oddly, there was not a single mention of the genocide of the Jewish people through the global and local media, and I'm not sure how many people around me were aware of the systematic depths to which Hitler would go to destroy those he deemed undesirable, inferior. I did pray, my eyes fixed on the dusty crucifix above the school altar, a Buddhist girl praying for strangers in a far away land hoping that someone, somewhere, would pray for the Burmese, too.

In April 1940, Aung San and the Thakins sought armed assistance, which Phay Phay considered with a heavy conscience. There were more secret meetings in the back room of our house, my father in constant shouting mode with the younger revolutionaries. They were ready for guns, bloodshed, bombs and heroics that they had read about in newspapers and history books, but had never seen or ran from in person. Aung San and Thakin Than Tun suggested contacting the Chinese due to similarities in ideology, an impossibility in my father's eyes. The Chinese had partnered with Great Britain on the global war front; how could the Burmese possibly ally with those who were in cahoots with their colonial government? Would the Chinese risk their arrangement with Great Britain for the sake of little Burma? And what would they really expect of Burma in exchange for help?

There was only one other way to acquire guns and that was to reach out to the Japanese. We were in awe of the Japanese during that era, conjuring images of brave warriors, a fortified kingdom, and vast armies. As a child, I learned about Japan's great victory during the Russo-Japanese War, a legacy showing that Asians, deemed an inferior race, could militarily dominate a western power. It remained the only unconquered kingdom in Asia, fending off foreign military and commercial advances when so many of us could not. Children used to play the *samurai game* in which boys slung makeshift swords made of bamboo sticks and fought each other, with the winning side declared as samurai and the losing side European.

Thakin Than Tun and Thakin Soe were ardent Communists whose deepest loyalties were with China. They warned the others about the Japanese Imperial Army's desire to conquer the whole world, that they should not allow for their message of "Asia for Asians" to mean anything other than there would be one Asia under Japanese command. "Look at what they've done to Manchuria and Korea, regions far stronger than us. Their warlords will enslave us, the Burmese only fit to wipe the shoes of the Manchurians, who wipe the shoes of the Japanese," lamented Thakin Soe.

My father wrote to Governor Cochrane one last time, extending a final offer to discuss Burma's independence as diplomats, as gentlemen, and to broker a deal that would suit both sides. *Thousands, if not millions, will die if we go to war on opposing sides. As we have mentioned before, we will not fight for you if the Crown refuses independence. Please consider this*, he pleaded the Governor.

Cochrane never replied. The Freedom Bloc contacted our physician, Dr. Suzuki, in April 1940. The old man's hands quivered as he delivered a message to the Japanese embassy. We prepared for war.

* * * * *

U Nu and Thakin Than Tun went missing the following May, the absence of their booming laughs carving a void in our home. The government had long suspected clandestine operations and arrested them after the final Thakin Party Conference in which they declared armed uprising. They were tossed into overcrowded jails festering with rats and cholera with the likes of bandits and murderers. The others went into hiding while my mother sent parcels of food, medicine, money and clean clothes to them through secret messengers.

I will never forget the one-eyed man who arrived in Rangoon amidst the chaos. His name was Colonel Suzuki, later to be immortalized as Bo Mogyo (General Thunderbolt) after an ancient fable that a strike of lightning would hit the Burmese king's palace and disrupt the course of history. A slim man with refined, sharp Japanese features, he had a habit of scurrying about town as if in a perpetual hurry, with his fingers anxiously twisting the right tip of his moustache. Suzuki became famous for showing up at teahouses and asking patrons if they would like to hear about the origins of his glass eye. "Look! Look!" he would point to his right eye. "Do you know who gave this to me?"

The men of Rangoon shook their heads no in confusion, wondering who the drunk Japanese man was who was shouting at them. "The Chinese did this to me. And they can all rot in hell!" he would shout into the night, street dogs howling in unison with him.

While Suzuki trolled teahouses and cafes for intelligence, my father and the Bloc struggled to hold on. The remaining members were detained or went underground, hunted like dogs. The Freedom Bloc held its last conference in Mandalay in the wet of June, 20,000 supporters coming to see Dr. Ba Maw, the last man standing. He knew that the government was watching and that there were spies interspersed in the crowd. My father sermonized the Bloc's manifesto one last time and uttered the words that sealed his fate, the declaration that the government had been waiting for. *We will use all means necessary to defend our country, including armed means.* Phay Phay's Mandalay Speech ended his cat and mouse game with the Governor, who had been waiting to arrest my father on charges of sedition.

They finally took my father away on August 6, 1940, the most high-profile Freedom Bloc member saved for last. On that day, Zali, Mala and I were playing hide-and-seek in the garden, camouflaged in the wild rose bushes. I was particularly proud of my hiding spot, a nook no bigger than three feet in diameter nestled in the heart of a dying *Chinensis* bush. My excitement turned to worry when I stopped hearing Zali's footsteps on the dry grass and Mala's heavy breathing from her hiding place, two bushes down from my own. I managed to crawl from beneath the bush without encountering any thorns, but the *Chinensis's* rotting fuchsia petals stubbornly clung to my hair and cotton shirt. Realizing that it was almost dinnertime, I ran to the front of the house leaving a trail of broken rose petals behind me, in time to see dozens of mounted policemen trotting to our front door.

I had never seen officers in such grand uniforms before,

their gold medals and pennants jangling a step behind the tempo of their horses' footsteps. The horses were the size of three water buffalo and I was amazed at how placid and docile the great beasts remained under their masters' command. One of the poor beasts, a mare with an auburn coat, looked at me with great sad eyes and was straining beneath the weight of her portly rider. I wondered why, with all of her strength, she did not kick the fat man off her back and run away.

A lone officer broke from the line to address my parents, who also heard the commotion and had come outside to meet our unwelcome guests. Our maids, who had also never seen such a grand display of militarism before, had pushed the front window curtains aside to stare at the scene from the safety of the indoors. The officer, whom I presumed to be the captain judging by the ostentatious plumage of his hat, greeted us with stoicism. "Dr. Ba Maw, you are hereby to be tried under the Defense of Burma Rules for sedition," he exclaimed, spittle flying from his lips as he read a directive. "You will come with us peacefully and stand trial, or we shall be forced to detain you under the orders of the Governor."

At the sound of the word "Governor," the officers raised their revolvers and pointed them at Phay Phay's head. He did not blink at the sight of guns. Instead, he grinned in the midst of the standoff. My mother, on the other hand, placed herself in front of her husband and chanted Buddhist prayers under her breath, willing it all to go away. Even though I knew that prayers could not physically stop their bullets, I began to chant with her in a show of unity.

"As gentlemen, I will ask that you not point your guns at women and children. You know better than that," my father chided the captain. Several tense moments passed before the captain waved his hand as if he were holding a magician's wand, the revolvers disappearing instantaneously.

"You will come peacefully, Dr. Ba Maw."

"Indeed, because I have done nothing wrong." Phay Phay placed a gentle hand on May May's shoulder, their eyes locking. "We both knew this was coming. Remember what I told you…" He whispered something in her ear, my mother's eyes dancing with sorrow, rage and vengeance.

May May continued to stand in front of the door after they took him away, looking out at the expanse of Rangoon as if she were expecting someone. Aunt Kinmimi, who had quietly appeared at her side, dared not touch her sister, afraid that she might break. "What can we do to help?" was all she could ask.

"They're taking him to Mandalay and will try him for conspiring with the Japanese. We haven't even heard anything from the Japanese." My mother was speaking to herself, Aunt Kinmimi with no knowledge of politics as she kept her nose out of her brother-in-law's dealings. My aunt asked me to take my siblings upstairs and to keep them occupied until dinner. I did as I was told.

When my brothers and sisters asked me where our father went, I replied tersely, "Mandalay."

"Where the kings and queens lived?"

"Yes, where the old palace is."

"Will you tell us a story about a king?" Mala pleaded, a child's game. I told them stories of many kings and queens who braved battles, mythical creatures, fierce enemies and dark magic in lands not so far away.

"Did they come back home after their battles?" inquired Binnya, the youngest.

"They did," I said with such conviction that I almost believed my own stories.

* * * * *

After my father's incarceration, Aung San and Bo Yan Aung[16] left the country when they did not hear from the Japanese. With a bounty of five rupees on his head, Aung San snuck on a cargo ship and landed in Amoy, sending a messenger to our home to confirm his arrival. The remaining

---

[16] A member of the Thirty Comrades, Communist Party leader, killed during Communist Party purge on December 26 1967.

holdouts – Bo Let Ya, Nagani Tun Shwe, Ba Hein and my mother – continued working in the back room. I held my head against the door listening to clandestine route plans, sourcing supply lines and lists of who could be trusted and who were spies.

My family and I were not permitted to contact my father during his initial weeks in detainment, so I followed his trial through newspapers. He was charged under the Defense of Burma Rules for collaborating with the Japanese and sentenced for an indefinite period of time beginning on August 28, 1940. His trial took place in Mandalay in what the government had hoped would be a final warning to the Burmese about the repercussions of dissent, but instead fomented nationalist outrage. The local police force and my father's armed escorts, who were employees of the Crown, saluted him as he walked into the courtroom. Hundreds of Bloc supporters stood in his car's path as it pulled away from the courthouse, the Governor sending additional forces to break up the protesters. Those who were arrested gleefully skipped to jail holding their handcuffs proudly above their heads, their jailhouse uniforms a source of pride.

The authorities transferred my father to the Rangoon Central Jail in September. If the Governor had thought that Rangoon would have been a more quiet prison for the former Prime Minister, the capital exploded in demonstrations and protests the day that my father arrived. Finally, he was transferred to a small jail in Mogok, a long forgotten hill station nestled within the most valuable ruby mines in the world. It was a quaint arrangement with only a handful of other prisoners who kept to themselves. Phay Phay was permitted to write to us and we received his letters once a week. My siblings and I would race to the bottom of our driveway for the postman and I would always win, holding the victorious envelope in my hand like a trophy. He asked us not to worry, that he was spending his days stretching his legs in the garden in the cool mountain air, reading whatever books or newspapers the guards decided to bring that day.

My father's absence took a toll on all of us. I no longer cared about my schoolwork and began daydreaming in my classes, concocting grand schemes to break him out of jail. My grades suffered as a result and I couldn't focus when the headmistress called me into her office to discuss my performance. I was grateful that she was concerned for me, but the thought of exams and composition books and uniforms seemed so frivolous when my father was sitting in a cell somewhere, his fate undecided.

May May suffered the most. On some nights, I heard her cursing at my father for the mess that he had gotten her into, how she should let him and the others rot in jail. Her cursing was followed by stifled wails, erased by the time morning came. With my father gone, there was no one that she could turn to with her deepest secrets. How lonely she felt. The strain of caring for their six children in addition to her sister and mother, who was in the early stages of dementia. During dinner one evening, Daw Sein entered the dining room covered in her most valuable jewelry, her life's work. Tears stung my cheeks as I stared at my grandmother, who was wearing a wrinkled nightgown beneath clusters of rubies, sapphires, diamonds, emeralds and gold, clutching in her hands whatever items she could not fit on her body. Daw Sein babbled nonsense about how the king's taxmen were conspiring to charge her additional fees in preparation for war, reciting a stream of outdated laws and regulations in a manic soliloquy. I continued to cry at the horrific scene, an eyewitness to my grandmother's nightmarish battle between her iron mind and the encroachment of her fate. While my mother sat frozen in her chair, powerless in her sorrow, my aunt Kinmimi gracefully stood up from her chair and took their mother by her elbow, escorting her upstairs to her room where she remained for the rest of the night.

The following afternoon, Mala and I came home from school and walked into the living room to see our grandmother with three iron trunks at her feet. Her eyes were lucid and cloudless. I could smell the rose essence in her clothes, pressed into the threads. May May sat perpendicular to her with bulbous moons under her eyes, lost in conversation with her mother. My sister and I arrived in the middle of my grandmother telling our mother, "Please, I want you to take these. You need them."

My mother put her hands up and waved no, defiantly. "I can't take these from you. It's too much. It's all," her voice broke as she said this, "too much."

"Take them before it's too late. I will be forgetting them, and everything else, soon. Do something useful with them. You know what I'm talking about." My grandmother flicked her eyes to look at my sister and me and I was not even aware that she knew that we were in the room. I held my breath under her leonine gaze, startling in its sharpness and determinedness. "Come, little ones," she beckoned us while unlocking the three trunks. The hinges screeched like crows as my grandmother pried the reluctant iron covers open. I gasped when I saw what was inside: every single piece of jewelry, precious gems, gold nuggets and silver bars that she had acquired over a lifetime. The sum total of her life's work was in those three boxes, capturing every step of Daw Sein's journey from a young widow to one of Burma's most powerful jewelers.

My grandmother dug her hands indiscriminately into a pile, pulling whatever item happened to catch her fingertips and placing it on the table. "Now, you are going to help me sort everything and I will tell you how to discern the value of an item. Tinsa and Mala, you need to learn how to appraise jewelry. It might be helpful one day, should it ever come to that. I hope that day never comes, but you should know regardless," Daw Sein said with just a hint of sadness, her voice quavering beneath the jangling of pendant chains and scattered stones. May May was too drained to argue with her mother, acquiescing and creating separate mounds of necklaces, rings, earrings, bracelets, watches, loose gems and precious metals. Mala looked longingly at the jewelry, the yellows, reds, blues, greens and brilliant whites bursting in the reflection of her welled tears. My sister sobbed as each piece passed through her hands like water, meant to be held for only a few grasping moments before it was to go on its way.

    I thought that my hands would shake while sifting through all of my grandmother's worldly possessions. They didn't, holding steady as I let the cool metals sit in my feverish palms. I took mental notes of each and every piece, recording its weight, the smoothness of the settings and finish, and how some of the pieces seemed to burn like ice. Millions of rupees, dollars, pounds passed through my hands yet I was not interested in their monetary value. I felt proud of my grandmother, that her will was stronger than gold or diamonds, and that she had persevered to collect such beautiful things yet was also unattached to them. I envied her last act of freedom in her final days, to be released of the anticipation of pain.

    Mala tiptoed to my bed at midnight not long after we had inventoried the contents of the iron trunks. I caught a glimpse of the full yellow moon from my window, the only time of the month when I could see a man's face staring back at me from that far away planet. He seemed to be smiling on this dark night, the sky an opaque navy. "Tinsa," Mala tugged at my shirt hem, "come downstairs with me. I want some water."

    I obliged and got out of bed, even though I knew that my sister was looking for an excuse to return to the living room and look at our grandmother's jewelry one more time. She took my hand and navigated us down the dimly lit staircase, refusing to carry a lantern. A recent growth spurt had left me with oversized feet and lanky, toothpick legs that knocked about as I hurried to catch up to my sister's speed. Mala let go of my hand when we crossed the threshold to the living room and she ran to the second trunk, carefully lifting its cover so as to not make a sound in the night. She did not need light to see through the darkness. As soon as she opened the trunk, the moonlight and jewelry collided, illuminating the room in gold, silver, ruby and sapphire rays.

    "Mala, don't," I warned my sister, but I was not quick enough to stop her from reaching into the pile. She did not need to search long; Mala pulled her hand back victoriously, holding a simple gold chain with a single solitaire ruby on the pendant. The stone was cut in a rough, antique fashion, jagged like the edges of a cliff. The gold hue was tinged with specks of brown and mustard yellow, inferior to the dandelion hue of the most valuable grade. The pendant was far from the most valuable item but its flaws did not matter to Mala. All that mattered to my sister was that it was the most beautiful to her for reasons that only she would know.

"Your turn," Mala goaded me as she clasped the chain around her neck.

"You're going to get in so much trouble!" I chastised her, yet I knew that I did not have the heart to reveal her secret to anyone.

"I don't care!"

"How are you going to wear that thing without anyone noticing? Especially May May," I reasoned with my sister, who was hypnotized by the ruby's eye, its magenta rays flashing in her irises. Mala did not respond to me, instead grabbing me by my hand again and dragging me outside to our secret hiding place between the rose bushes, where we had been when we last saw our father. She dropped to her knees in a crash of loose dirt and bones and began digging a hole in the center of her deigned hide-and-seek enclave. Her delicate fingers, which were so nimble and would later serve her well as a prominent doctor, attacked the soil with a surgeon's precision. She gouged a small crater so deep that I could no longer see where it ended under the bright moonlight. When Mala felt satisfied, she looked up at me exultantly with her hands, arms and white cotton nightgown splotched with pure earth. The silence that stood between us was interrupted by the click of the pendant's clasp. Before I realized it, Mala had thrown the necklace into the pit and began to bury the mound as furiously as she had unearthed it.

"Why did you do that? That didn't belong to you!" I hissed. I was enraged that she had violated our grandmother's wishes, going against the sacred act of an elder's final requests.

"Tinsa," my sister looked at me innocently, "what I don't understand is how you can let go of these things so easily. I just wanted to keep something for myself because everyone and everything keeps disappearing and I don't know where they go."

My heart ached for my little sister and I was angry with myself for judging her so harshly. Up until that point, I had assumed that Mala, being the younger sister and my shadow, had viewed the world through my eyes. Her act of burying an insignificant necklace was her way of coping with a fleeting childhood and past, whereas I saw liberation in the form of my grandmother giving away all of her earthly possessions. I was ready to let go of my childhood but my little sister, and perhaps my other siblings whom I did not consider, were grieving the loss of theirs, which had come too soon in our father's absence.

Mala and I never spoke of the buried necklace again, but I thought of her in the weeks following that incident. My family had not heard news of my father's status though my mother went to see him in Mogok. I was not allowed to join her on her visits but I noticed that the Freedom Bloc's care packages multiplied each time she returned. As care packages and supplies increased, the items in Daw Sein's trunks decreased, until finally there was nothing left. I had no real attachment to my grandmother's things so I did not grieve for them like Mala did. I only grieved when I stopped hearing the familiar clinking of my mother's heavy gold chains and when I no longer heard the sharp rustling of her beloved silk *longyi*s, now replaced with the soft chafing of thin cotton.

* * * * *

There was radio silence from Aung San for months. It has been theorized that he tried to strike a deal with the Chinese, no one truly sure of what happened in Amoy except for Aung San himself. I am inclined to believe that he did try to negotiate with the Chinese before approaching the Japanese, similar to my father's private letter to Cochrane asking for one last opportunity to discuss Burma's independence without resorting to war. I think that if my father or the other Freedom Bloc members were in his position, they would have done the same. In any case, Aung San did not manage to reach the Chinese. Stranded in Amoy, penniless, in ill health and in a poor emotional state, Aung San's messages were repeatedly intercepted by the Japanese until Colonel Suzuki's men managed to track him down in November 1940. There are no records of Suzuki and Aung San's first meeting but they struck a deal and Aung San took the next ship back to Burma in March 1941 to find recruits for a brand new army.

The new independence army was to be comprised of the brightest young minds. Lawyers. Doctors. Engineers. Activists. Aung San called on those already in the Freedom Bloc – Bo Let Ya, Bo Yan Naing[17], Bo La Yaung, Bo Mo – to form the first batch as Burma's best revolutionaries. They left with the clothes on their backs, crumpled photos of loved ones and pockets filled with Burmese soil as a promise to return one day. Bo Let Ya in later years would reminisce how the only food they had during that arduous trek were the biscuits and meal packets that my mother prepared.

Everything fell apart after the original batch departed. Countless hand-selected recruits dropped out one by one and Aung San struggled to find anyone he could to be a part of his nascent revolutionary force. Desperate, he sent a messenger to my mother and begged her to find more recruits, risking his life and hers in the passage of this note. Again, fate intervened and she did not receive the note until long after he left. Aung San took whomever he could on the last ship leaving for Hainan on March 27, 1941.

These men would make history as the Thirty Comrades.

---

[17] Tinsa's husband. A member of the Thirty Comrades, student leader, hero of the Battle of Shwedaung in 1942, formed insurgent group in 1965 until 1980, returned to Rangoon after the 1980 amnesty.

Aung San, Setkya[18] and Ne Win led the staff because of their seniority and experience. Let Ya, La Yaung and Ze Ya were in charge of regular combat duty, to lead future troops into battle. Yan Naing, Lin Yone and Min Gaung were the youngest members and gifted with individual fighting skills, placed in charge of clandestine and guerrilla tasks. The Comrades finished their training in September 1941 just after the Atlantic Charter declared that the Allied powers would "…respect the right of all people to choose the form of government under which they will live, and sovereign rights and self-government returned to those who have been forcibly deprived" (Article III). Winston Churchill clarified that Article III did not apply to the British colonies.

In their final moments as civilians, each Comrade sliced his hand and dripped his blood into a bowl in an ancient blood drinking ceremony called *Thwe Thauk*, once a rite of passage for royal soldiers before serving their kingdoms. There is much controversy over who sat in for the ceremony, some in later years claiming that others were not present. They took this secret to their graves, bonded in silence. The Comrades passed the bowl until each had a sip; brothers in blood, brothers in war.

---

[18] A member of the Thirty Comrades, went underground after 1962 coup, joined Yan Naing in his insurgency and died before U Nu's arrival.

Dr. Ba Maw in BIA uniform

CHAPTER FIVE

On Monday, December 8, 1941, I took my usual route to school walking along the edges of Kandawgyi Lake until I reached Prome Road which was the primary artery linking upper and lower Rangoon. I felt serene for the first time in a long time, taking slow steps on the cracked sidewalks and studying the trees and plants that had bloomed for the winter season. Christmas was nearing and I made a mental list of all of the books that I wanted to read over my holiday break. Dickens, Bronte and Sun Tzu's *The Art of War* were on my list by recommendation of my father, who had written to me from prison. Phay Phay sounded in good spirits and hopeful that he would be released soon. Though my family and I were unsure of his release, it was a relief to hear his optimism.

I entered St. John's and breathed its musky smell, a combination of aging wood and old books. It was a cool morning but I was sweating from my walk. I self-consciously dabbed my neck and underarms with talcum powder to mask my body odor, an uncomfortable and unwelcome hallmark of puberty. Flecks of rose-scented powder flew about me as I dashed to the chapel room, which was the new location of our school meetings instead of the large convocation hall due to the dwindling number of students. Two dozen of the holdouts were sitting in front of the altar with their hands clasped in prayer, including my bespectacled friend Marie and Mala, who had arrived earlier that morning for her music lessons. The headmistress was in the middle of morning prayers and she appeared more solemn than usual. She closed her eyes tightly, painfully, as if she were trying to hold back tears. I looked to the nuns at her side who were equally grave with their expressions, clutching their rosaries so firmly in their hands that I could see dull blue veins bursting from beneath their thin ivory skin. "And let us pray, let us pray," the headmistress stammered, "for the souls lost in war. May they rest knowing that the innocent shall always find salvation in the end."

Amen, my schoolmates and I whispered in unison. I had heard the headmistress say that prayer many times before, but the severity of her melancholic tone stayed with me for the remainder of the day. It was not until the day's end when I found out what had transpired. Marie, Mala and I were standing in front of the school's iron gates waiting for our mothers to fetch us when a young paperboy walked by with a bundle of newspapers in his arms. He caroled through his betel-stained teeth, "The Japanese have attacked Pearl Harbor! The Americans rally to war! Get your papers! I repeat, the Japanese have attacked and America is now at war!"

I chased after him and grabbed a copy from the stack, thrusting whatever money I had in my coin purse in his inky palms. His eyes went wide at the wad of crumpled notes in his hand. "Keep the change," I mumbled as I scanned the front page. I did not want it to be true but the grotesque photos of the attack on Pearl Harbor were splashed all over the front page. Burma had so far escaped the ravages of modern warfare and I could not picture what war looked like until that moment. Moreover, I was stunned to learn that the Japanese had attacked on American soil, evoking lessons of the Russo-Japanese War that I had learned about when I was younger. It was unthinkable that anyone could have dared to provoke the United States of America and succeeded in paralyzing its Pacific fleet, behemoths now lying dormant at the bottom of Hawaii's paradisiacal waters.

Shocked, I called out to the newspaper boy and asked naively, "What does this mean? What does it mean for us?"

He stopped in his tracks, looking at me with an amused grin, as if he were addressing a young child and not an older girl. "Sister, sister...Burma is going to fight now. Don't you know that?" He bared his cherry red teeth at me again before continuing on his way.

I couldn't breathe. I had foolishly assumed that everything, even politics, would wait until my father came home. If Burma were to fight, then who would protect our family if not him? How would we survive when almost everyone we knew was missing or in jail? I couldn't inhale, my lungs refusing to obey my mental command of *Breathe! Breathe! Breathe!* I gripped my throat with both hands, preparing to faint on the sidewalk.

"Tinsa, are you okay?" Marie rushed to my side, her alarmed eyes magnified by her glasses.

I shook my head *no, no, no*. At last a gulp of oxygen fought its way down my throat, kicking my lungs and releasing me from my panic.

Hearsay ran rampant in the days following the attack on Pearl Harbor.

The Japanese are mad to have attacked the Americans. How foolish they are!

They are not crazy – Japan would not have attacked such a great power if they were going to lose!

Asians must unite behind the Japanese...God must be behind this victory!

Warplanes rained pamphlets from the skies, igniting the Japanese Imperial Army's propaganda campaign in Burma. Children ran to dance in the streets beneath showers of newly printed paper. It was a parade, a supposed celebration for all. The air smelled of cheap ink and engine exhaust, the scent of encroaching war machines.

The Japanese will die for Burma's independence.

Asians are united as one. Asia for Asians!

The Japanese are your friends! They are loyal to the Burmese cause!

Propaganda messages swept the radio waves, the same mottos chanted with brutal conviction. Japanese voices crossed with British sources documenting the war in Europe and denouncing Japan's attack on Pearl Harbor. It was one man's victory and another's despair.

The remnants of the Thakins burst into our home on a balmy evening in the cover of darkness, seeking my mother's help. My father, Thakin Than Tun, Thakin Soe, Thakin Nu and all of the major leaders were in jail. I did not recognize their panicked faces or their worried voices, deducing that they were with Than Tun's Communist faction while eavesdropping on their conversation. "Did you see what the Japs did to the Americans? They've dragged us all to hell!" the faceless de facto leader screamed in frustration. My mother asked him to lower his tone as children were in the house. "This was a terrible mistake and we will pay for this. We said yes to the Japanese because we were against the British and them alone. Now we are to fight the Americans too and we don't stand a chance!" His cries turned into racking sobs, desperation reeking in the night air. May May did nothing to comfort the young man shaking with fear, letting him cry until silence filled the room again.

My mother was keeping a secret from us, from everyone she knew. At that very moment, Aung San and the Thirty Comrades had crossed the border into Burma, hundreds of men entering Rahaeng through Mae Sot, Tavoy and Victoria Point. Villagers supporting the Freedom Bloc cheered as they saw the distinct green uniforms, leaving meal packets and notes of encouragement for their heroes. Village boys, desiring adventure and with a bone to pick with the colonial government, followed after them, their mothers only too willing to let their sons fight. In the midst of this, Bo Let Ya sent a scrap of yellowed parchment hidden in coffee grounds to our home: *Landfall. Get out. Go north.*

* * * * *

I remember the day that Rangoon went ablaze, each fleeting second still fresh in my mind after seven decades. On December 23, 1941, my mother announced that we would be going upcountry to Mogok where my father was imprisoned. It was an ideal time to leave. U Saw, the third and last Prime Minister, had been arrested for treason and the entire local government was dismantled, yet the country's affairs went on as usual under the Governor's orders in spite of this. Rumors of a pending attack grew by the hour through word of mouth and escalating radio broadcasts, convincing my mother even more that leaving Rangoon would be in our best interests.

The Burmese Independence Army (BIA) enters Rangoon

It was a calm, dry day, the peak of winter that brings cool and arid winds. I tiptoed about the house, boarded and lifeless in the thick of the trees. Everything was shut away, packed, static. I noticed how alien our home looked without the usual flurry of nannies chasing after the children or vines breaking against the gardener's shears. Most of the household help had returned to their villages, my mother having given them advanced wages knowing she could not save them all when Rangoon was eventually attacked. Our family – my mother, aunt, grandmother and six children - was minutes away from leaving for the railway station when I heard a buzzing noise in the air. It sounded like a pack of fruit flies eager to attack uncovered plates of fresh, syrupy fruit. The buzzing, at first dull, became sharper and louder until my eardrum pressed against my temple, the drone of airplane engines in the skies above Rangoon. They circled once, twice, pirouettes spinning in the clouds. I ran outside to the garden to look up at the sky, agape with naïve wonder.

Smoke began to rise from every strategic corner of the city, thick plumes of charcoal and lavender dust. The port. Bridges. Major roads. Most importantly, the railway station. We were due to take the train to Mogok, a two-day journey through the dry zone and through the mountains. We would have been bombed to pieces had we left the house ten minutes earlier. My mother, who had been standing on our porch, scrambled to the car and jammed the keys into the ignition to turn on the radio. Every station confirmed that the Japanese bombers had destroyed all of the major transportation links. We were trapped in Rangoon.

The radio messages snapped me from my daze and my first instinct was to make sure that my younger siblings were safe. I struck our front doors open and ran through every room on the ground floor, my footsteps racing to beat the rhythm of the crashes outside. I found my five younger siblings huddled underneath the dining room table, holding one another and covering their ears. Binnya, my littlest brother at just four years old, was curled in a fetal position on Mala's lap with a river of tears flowing down his plump cheeks. "Are you okay?" I screamed to compete with the explosions outside. Zali and Mala nodded yes. I realized that my younger siblings' nanny, Mee Mee, was not in the room with them. "Where's Mee Mee?" I shouted at Zali and Mala, who threw their hands in the air and shook their heads no. "Stay here until May May comes!" I ordered while I ran to get our mother.

Little black oblong objects continued to sprinkle on my city like flakes of pepper, nimble droplets of carnage. Smoke came before the sharp blasts, and amidst the chaos I spotted Mee Mee standing beneath the large guava tree next to the front gates. She was smiling euphorically at the sky and there was a thin line of blood trickling from her ear down to her chin, her eardrum ruptured as a result of the bombings. She clasped her hands in a prayer hold, fingertips grazing her chin as if some heavenly deity were looking down on her from the clouds. I approached her cautiously, careful to intrude on what I believed to be a sacred and religious moment. I got close enough to smell the iron in her blood mixed with the cloying aroma of fallen guavas. "Mee Mee, are you all right?" I asked gently.

She did not turn to address me, continuing to stare off into the heavens. "The Japanese have finally come. We are saved," she wept with joy.

Mee Mee's words were the last thing I remembered before everything blurred. I did not lose full consciousness but I drifted in and out of awareness, seeing things as if I were watching filmstrips or a moving slideshow of someone else's life. I saw my mother arguing with the drivers and pointing at unmarked roads on yellowed maps. Then my observations cut to a scene in which my aunt Kinmimi walked out of the house linked arm-in-arm with my grandmother, Daw Sein, while my siblings followed them like ducklings. I don't remember getting in the car or driving away from our home, only that I regained my awareness two days later while our convoy was passing through Phyu. I had been holding my grandmother's warm hand in my lap, the sensation of which jumpstarted my nerves and awakened me.

My family and I arrived safely in Mogok after five long days traveling through back alleys and country roads, avoiding all coastal areas, highways, landing strips and city centers that were of strategic importance. Our path was a cemetery; what used to be green hills, carefully tended farmland and solitude was now the site of a massacre. The countryside was completely scorched, dead, not a hint of green to indicate signs of life. Bodies were strewn along the road, faces burnt beyond recognition, hands frozen and clutching at the earth in a final act of desperation. "The British are burning everything in retreat and the Japanese are bombing everything's that left," our driver croaked, unable to register the scale of destruction that had only just begun. He did not say anything for hundreds of desolate miles, his eyes flushed with tears.

Our family friends, Daw Pu and U Lay Kyi, waited for us at their hilltop ranch in Mogok with my uncle Ba Han and his family who had arrived several weeks before us. Daw Pu and U Lay Kyi did their best to accommodate our enormous brood, converting their formal dining and living rooms into a makeshift campsite. We settled in as best as we could by choosing our own corners and unpacking what few belongings we brought in our respective spaces. Aunt Kinmimi drew up a daily school lesson schedule for my younger siblings in order to create a sense of continuity in their lives. Zali, Mala and I took turns quizzing each other on history, mathematics and science, keeping our minds sharpened for whenever the schools reopened. It was the Christmas break period and we remained hopeful that things would be back to normal in a few weeks.

It was impossible to hide from what was happening below the hills no matter how hard we tried. Thick mushroom clouds appeared on the horizon, inching closer each day. The smell of distant rot and burnt gasoline hung in the air, the crisp mountain breeze the only thing preventing us from suffocating. The once vibrant reds, oranges, greens of the forest gave way to a murky brown landscape, the unmistakable hue of waste and death. At fourteen going on fifteen, I was allowed to sit with the adults in the evenings and listen to the news on the small brown transistor radio. We could not hear anything on most days except for empty static. The news was macabre on the rare occasion that we did. "The British are killing all Burmese on sight. Do not trust them!" the Japanese propaganda station railed.

"The Japanese will murder all of you! They want you as their slaves!" cried an Allied propaganda operator. Both sources would go on to describe mass executions, rapes, looting, the incineration of villages, fingers pointing at the other like daggers. It was a guessing game as to who had really committed them, impossible to know the truth from the blurred transmittals.

During my sleepless nights, of which there were many, I would lie awake thinking about my life in Rangoon. I yearned for the everyday things that I used to take for granted: the occasional ripples of the grand lake across from my home, the quiet shuffling of monks' robes during their morning alms on my street and gusts of sandalwood and jasmine blowing down on the city from the Shwedagon Pagoda. I suffered from night terrors, jolting awake every time that I thought I heard bootsteps. It seems ridiculous to me now, but the whole family would run and hide underneath mosquito nets whenever we thought we heard sirens or soldiers' footsteps, curling at the corners of our mattresses and hoping that the sheer fabric would somehow save us from bullets, a bayonet, or worse.

The person who suffered the most remained silent. My grandmother, Daw Sein, was in her late seventies but looked older than her years. Her hair had turned completely white during the arduous journey from Rangoon, bombs and gunshots too much for her to cope with. She sat in front of the bay window all day long, clutching her earth green meditation beads and staring at the distant hills that were so familiar to her. Mogok was and continues to be the source of Burma's famous rubies and sapphires. The precious stones and metals that had made her into one of Burma's wealthiest women came from the very ground that we stood on, being destroyed before her eyes. I could not hold conversations with her due to her deteriorating state, so I would sit next to her and stare out the window with my grandmother because I didn't want her to be alone. And maybe I didn't want to feel alone, either.

My grandmother passed away peacefully in her sleep about two months into our stay at Mogok, her remains wrapped in a clean white cloth and laid to rest amongst the ruby mines and Shan ruins. Her burial day was one of the loveliest spring days in years, the mountain air blowing against traditional incense, hints of sandalwood wafting between Buddhist chants. My mother and Aunt Kinmimi sat at the edge of the burial bed, reciting melodious prayers that would carry their mother to the next life. I did not hear a single bomb or airplane that day, just the wind that tapped on palm leaves, the telltale sign of the approaching monsoon season.

My mother was the most courageous person I knew, even more so than my father, but my grandmother's death catalyzed an element of ferocity in her normally subdued valor. With only her sister and children left, her thoughts immediately turned to my father, her anchor in this world. He had been in jail for over a year in the Mogok hill station, long forgotten by the British and the Japanese. The jail was more of a rudimentary holding cell than a maximum-security fortress, with a well-tended garden and community areas for the prisoners to exercise in. My father charmed and befriended two of the jail officials – Dr. Thein Pe, the medical assistant and U Myint, the senior jailer – both of whom were secretly loyal to the Freedom Bloc cause. The two men did what they could to pass information to my father, while he kept up their spirits with jokes and stories in the otherwise isolated outpost.

On March 22, 1942, six days after my fifteenth birthday, the Japanese Imperial Army and ten thousand men from the newly formed Burmese Independence Army (BIA) marched through the streets of Rangoon after capturing the city, the wide avenues glistening with a hint of new year rain. A week and a half later, without any warning whatsoever, my mother suddenly vanished to May Myo[19] which was about a day's drive from Mogok in war conditions. My siblings and I panicked, worried that May May would not survive the treacherous road to the resort town, the lush hillside peppered with empty plantation homes. Aunt Kinmimi was left in charge of the children and did her best to cope with the crying, screaming, weeping and confusion in the wake of our mother's disappearance. I was absolutely petrified, unable to sleep. In the rare times that I did, I dreamt of an apocalypse, of the Shan hills erupting in flames and engulfing the low-lying lakes of the region, leaving fish to flounder amidst the scorched earth. My

---

[19] May Myo is now called Pyin Oo Lwin.

heart told me that May May was strong and would make it back to us, yet my logic reasoned that it was war and we were on neither side. It was only a matter of time before the rustling of the leaves outside would one day turn into the clicking of boots and the whirring of warplane engines.

My mother arrived in May Myo under the pretense of withdrawing money from one of the three banks still operating in the country, but what she had really gone there for was to obtain new information on the war front concerning my father. She got her wish. Her network found her the moment she stepped inside the city limits, giving notice that the British forces were to move our family, including my father, to Chungking to use him as a bargaining chip against the Japanese and the Comrades. The Imperial Army and Comrades had captured nearly every stronghold in the country and they wanted the leader of the Freedom Bloc, Dr. Ba Maw, but the British would not let their most valuable prisoner out of their sight.

My mother rushed out of May Myo with the news but not before purchasing a crucial ingredient for her plan. May Myo attracted food vendors from all over the country as one of the major trading cities, its supply line surprisingly undisturbed in wartime. She paid a visit to an Arakan shop on a side street, its canteen blooming with fragrant steam from black pepper soup and fish bathing in turmeric sauce. "Uncle, do you have any chilies from Arakan? Fresh?" she asked the shop owner, a man as old as her father would have been.

The ancient shopkeeper looked at my mother, her skin as white as the sun, wondering if she had the stomach for such spices. "I presume you want the mild ones. We just received them today." He proceeded to count small green bird's eye chilies in a paper bag, a common variety used in Bamar dishes.

She waved her hand, dissatisfied. "No, I want the other kind. The rare ones."

His eyes went wide at her request but it did not deter him from reaching for a hidden pouch and handing her its contents. "Are you sure? These can burn a man's stomach clear through."

My mother smiled and counted the money in her coin purse. "That's perfect."

While my mother was in May Myo, Freedom Bloc member Kyaw Nyein[20] bribed the jail officials to let him see Dr. Ba Maw. The young man confessed to my father that he had plans to rescue him. "Sayar[21], my team and I have two revolvers. We can shoot our way out if necessary." My father did not take Kyaw Nyein's offer seriously, an ill-advised plan to shoot their way out of Mogok which was crawling with British, Chinese and Japanese agents. Phay Phay changed his mind when he learned that he would be shipped to Chungking to be used as a pawn, a position that he had never been in before and did not intend to be in ever. He had to leave at once, asking Kyaw Nyein to alert my mother and their associates. Luckily for my father, my mother returned from May Myo the day after Kyaw Nyein's visit and went straight to see her husband at the hillside jail. My mother agreed that he needed to leave at once, handing him the bag of Arakan chilies. Dr. Ba Maw looked at his wife with one eyebrow raised. "Are we cooking something?"

After seeing my father, May May came to the ranch house, my siblings and I running to greet her car at the bottom of the hill. She was cheerful, handing each of us a pebble of palm sugar candy that she had brought from May Myo. There was an air of contrived nonchalance about her demeanor, her brief appearance calming my siblings' worries but not mine. The look on her face said it all: determined, steely eyes focused on the future and not quite fixed on the present moment. Her quiet resoluteness meant that she was facing great danger, though what exactly I could not figure out. "Off you go," she said to the younger ones, who skipped and twirled in the fields secure with the knowledge that our mother was back.

I followed May May into the house where she was packing

---

[20] Later to become Deputy Prime Minister under the AFPFL.

[21] *Sayar* is the honorific term for an elder man or teacher.

a small rucksack with two *longyi*s, two clean shirts, toiletries and a spare pair of sturdy leather boots. I saw her hands feel for two sets of Shan clothes in the bottom of her canvas travel satchel – one male, one female. "Are you leaving again?" I asked her, though I already knew the answer.

My mother stopped for a brief moment, contemplating whether to give me an excuse or not, but she knew that I could not be fooled. "Tinsa, I'm coming back. I came back from May Myo, didn't I? Have I ever lied to you?"

I shook my head no.

"Then you must trust me. And please help your aunt in the meantime, because she has her hands full with your little brothers and sisters. If they ask you where I've gone, just tell them that I'm with your father and that I'll see you soon. Understand?"

* * * * *

Daw Kinmama Maw waited on the outskirts of the hill station on April 13, 1942, dressed as a regal Shan woman, her *longyi* made of the finest cotton and embossed with a traditional zigzag pattern reserved for nobility. She held her breath hoping that her husband would make it in time, the hands of her watch beating against her rapid pulse as she clutched a second set of clothing for her husband. Soon they would disappear into their new identities: a high-ranking Shan noblewoman and her male bodyguard, his presence necessary for her travels through the treacherous mountains.

As a special treat for the prisoners before Thingyan, Burmese New Year, Dr. Ba Maw asked the jail cook to make a dish with the chilies. The cook, a slight, translucent-skinned Shan man from a neighboring village, thought nothing of the red bulbous peppers in his hands. Since Mogok was not a major trading center and Shan cuisine did not call for extraordinarily spicy peppers, there was no way for the cook to know that they were Bhut Jolokia peppers, otherwise known as Ghost Peppers. Cultivated in Assam, Nagaland and Manipur, the Ghost Peppers had crossed the border into Arakan state and into the palates of the Arakanese, who ate the chilies raw as an accompaniment to their main dish. Those who had heard of Ghost Peppers knew of the dangers of cooking them over an open fire, which would cause the chilies to burst and emit a stinging odor and irritant that could incapacitate anyone in the vicinity. In later years, the Indian National Army would weaponize the Bhut Jolokia in the form of non-lethal chili grenades, similar to tear gas.

Upon hearing the crackling of the peppers' skin against hot oil, my father ran to the door preparing for his exit. The cook's concoction released a noxious cloud of pepper smoke that infiltrated the windowless kitchen and dining areas. My father, feigning extreme illness and choking, asked to be let outside into the garden to gather his breath. The prison guards did not mind, far too busy tending to the other prisoners who had been waiting in line for their meals and were caught in the epicenter of the chili smoke. My father felt the weight of an iron key in his hand that he had acquired from a junior jailer for a small fortune. He unlocked the outer door and ran to my mother in the waiting car, the fat warden tumbling after him but losing his breath halfway down the hill.

My parents made their way through the Mogok hills where Kyaw Nyein had arranged for them to meet with U Aung Ba, Chief of Maing-lon state and a former student of my father's at Rangoon College. He offered shelter in one of his villages, a desolate mountaintop hut where no one would think to look for them, but what they had not anticipated was to attract crowds with their refined features and city manners. The perplexed locals could not help but stare at the sight of them; Rangoon was as alien as Antarctica as far as they were concerned. My parents decided it was time to trek through the Palaung hills when the staring and attention became a little too intrusive, despite Chinese troops closing in on the territory.

In May 1942, more than two weeks after my parents' disappearance, we received a letter notifying us that they had arrived in Mandalay and that my father was officially out of hiding. I hugged my parents for as long as I could in Mandalay, the ruins of the old teak palace looming over us as we reunited as a family for the first time in over a year. Phay Phay was noticeably thinner, his cheekbones jutting like canyons. I inhaled his scent, a mixture of clean soap, earth and perspiration. My mother's skin, normally chalk white, was the color of almonds. She was beaming and while I was sure that she was happy to have her husband back, I couldn't help but suspect that her triumphant smile was due to her engineering the most cunning jailbreak of that period.

The basic military campaign ended in May and the British were in retreat, the campaign bloodier and more entangled than we had imagined. The Japanese had temporarily appointed Thakin Tun Oke as the head of the civil administration, but there were two main issues rising to the surface. The BIA had left a trail of wanton destruction upon invasion and the Japanese higher command was equally destructive with its unraveling superiority complex. The BIA, originally composed of the Thirty Comrades, had managed to draw some of the worst elements of society to its ranks when it entered Burma. Like the original Thirty, the army intended to attract the finest young men who would serve and protect their country. Though they did attract some of them, the vast majority were essentially young hoodlums looking for a thrill. The Japanese and Comrades did not have the foresight or time to implement a thorough recruitment plan before landing, instead relying on word of mouth to attract new soldiers. When word of mouth failed to attract an elite force of educated, dignified, humane soldiers, they took any young man with two legs, two eyes and a shooting arm. The new army also drew convicts who had been recently released from prison, or rather, took it upon themselves to break out of jail during the British retreat. They terrorized villagers, extorting tea money from the very people whom they swore to protect. The Comrades tried to discipline the wild ones under their command, but justice only went so far when the accused happily disappeared into the jungle with their ill-gained riches.

The errant BIA rank-and-file soldiers butted heads with the Japanese command, which was experiencing its own problems. What we had thought was going to be a fully supportive partnership turned out to be fragmented promises. The best of the lot came in the form of men such as Colonel Suzuki, more loyal to the Burmese cause than the Burmese themselves. When meeting U Nu for the first time, he famously declared:

> Don't be worried about independence... Independence is not the kind of thing you can get through begging for it from other people. You should proclaim it yourselves. The Japanese refuse to give it? Very well, then; tell them that you will cross over to some place like Twante and proclaim independence and set up your own government. What's the difficult thing about that? If they start shooting, you shoot back.[22]

The majority of the high command and officers were respectful and well-mannered, products of a noble and proud lineage of warriors. However, the Burma theater also attracted the dregs of the Japanese forces from their Korea and Manchuria campaigns, some of the most brutal combatants to come from their quest westward and these men knew no life outside of war. Though I was at the center of the political storm, I was blind to their brutality in Asian nations far more strong-footed than us, impervious to seeping reports of fanaticism and manic killings. There was no way to know the truth with contradictory Allied and Axis reports bombarding the airwaves to the point where I simply stopped listening. I passed these soldiers every morning on the way to the market, striking in their ironed uniforms and bashful smiles. There was nothing about their humanly forms that hinted at Nanking, the Manchurian Incident and the demolition of Korea.

There was a key element missing in this chaos: a figurehead.

---

[22] U Nu. *Burma Under the Japanese: Pictures and Portraits*. London: Macmillan & Co Ltd, 1954. Print.

The Comrades had the heart but lacked the experience and knowledge to manage an entire government and country. There were exaggerated reports of tensions between my father and Aung San at this stage, purporting that the Japanese actually favored Aung San over Dr. Ba Maw until some inexplicable turn of events changed the tide of war. There was nothing surprising about my father's appointment to those who were there. Prior to our arrival in Mandalay, my father was in prison and the plan to ship him to Chungking was well known in political circles. Taking this into account and also the fact that U Nu and other Freedom Bloc luminaries were scattered in prisons across Burma, the role of figurehead fell to Aung San, who was second-in-command of the Freedom Bloc and the sole link between the Bloc, Comrades and the Japanese. When my father escaped from jail, it was only natural for the leader of the Bloc to serve as the figurehead of a new government and Aung San deferred to my father as the continuing leader of the Freedom Bloc and his superior. There were lingering ideological disagreements but none serious enough to warrant a power struggle. This was evident in June 1942 when Dr. Ba Maw, Aung San and U Nu entered provisional talks with the Japanese Army Command in May Myo to determine the outcome of the future government.

The next two months were a languourous stretch for me despite knowing that whatever was happening between the Freedom Bloc and the Imperial Army would change the fate of Burma forever. I was lulled into a deep sense of calm, my father at finger's reach and my family intact. Even when he was buried in meetings barricaded by rows of army uniforms, at least I could see my father, speak to him, hug him every day. My aunt and I spent our days wandering the ancient capital, slipping in and out of alleyways no bigger than the width of a single oxcart. The streets were still as vibrant as I remembered from my childhood, hiding in between cracked stone pillars and the soot-covered walkways of the old palace. The wet market brimmed with throngs of customers waiting for their daily ration of broken rice and wilted kale. Rotund vendors shouted *Dandelion stew! Carnation salad!* The once omnipresent red orange of fish cake and tomato curry was replaced with steaming piles of yellow, magenta and orange hibiscus flowers. I saw then the reality of war for the rest of Burma, people reduced to eating weeds for other men's ambitions. Did my father, Aung San and the Bloc see what I was seeing? That the lives and deaths of millions of people were at their mercy, of no volition of their own? Our family, our friends, we thought that we had nothing at that point. But our nothing was greater than the majority's everything, a lesson that has stayed with me my entire life.

The Burmese Provincial Administrative Committee elected Dr. Ba Maw as the temporary head of state on June 4, 1942 with Aung San as his War Minister. Relieved to learn that we could leave Mandalay and return to Rangoon, my family and I drove home via the Mandalay Road. Our convoy stopped in Mogok to collect Dr. Thein Pe and U Myint who had so generously helped my father at the hilltop jail. The city no longer existed when we arrived. The enormity of the destruction was far too great for me to comprehend, nor did I want to comprehend it at that point. Mogok, the final battleground of the British retreat, was flattened. The mountains were split open, craters spilling with uncut rubies, sapphires, minerals. We found Dr. Thein Pe and U Myint huddled in a bomb shelter on the edge of the jail, visibly shaken but in remarkably good spirits. True to the Burmese sense of humor, they made light of the situation, joking that the only way to get the fat jail warden up from his seat was for the Japanese to blow it out from beneath him.

The road to Rangoon was just wide enough for us to weave through potholes and shrapnel for hundreds of deserted miles. I pushed the mental images of war out of my head as soon as I saw the front gates to my childhood home, my fifteen-year-old mind unable to absorb more distress. I ignored everything for the time being, simply opening the door to my bedroom and crawling silently into bed. I dared not to dream that night or many nights after that, letting the silence of my room envelope me like a warm bath.

CHAPTER SIX

I turned sweet sixteen at my childhood home at Kandawgyi Lake, surrounded by my parents, aunt, siblings and neighborhood friends after months of isolation in Mogok. My St. John's friends had returned from similar evacuations to Tavoy, Pegu, Putao, Moulmein and Taunggyi, our collective paths traversing the pebble sand beaches of the south to the snowy peaks of north. All of the schools were closed indefinitely and I was beyond relieved to see them in the flesh, to know that nothing had happened to them. I gathered everyone in the living room for traditional bitter tea and grainy semolina cake. My birthday cake was half of a watermelon with a single candle, its dripping wax sitting uncomfortably atop the melon's syrupy, peony-colored juice. "Make a wish!" everyone chanted in unison, goading me with their cheers and clapping. I closed my eyes and blew out the candle but I did not make a wish that day. Everything was perfect in that moment, to be with my loved ones and nothing more.

Sixteen is the traditional entrance to adulthood in our culture, the golden threshold to maturity, career prospects and love. I waited for my birthday superstitiously believing that reaching this magic number would open the door to a cathartic new phase in my life. I decided to put my superstition to the test in my first act as a supposed adult. The day after my birthday, I asked our driver, U Win, to take me to my father's law office on Barr Street. U Win was an elderly Bamar man with three missing teeth as a result of his former boxing career and was placid and discreet. I knew that I could trust him. "Shall I fetch your mother?" he asked, the normal protocol when any of the children were going into town.

"No, U Win, it will just be me," I replied, stepping into the backseat and shutting the door before he could argue with me. I was feeling quite good about my newfound confidence when I heard the pitter patter of delicate feet running up to my passenger window, followed by the sight of Mala's oval visage in my window. Her eyebrows looked like angry caterpillars, curled in fury.

"Where do you think you're going?" she demanded, and I laughed when I realized how she was becoming a stern busybody just like our aunt Kinmimi.

"To town." My voice was cool and immoveable.

"Without May May or a chaperone?"

"Well, May May's in town with Aunt Kinmimi and I'm going to see Phay Phay at his office."

"I'm telling!"

I rolled my eyes at my sister. "Just remember, you owe me," I said flippantly while rolling up the window, mouthing the words *ice cream* to remind her of our dangerous excursion a couple of years ago, which had been her idea after all. U Win shrugged his shoulders at our bickering and started the engine, turning the radio on in time to hear an announcement that the British government's new aim was to guide Burma to self-government within the Commonwealth. The broadcaster's Belgravia drawl crackled through the speakers, cut short when U Win turned the dials to another news source.

"Rest assured that the Japanese Imperial Army and Burmese nationalists have formed the Independence Preparatory Committee, dedicated to the promise that Burma will be an independent state by May of this year, 1943," read a bored announcer, yawning through his message.

The competing reports normally would have frightened and confused me, but I was no longer afraid. I was tired of being trapped in limbo, feeling vulnerable all of the time. While it was comforting to be back home and together with my family under one roof, I felt that staying inside all day and feeling scared was not going to solve anything, not least the country's affairs. Not having made my birthday wish the previous day, I wished for the courage to help my parents and my country, because it was about time.

U Nu, Thakin Than Tun, Thakin Mya[23] and Aung San were in my father's meeting room when I arrived, the strong aroma of thick jasmine tea greeting me as I opened the teak doors. Given that I was a young woman and the daughter of Dr. Ba Maw, their warm smiles turned to mild panic when they saw that I was unchaperoned. Thakin Than Tun and U Nu were smoking verdant green cheroot cigarettes and Than Tun blew smoke politely to one side and asked me, "Tinsa, it's not safe for you to go around on your own. What's the matter?" He treated me like a younger sister after spending so much time in my home, seeing me grow up before his eyes. Yet I would always remain the little girl asleep at the top of the staircase to him.

Cheroot fumes covered U Nu like a cloud, giving him a phantasmic aura. He raised an eyebrow at Than Tun and interjected, "She's old enough to do what she wants, not least visit her father's office. Doesn't make a difference if we all get bombed in our homes or on the road, they're everywhere. Sit, Tinsa." U Nu pointed his right hand towards a rattan chair behind Aung San, who looked forlorn and pensive. Aung San was sipping his tea quietly, his thin lips perched on the edge of the floral porcelain cup. In contrast to Thakin Than Tun and U Nu, who bickered like an old couple, Aung San seemed to perpetually live inside of his own head. When he did speak, he did so with the might of a tiger, forceful and methodical, yet I was more uncomfortable during the times in which he stayed silent, removed from his surroundings and immersed in a world that only he could understand.

---

[23] Minister of Home Affairs in Myanmar's pre-independence government. Assassinated July 19 1947.

"No thank you, Uncle, I won't be too long," I replied to U Nu's offer. I heard the doorknob turn and my father stepped inside the room, stopping in his tracks when he saw me.

"Tinsa, where's your mother? Is something wrong?" His forehead was creased with concern, his mouth locked in a deep frown.

"Phay Phay, can I speak with you? I won't take up too much of your time," I asked as politely as I could, anticipating his reaction to my following request. He nodded to the Thakins, signaling that they should begin their discussion without him and led me to his office that was adjacent to the meeting room. I squinted my eyes to see him, his office bathed in darkness. The bay window, the room's only source of light, was boarded with cheap planks of pine wood, indiscriminately nailed into the ecru plaster. The air was stagnant and aged like the pages of an antique book. Every line, wrinkle and sag on my father's face was exaggerated by the darkness.

"I want to help you and May May. I know that I can help. Please, let me do something, anything, because I've seen enough and it's not right that I'm sitting at home all day while everything goes to pieces," I declared.

My father assessed me through the dim light and I could not tell if his quizzical expression was judging me, pitying me, or both. "You think you've seen enough?" he asked incredulously.

I nodded my head assuredly. "I'm sixteen. I'm an adult now. People my age are supposed to attend university, or begin their first jobs. I can't be treated like a child anymore. You need help, this country needs help, so let me do something." I was not angry or accusatory. For once, I simply wanted to say the things that were on my mind.

Phay Phay did not flinch at my declaration, to my chagrin. He stood there like a rock, a mountain. "I know that you want to help and that you want to start taking control of your own life at this age. Your time will come and I have a feeling that you will be a part of history, much bigger than a postscript in my biography or as the girl who was always in the meeting rooms. But, this isn't the time. There is so much more that you need to learn about the world, Tinsa, and I don't mean bombs and guns and evacuations. It's the silent cruelties, the things that men and women say in their hearts but never aloud. Those are the dangers that I fear for you and your siblings. What you think you're seeing now is just a small percentage of the truth and this isn't the time to go rushing into these things."

I recoiled at his words, at their startling clarity. I was angry now, the bitterness of being treated like a child rising in my chest. My father watched my face and fists tighten and relaxed his tone at my evident anxiety. "I don't mean to be condescending, or to upset you. It's just that you are my daughter and you will make it through this if I don't. That is promise that I made to myself a long, long time ago."

At that moment, the door creaked ajar and I saw Aung San's onyx eyes peeking through. He was rarely shy or bashful, but he lowered his head on the account of interrupting an intimate conversation between a father and daughter. "Excuse me, Sayar, but we really need you in the meeting room." He smiled at me and shut the door behind him. Aung San had married his wife, Daw Khin Kyi, in 1942 and I wondered if marriage had softened him, in a good way. Thakin Than Tun had married Daw Khin Kyi's sister, thus making him and Aung San brothers-in-law, but Than Tun had always been fatherly and doting.

My father sighed and threw his hands up in the air. "You wait right here and don't sit near the window." He placed one of the rattan lounge chairs next to the entryway and I sat down with my arms crossed, intent on staying there until we could resume our conversation. I thought that I would be bored for several hours, but the walls were very thin and I could hear everything going on in the war room. Thakin Than Tun had taken the floor, his voice subdued as he described a growing number of reports on the Imperial Army's torture tactics. The Korea Men had infiltrated the upper echelons of the Kempetai (the secret police). The Kempetai, though small in number, were more powerful than the Imperial Army's standing forces in Rangoon. Their foot soldiers had a very nasty habit of slapping those whom they deemed inferior, racial or otherwise, but that was not the worst of it. It was said that the Kempetai tortured anyone suspected of working for the Allies with techniques perfected in Seoul, Manchuria, Nanking. Hanging upside down until blood collected in your head, the brain on the cusp of explosion. Beaten with steel rods. Pouring boiling water repeatedly on one's head until every last strand of hair fell out. Pulling nails out with rusty pliers.

Thakin Than Tun reported that General Oseka of the Home Office sought the most pro-Japanese Burmese to fill the ranks of the Independence Preparatory Committee in order to counteract the Freedom Bloc's influence. My father and the Thakins were the most high-profile members of the committee and their participation only encouraged sycophants to flock to Oseka's side. Oseka and his followers were making it very clear that my father and the Thakins were completely replaceable should they step out of line. Than Tun, an ardent Communist, urged my father to make contact with the Chinese and to reverse the tide of war. "You cannot trust the words that come out of the Kempetai's crooked teeth," he snarled. "They speak so sweetly to us while stabbing us in the back."

"Maung Than Tun, do you prefer to be stabbed in the back by the Japanese, or in the front by the British?" my father retorted. "We cannot turn our backs on the Imperial Army. I do not like them any more than you do, but it is too late to go back now." He reasoned that the Allies had lost their footing in Burma after the retreat and they could not count on when the Chinese would return. No one had received messages from Chinese intelligence or news from the Allies since his escape from Mogok. Their silence was enough to doubt the Allies' positioning in the country and their military capabilities at that point.

Aung San agreed that they should stay the course. "I concur with Dr. Ba Maw. We are not in a position to switch sides at this point. I know the Japanese command in and out and we can still work with some of them as long as they are not

Kempetai." The others relented in the face of Dr. Ba Maw and Aung San's united front, grunting in exasperation while Than Tun slapped the table in frustration.

"I shall be loyal to you, Sayar, but I will not swear my allegiance to any of those dimwitted brutes," Than Tun promised. It was evident to anyone in the war room that he would continue to tow the Communist mission underground, my father not pressing him further. Thakin Mya mumbled his way through the meeting in weary acquiescence, and I could tell that he felt morally obligated to stand with his comrades but was perhaps tempted to run off to neutral territory and lead a quiet life with his family.

Next, Phay Phay called on U Nu to draft the constitution before Oseka and his cronies could submit theirs. "What?! WHAT?!" U Nu shrieked. U Nu tried to wriggle his way out of his new task, his chair squeaking beneath him as he shifted uncomfortably in his seat, pleading until he ran out of oxygen and excuses. "I'm not prepared for this. I've never written something like it, just short stories, articles and god-awful novels. There are more experienced men to do this." I was taken aback by the severity of his reticence because I had read his newspaper articles and theses, and he was one of the most talented writers that I had ever read. His simple voice and tone appealed to readers from all walks of life, a rare skill even amongst the most dedicated and talented writers.

My father had little patience for U Nu, who was always doubting himself and his brilliance. In U Nu's memoirs, he recounted my father's stern lecture, which I heard through the thin plaster walls:

> Thakin Nu, you are always running off the track. Politics does not consist merely in pulling things down. It also means building them up. I shan't be able to carry on for very much longer. And then there will only be Bo Aung San, Thakin Than Tun and you. Now that you have a chance, do try to learn the work

and let me give you a good practical training.[24]

A hush fell over the room after my father uttered the words, *I shan't be able to carry on for very much longer.* Even U Nu sat still in his seat, not a peep from him until the meeting ended.

My father remained in the war room with Thakin Mya and Aung San after the others had adjourned. Thakin Than Tun and U Nu appeared at the doorway to my father's office, looking at me with sympathy. I did not need to ask if they had overheard my conversation with my father. U Nu pulled a cigarette from his left breast pocket, dangling the fresh roll between his lips but too fatigued to search for the matches in his pocket. He asked through his clenched jaw, "Tinsa, what do you want to be when you grow up?"

"A doctor," I responded as if on cue, the quickness of my reply surprising to me. It was true that I had always dreamed of attending medical college because it was reserved for the brightest students, its prestige unchallenged in the university system. However, if one were to ask me what specifically about medicine drew my passion, I wouldn't have known what to say. It was simply how things worked, that if a student had high marks then he or she would enter medical school according to the assumptions of our society and culture. I prayed that they wouldn't ask me for my reasons.

U Nu balked at my response, disappointed in me. "We already have too many doctors in this country!" He grabbed the cigarette from his lips, flicking it by force of habit even though it was unlit. "Tell me, is that what you really want to do? Does your heart beat for medicine? Does it drive the blood in your veins?"

I giggled at U Nu's interrogation because his assessment had bared my ambitions, or lack thereof, for my future medical career. "Well, I like working with people and I suppose I'm

---

[24] U Nu. *Burma Under the Japanese: Pictures and Portraits*. London: Macmillan & Co Ltd, 1954. Print.

quite good at looking after others. Being a doctor wouldn't be so bad."

U Nu waved his cigarette hand at me, dissatisfied with my tepid response. "Tinsa, I want you to think about becoming a teacher. I know that the medical college is the most prestigious school, but there's no point if your passion is not with pills and prods and stethoscopes. What I mean by passion is not money, fame, or prestige. It's an explosive chemical in your body, the dynamite that jolts you awake in the morning to go to work and keeps you awake at night with wonder. It cannot be feigned." He at last retrieved his matches, the cheroot leaf wrapping of his cigarette sizzling as he took a well-deserved drag.

Thakin Than Tun bumped U Nu's elbow in jest. "Thakin Nu, you write such passionate novels and you shall write a passionate constitution!" he teased.

"Burma is my great love and writing is an exciting mistress," U Nu bellowed as he walked away, leaving a trail of blue and gray smoke curling behind him.

Than Tun laughed at his companion's dramatic exit, difficult for anyone to upstage U Nu's charisma. Before he left, he imparted some wisdom that was oddly prescient. "Despite U Nu's theatrical lecture, he's right. You ought to look into teaching, which I think is one of the most noble professions. It may not be as glamorous as a surgeon's life, but you're not one for glamour, are you? You want to make an impact, so think about sharing your knowledge with future generations. Your father's also right, too, you know. We've made a bloody mess of things and this war…it isn't your time. The future is yours and you must do everything in your power to prepare for it. Do you understand?"

"Thank you, uncle," I said to him, and I meant it. Thakin Than Tun gave me a short salute and went on his way, his shadow growing smaller on the wall until he disappeared from my sight.

Thakin Than Tun's advice haunted me during my drive home with my father, who said nothing to me when we left his office. I could tell that he was deep in thought but not angry, because when he was angry he had a funny little way of squinting his eyes to the point where one could no longer see the white bits, the blackness of his stare penetrating the source of his fury. Phay Phay's eyes were bright and alert as we sat in the backseat, U Win humming a folk number to himself and probably grateful that my father had not reprimanded him for his complicity in my solo trip to town.

The more that I thought about the Thakins' advice, the more I become convinced of their suggestion. I had never thought about teaching or academia before, but I was a bookish child and relished being in a classroom. Most of my treasured childhood memories were of reading books at my mother and father's feet in our sitting room, my siblings running around me while I lost myself in *Oliver Twist*, traditional Burmese stories and the *Ramayana* epic. Teaching was the bridge between my passion for literature and making a greater impact on the world around me, and to be honest, my right hand was better suited for a pen than a scalpel.

It also occurred to me during my epiphany that I was perhaps being unfair to my father. I was seeking his approval and energy on a decision that I alone needed to make, if I did truly consider myself an adult. How could he, or anyone else, have known what to do with me if I did not even know myself up to that point? It was the first time in years that I could picture myself on a solid trajectory towards the future, a discovery that shone a light through the haze of the war years.

"What's on your mind, little one?" Phay Phay inquired through a stretching yawn. He always had the gift of timing, able to read others' thoughts in anticipation of a potentially lethal discussion.

There was no point in being coy. "I want to be a teacher, Phay Phay." I said nothing more than that because it was, at last, a decision.

A long silence passed between us, loose gravel spinning between the car's tires as we drove around the lake road leading to our home. A pack of boys ran after our car, their spindly legs racing against our speeding vehicle. I couldn't help but smile at the boy at the head of the pack, whose chocolate skin peeked through crumbling layers of thanaka paste on his cheeks. He huffed and puffed and thrashed his toothpick legs until he raced past the hood of the car. Phay Phay asked U Win to stop the engine, stepping onto the middle of the empty road and going up to the boy, who was standing on the sidewalk and pumping his hands victoriously in the air. My father laughed and took the boy's sweaty palm, shaking it vigorously in congratulations while the champion's scrawny frame quaked at the force of the elder man's handshake. His friends caught up with their triumphant winner, their palms slapping his shoulder in a hearty celebration. They ran off like wild young puppies, living for the day's next discovery or adventure.

Phay Phay returned to his seat, still smiling at the young boy's feat. His good mood jumpstarted his sense of conversation and he said to me, "If you want to teach, then you shall teach."

"Thank you, Phay Phay." My voice was calm and collected though I was squeezing my hands with delight.

"You know, some of my happiest days were when I was a teacher at Rangoon College. I hadn't even met your mother yet, but sometimes I think back and wonder if all of this hadn't happened," he stopped to point out the window, out at the great expanse of Rangoon, "that I would have been better suited as a university professor or as a school rector." Phay Phay's nostalgia sent him into a pensive mood, no trace of his smile from seconds before. "Just promise me one thing?"

I nodded my head, ready for whatever he would ask of me.

"I want you to remember all of this, everything that's happened to us and this country and never forget it. Teach your students the truth because that is the most important responsibility you have towards them. I don't know if the Japanese or British will win this war, but the people who lived through these events must make sure that the Burmese version of history is not lost. I assure you that many will try to rewrite or erase what has gone on, and your voice can and needs to be louder than theirs."

There was a brief pause. "That, Tinsa, is how you can help."

* * * * *

At sixteen, I began preparing for a career in teaching, aided by my father's meticulous lecture notes from his teaching days and by my mother's support. May May was the head of the All-Burma National Women's League, which at the time was doing more for the public than both of the armies and the administration combined, the brains and womanpower behind civilian relief operations. Hundreds of League volunteers maintained civilian hospitals, provided shelter for homeless people, distributed supplies to remote townships, and helped struggling monastic schools and orphanages by assigning volunteer teachers and guiding the curriculum to meet exam standards.

I joined the Women's League as a volunteer curriculum advisor on my parents' condition that Aunt Kinmimi would accompany me on all of my visits to four monastic schools near our home. War aggravated my aunt's existing fear that something untoward would happen to us children, and with good reason. During my visits to the schools, we passed through neighborhoods that had been shelled, decimated, leveled. Shantytowns grew above the rubble, people left with nothing but to rebuild their lives with the barest survival instincts. When our car drove through the cracked dirt roads, rolling carefully between the makeshift homes that had been cobbled together with scrap metal and burnt wood, the residents of these neighborhoods flicked their crooked shutters open to stare at us. I never felt unsafe but it was a curious thing to be stared at, particularly by the houses in the far-flung corners of the streets where uniformed men went in but the women never came out. Sometimes these women smiled at me through the broken shutters, shards of the yellow and pink flowers in their hair visible through the cracks.

Daw Kinmama Maw (far left) and Tinsa (second from left) witness the declaration of Burmese independence under the Japanese

Aunt Kinmimi did not approve of my new work, preferring that I remain in the house until the remainder of the war, but she would always grab her pocketbook and chaperone me to these schools without protest. They were all less than two miles from Kandawgyi Lake yet they could not have been in a more different world. Hundreds of bubble-cheeked schoolchildren, mainly orphans or children whose parents could no longer look after them, were crammed into teaching halls that should not have held more than fifty people at a time. When I asked the children what they wanted to learn, their hands shot up at once and they screamed *Arts! Reading! Science!* with a few murmurs of *Mathematics!* here and there. The children ranged from three to twelve years old and I found it peculiar to think of the older ones as children since I was only a few years older than them. Sometimes the younger girls of elementary school age would circle me and giggle, telling me that I was the strangest teacher that they had ever met with my too proper of an accent, mimicking the way in which I drew out my *ahs* and my *oos*.

I worked alongside the young teachers who were in charge of the curriculum for hundreds of pupils. They came from the surrounding neighborhood, were no more than thirty years old and tough as the nuns at St. John's. I was thankful that they welcomed me, afraid that they might sneer at my "tea salon" posture, but the teachers were wholeheartedly dedicated to the children, not caring who walked through the corrugated iron doors just as long as they were there to help. So, twice a week, with Aunt Kinmimi always parked in a corner of the darkened schoolroom, I met with the volunteer teachers from these four monastic schools to discuss class lessons. In their words, they wanted to replicate the standard of teaching at the best schools in Rangoon, like St. John's and St. Paul's. I was in awe of the way that they selflessly created and revised lesson plans for their students, working by candlelight well into the evenings.

I taught basic English to the younger students, aged four to six, who giggled even harder at my British-English lilt. I found an immense sense of purpose within those faded schoolroom walls, reading stories to the children and having them practice the alphabet. Every week, my students would hand in their homework with their crooked ABCs a little straighter each time.

I matured as Burma prepared for its own independence. My family and I had returned from Mandalay exactly a year earlier and my father and the Thakins had spent the entire year negotiating with the Imperial Army. The independence committee, consisting of my father, Aung San, Thakin Than

Tun, U Nu and other nationalists, finished the final constitution by July 1943, followed by elections. The man who doubted my father the most during his political ascent was the first to call on him. "I nominate Dr. Ba Maw," Thakin Ko Daw Hmaing, the poet and writer, asserted, saying nothing more than those few words. He gave a nod at my father's direction, showing his support but also daring him to succeed at the role.

At 11:20 AM on August 1, 1943, Burma became an independent state and my father was sworn in as *Naingandaw Adipadi* (Head of State). I read newspaper reports stating that the Japanese did not want to confer the title of President to Dr. Ba Maw, thus they agreed to call him *Adipadi*, the Pali term for Chief and also the title of a university rector. The term *adipadi* has often been misconstrued as dictator but it was a controversial slight of hand, a political checkmate against the Burmese in a continuation of the power struggle between the nationalists and the Japanese command.

At 4:00 PM, Burma declared war on the Allied Powers. At 4:30 PM, Dr. Ba Maw signed a Treaty of Alliance with Japan, followed by his first press conference at 6:00 PM. Aung San, the War Minister and Commander-in-Chief, stood next to my father and scanned the room for his troops. I watched him cheer earnestly for my father, weary of the circus but vowing to continue for Burma's sake. I observed a particularly belligerent, difficult and sadistic Japanese officer sidle next to Aung San, who turned his back to the odious character. The officer could not resist jibing the young Commander-in-Chief, standing so erectly and proudly in the midst of the spectacle. "Thakin Aung San, you look awfully happy. Is it so?" He grinned ear to ear, eyes squinted, a juvenile game. "Our commanders discussed putting you in charge instead of Dr. Ba Maw. What do you think of that? But since you are such a physically small man, so meek, you hardly attracted any attention. You are almost...unnoticed."

Aung San, notorious for his temper and caustic wit, clenched his fists and prepared to deliver a satisfying punch to his smug little nose. I squeezed my eyes shut in anticipation of his right hook slamming against the officer's cheek, waiting for the crack of impact to ripple through the room.

Instead, he looked at my father, whose eyes pleaded with him to keep a cool head. Aung San disappeared into the crowd, his shoulders bumping against the current of spectators clamoring to take a photo with Adipadi Dr. Ba Maw.

* * * * *

In October 1943, Governor Dorman-Smith, the penultimate Governor of Burma from May 1941 to August 1946, reflected on the Burmese nationalists' decision to side with the Japanese and acknowledged Britain's role in driving us to the enemy:

> Neither our word nor our intentions are trusted in that part of the globe... We have fed such countries as Burma on political formulae until they are sick at the very sight and sound of a formula, which has come, as far as my experience shows, to be looked upon as a very British means of avoiding a definite course of action.

It was too late for Dorman-Smith's words. The Japanese had finally given us the formal independence that we sought for nearly six decades, but the true battle had yet to be fought.

It was clear by September that the deal with the Imperial Army was a sham all along. The humiliations were trivial at first, beginning with the placement of our family. Major General Isamura, Head of the Burmese-Japanese Relations Department, made it his personal mission to undermine and degrade my father and the Burmese cabinet as often as possible. Isamura was living at the Government House in Rangoon for years, fashioning himself a kingdom built on bomb dust. He thought little of the Burmese no matter the rank, a small-minded and slap-happy man who took immense pleasure in turning someone over to the Kempetai if they looked at him in a suspicious manner. When it came time for the Japanese to move from the official residences to make way for the Burmese cabinet, Isamura blocked every attempt for our family to move into the Government House. My father scarcely cared about moving into the cold and clinical walls of the colonial monstrosity, but General Suzuki, the man who had sourced the Thirty Comrades, took great issue with it. Suzuki went straight to the military command in Tokyo and they ordered Isamura to relinquish control of the house immediately, to which Isamura feigned concern for the building's structural safety and delayed his exit. He could not bear to see a Burmese person, even the Adipadi, seize his self-appointed castle.

Isamura was not the worst of the lot. Bo Saing-gyo of the Kempetai delighted in torturing the Burmese. He was famous for extrajudicial torture and killings, making innocent men disappear, never be heard from again. When my father asked Aung San to reprimand Bo Saing-gyo within his powers as War Minister, Saing-gyo laughed in Aung San's face. "If I call them criminals, thieves, spies, then that is what they will be called."

There were a great many men who were decent and honorable in the Japanese command, such as Commander-in-Chief Shojiro Iida, General Nasu and Colonel Hiraoka, the liaison officer assigned to protect us and remained unfailingly loyal to our family. Hiraoka was an unusual character even among the eccentrics of the Imperial Army and Kempetai. Discreet, calm and quick to tend to his duties, he never flinched in the most difficult situations. He was the only man that my mother and Aunt Kinmimi trusted to look after my siblings and me, accompanying us in the front seat of the car as a silent chaperone and standing guard on the porch when my younger siblings played in the garden.

Hiraoka was at odds with Colonel Suzuki, whose brash and outlandish tactics conflicted with his own subdued nature. Both competed for my father's attention like siblings, trying to outdo the other by impressing my father with new initiatives and taking on extra duties. Suzuki did this by becoming more Burmese than the Burmese themselves, shouting independence at every opportunity and empowering the Burmese Army to seek genuine independence at all costs. Hiraoka displayed his loyalty by keeping a watchful eye over the family as if we were his own. He warned my father of the dangers of publicly speaking about *real independence* and what he deemed to be Suzuki's attention-seeking overtures. "Think and do whatever you need to behind closed doors, Adipadi," Hiraoka warned. "But remember that there are eyes and ears everywhere, and not friendly ones."

By the time my father left for the Greater East Asia Conference in Tokyo on November 5, 1943, his government was in chaos. Burma was on the brink of riot due to corruption, increased banditry and violence, inflation, lack of consumer goods, and food and oil supply dwindling to feed the Japanese forces. Phay Phay had a noticeably heavy heart as he stepped on the plane, with deep purple caverns under his eyes and his normally erect posture turned down.

The administration came home without any concessions from Tokyo, but they returned with a solid ally. My father had previously met Netaji Subhas Chandra Bose in July 1943 in Shonan. Bose was the head of the Indian National Army, the Burmese Independence Army's counterpart across the border, and was the leader of the nationalist Azad Hind Government. His confident stature greeted my father on the landing strip as soon as he stepped into Tokyo's crisp haze. Bose had arrived early to meet with Tojo but unexpectedly ran into Dr. Ba Maw first. The two were physically similar to one another: tall, of similar age, with a natural manner of confidence and elegance and a way of softly imposing their presence on a room. They stood out in a sea of faces, drawing attention without ever demanding it.

It was apparent in my father's letters from Tokyo that he and Bose shared a kinship in Burma. The latter had been imprisoned in Mandalay in 1925 for plotting nationalist activities in India. Though his time in Mandalay was not a peaceful one (he contracted tuberculosis and other ailments), he identified with the Burmese and their struggle for independence paralleling his own. My father found Bose's pragmatic and cutting assessment of world affairs a fitting contrast to his own optimism. The INA leader had met with the Germans and Russians and saw the battlefields in Europe, holding a more cynical viewpoint of the conflict. He told my father that our independence would be earned through bloodshed and great sacrifice, that many would die whether we were prepared for it or not. There would be no clear path to independence but Bose was not the least bit downtrodden over his assessment.

Netaji approached my father after the Tokyo Conference and asked to move the Indian National Army's headquarters from Shonan to Rangoon. It was primarily an operational tactic, to be as close to India as possible for invasion purposes, but Bose had astutely noted the growing tension between the Burmese and Imperial Armies and wanted to show his solidarity with a fellow leader. My father's circle of friends, which in turn was my family's network of political allies, was growing smaller by the day, thus I welcomed the addition of Bose as a close confidante. If the Imperial Army would not implement true independence for Burma or India, then at least they would have two tigers to deal with in Rangoon instead of one.

* * * * *

It was not a question of if the Imperial Army would assassinate my father, but when. My father and his cabinet had ruffled the entire Japanese command in the span of a few short months. He was expected to source supplies for the entire country and both armies as the head of the civil government, but he balked at the audacity of Tokyo's initial requests, asking for ludicrous quantities of essential goods in a time of war. Two hundred cattle. Three tons of chicken. Truckloads of rice. One hundred and fifty viss of cloth. Unthinkable numbers to be delivered on a weekly basis while the Burmese went without supplies for days.

My family was not protected from the supply crisis. I remember fainting from anemia on more than a dozen occasions, one time splitting my head on my bedpost during a fall. I do not mean to sound maudlin about these times, because we were lucky to have one gourd a week as a vegetable ration among the whole family when others had none. In the words of my mother, "Rations, even presidential rations, are just pieces of paper when nothing is growing from the ground."

Phay Phay negotiated the orders down to half or even a quarter of their size at best, but the Burmese public became rightfully enraged with his government as they were appropriating supplies from people in need. In an attempt to thwart the Imperial Army, he and Aung San called on my mother as the head of the Women's League, who found a simple solution to the supply issue. May May asked that my father alert her when the supply orders came in so that she could creatively reallocate resources for civilians. Meaning, she would hide and redistribute clothes, food and oil at the League headquarters before the Imperial Army could get to them. As a League volunteer, I used to wake up at three in the morning to my mother's gentle nudging, May May cloaked in black like a Victorian lady-in-mourning. Her covert operations could have put both armies to shame, gathering dozens of women together in the cover of darkness to hide supplies. I happily joined the League ladies in the assembly lines, willing the sleep from my eyes and packing emaciated chicken carcasses, wilted kale and traditional medicine into the trunks of civilian vehicles. I hoped that some of the boxes that I had assembled would go directly to the schools that I worked at, one more connection to my young students.

Allied propaganda took full advantage of my father's decline during the supply crisis. *Ba Maw Crazy for Clothes! Burmese Leader Demands Cloth by the Tonne For Personal Use! Burmese People In Tatters as the 'Emperor' Commissions New Clothes*

Daily! DBM Gorges on Seven-Course Meals While People Starve! May May was particularly amused by the headlines, reading them aloud as she folded each of the children's moth-eaten sets of clothing, proud to wear her own heavy black cotton sarong that later outlasted the war by a decade. The Imperial Army did nothing to counter these claims, as doing so would have revealed their complicity in the supply scandal.

I was not as amused as my mother. I read the reports with disgust and disdain not because they targeted my father, but because of their glaring racism. If I was too young to have known my political views before, then seeing my country in ruins lit the nationalist fuse in my Burmese heart. I saw how cruel it was for empires to fight over us, for the British government to siphon our resources to better their people at the expense of ours, and for the Japanese government to aspire to do the same. Those who dared to stand up for their small nations were called arrogant, uppity, selfish and mad.

I supported the Freedom Bloc for their mission of independence, but I also questioned the cost of such independence. Was chaos truly acceptable as a means to an end? I decided not to choose politics like the men around me did, through the strength of armies or the size of ships or the ferocity of war engines. I chose to be on the side of Burma, pledging my allegiance to whomever would do his or her best for my country.

The cloth scandal cruelly jabbed at my father and Bose's friendship, assumedly its intention. Bose was essentially a guest in a foreign land after relocating the INA command to Rangoon in January 1944, his operations at the mercy of my father and the Japanese. Though they were great friends, the reality of their individual war situations became all too real in Rangoon. Whilst my father, the Thakins and the Burmese had realized their goal of self-governance and so-called independence, Bose and the INA had yet to accomplish their task. Theirs was the most difficult of all; invading their homeland from a foreign country, India still the military stronghold of the British forces in the South Asia theater.

The Azad Hind government's great strength was its support base, comprised of thousands of merchants, traders, businessmen and farmers who sent massive shipments of essential goods to Rangoon. Rice, cloth, tinned meat, gold, reading material and other desired consumer goods arrived by shiploads at Bose's feet. The public began to compare the two governments. Though we were technically independent, the Burmese administration was dealing with two different foreign invaders in our country. We were free on paper but the scorched-earth destruction of crops, transportation links, communication lines and pertinent industries left Burma a shell of her former self. She could produce nothing and was utterly immobilized.

The public and Japanese command pressured Dr. Ba Maw to demand supplies from Bose. Phay Phay, on one hand, thought it only fair that the Azad Hind government willingly donate some of its supplies. Bose, on the other, felt that the INA needed the supplies more, as Burma had already achieved its dream of independence. In the end, the Burmese received a small stream of goods without my father and Bose coming to blows, but their friendship was never the same again.

Cracks also deepened in Dr. Ba Maw and the Thakins' relationship. When my father formed the civil administration, he had two weeks to build an new government. There were one hundred and twenty-five positions to fill, ten of which went to the Thakins and the BIA. The Thakins resented their lack of representation, throwing accusations of nepotism at my father. There were only so many men to choose from, the majority of BIA leaders showing great irresponsibility in the early days of the war, unable to control their troops let alone an entire nation. Dr. Ba Maw had appointed people with whom he had worked with closely in the past, just as Aung San had filled the ranks of the military with those closest to him as War Minister. Who else was there? "Just because you know how to fight with a gun, know how to kill a man, does not mean that you know how to build a country," my father said to Thakin Than Tun one day as he tried to push the appointments of several untested, pro-Communist guerrilla fighters.

"Then a government cannot be true if it does not represent the people," Than Tun philosophized.

"Don't you see? The entire nation is crooked, the whole lot! My party, your party, the army, the Japanese, all hands reaching into an empty pot!"

Demoralized, fatigued, disenchanted. Phay Phay, Thakin Than Tun and U Nu vowed to resign at this point. My father told Isamura that he wanted to resign, to which the latter feigned ignorance, setting the issue aside. Colonel Hiraoka was aware of my father's desire to leave office, but he had grown attached to our family and encouraged him to remain in his post. My mother implored them to stay on, asking them to imagine what would happen if real Japanese puppets were to step up to the plate, combined with mounting suspicions that the British would launch an offensive within a year and recapture Burma. If things should end so soon, then at least they could stand their ground and wait with honor instead of running for the hills. She was beginning to sound more like a seasoned general than the generals themselves. I sided with my mother, believing that it was better to have one enemy than to have two as the war was closing.

The Imperial Army dealt yet another blow. Tokyo demanded that the civil government eliminate English instruction from schools and replace it with Japanese exclusively, designed to test my father's loyalty to their cause. What leader in his right mind dealing with food shortages, civilian deaths and economic implosion, would rationalize such a request? In an attempt to smooth relations with the Imperial Army, Aung San cleared an order to make Japanese the official language of the military schools, but it did little to allay suspicions of my father's loyalties. The Kempetai believed that our family was working for the Allies given our perfect command of British English, penchant for reading Western philosophers and frequent quoting of American films. My father's unwillingness to implement Japanese language teaching in schools surely meant that he was working for the enemy.

Professor Iwama, the Japanese Advisor in the Education Department, asked U Nu about a "treasonous" framed document in our living room[25]. When my mother and father attended the King's coronation in 1937, the Mayor of London had invited them to a special reception for heads of state. The framed invitation hung in a darkened corner of the room, a long-forgotten relic of days gone by. We hardly paid attention to the yellowed parchment, its calligraphy fading behind glass. Apparently the Kempetai thought better of it, assured proof of our Anglophile leanings and betrayal.

My name was breathed across the lips of the Kempetai. During breakfast one morning, my mother waited until Colonel Hiraoka had left the dining room to whisper in my ear, "Congratulations, Tinsa. Your name is featured in the intelligence reports as a potential spy, on the suspicion that you have been teaching seditious material at monastic schools."

I choked on my slice of stale bread, flecks of wheat trapped in my throat as I wanted to laugh and cry at the same time. "Me? A spy?" I gasped. My mind grappled to figure out what I had been teaching my students. The English alphabet? Lullabies?

Her eyes opened wide in feigned shock. "Oh yes, yes, once you begin teaching those children the ABCs, they're well on their way to becoming enemy sympathizers." She chuckled, the first time in a long time that I had seen her in such a jovial mood.

"Has your name ever been in the reports?"

Her chuckling stopped and she looked at me, surprised. "Oh heavens, no. No, no, no."

We laughed about these accusations until the Kempetai decided to get rid of my father once and for all in February 1944. They had enough assassins and resources to remove any man from Burma but they could not get rid of my father so

---

[25] U Nu. *Burma Under the Japanese: Pictures and Portraits*. London: Macmillan & Co Ltd, 1954. Print.

easily. He, Bose and Jose Laurel from the Philippines operated as a triad and his removal would have sparked a wildfire in East Asia during its most critical phase. Thus, they attacked from within, approaching U Nu and asking him to take the reins of leadership. He was decidedly more anti-Japanese than the Allies at that point, balking at such a request and never speaking a word of it again.

Their next plan involved my cousin-in-law, Taw Payagyi, the eldest grandson of King Thibaw who was married to my distant cousin. Lanky, timid and of an easygoing disposition, he was the central character in an elaborate plot to revive the monarchy, the Kempetai hoping that his royal blood would evoke the sympathy of the masses. Some accounts report that Taw Payagyi was initially interested in a plan to resurrect the monarchy, drawn to the romantic notion of playing savior to a fractured wartime country. But Taw Payagyi withdrew from any further talks with the Imperial Army, realizing that he was not politically minded after all. He approached my father and Aung San to apologize for his brief foray into murky politics, his head hanging low. "Uncle, please forgive me for my indiscretion," he said with great shame, a child asking for clemency. "I don't know what came over me. I would never do anything to betray you or the family." There was no more talk of royal ambitions after that, nor did my father bring it up again. Despite the young man's voluntary retreat from politics, the Burmese Communists later assassinated Taw Payagyi in 1948.

One option remained. Air raid alarms rang throughout the city on an impossibly hot day, steam rising from the concrete roads. I was reading *Wuthering Heights* for the seventh time when our sirens echoed, but my nerves no longer jumped at the shrill sound. My body naturally rose to walk to our front yard and into our underground bomb shelter. My siblings and I formed an efficient line to the shelter doors behind my mother and father, an ingrained habit formed from a childhood spent in the thick of war. The nannies were the last to arrive at the shelter, one carrying a plate of strawberries that we had planted in the garden. I was not very hungry but I took a handful of strawberries, letting them sit in my mouth as their tart juice pricked my taste buds. The berries were not made for Rangoon earth, the city too humid and at too low of an altitude for the fruit to fully blossom. I had flashbacks of our family trips to May Myo, where my parents took my siblings and me to the famous strawberry fields, acres upon acres of equidistant patches running until they reached the horizon. Zali, Mala and I used to race in between the patches and the last to reach the finish line would carry the basket of picked strawberries back to the car. Mala was always in last place, Zali and I laughing at her with clumps of garnet red juice smeared across our mouths and cheeks.

The air raid turned out to be a false alarm and my father opened the door slightly ajar, letting sunlight creep in. We exited the shelter in a steady stream, the younger ones spinning cartwheels on the lawn to stretch their legs with the nannies chasing after them. It was nearly dinnertime and the activity of the house centered on the dining room where my father was reading the day's intelligence reports. All of a sudden, the maids shouted that a drunk Japanese soldier had wandered into our front yard and was attempting to pry the doors of the bomb shelter open. "Dr. Ba Maw! Dr. Ba Maw! There is a strange Japanese man out there. Come look!" The girls hid behind the curtain, their eyes shut tight but fingers pointed at a faceless shadow in the garden.

My parents rushed to the window, worried that the Japanese soldier was of a poor lot and would harass the women and children. I crept to the side of the window next to the dining table, my heart stopping when I saw the soldier turn to see my parents' silhouettes in the backlight of our dining room. I tried my best to hold my breath, afraid that any movement would draw further attention, but I couldn't help but scream at the top of my lungs as he proceeded to run and slam the full force of his body against the heavy teak front door. Once. Twice. Ten times. I scanned the room and saw my seven-year-old brother, Binnya, curled beneath a chair with his eyes squeezed shut. Terrified, I scrambled next to him and put my finger to my lips to signal to him to remain quiet, trembling as I tried to make sense of what was happening.

Upon realizing that he could not open the door, the soldier shouted, "Spy! Spy! Spy!" Our gate sentries instinctively fired shots into the air, the neighborhood awash in flickering candlelight. My mother sprinted to the phone, calling Colonel Hiraoka who came running from his small wooden house just yards from our residence. He had forgotten to put on his uniform and came face-to-face with the mysterious soldier in his maroon dressing gown and soft slippers, bits of pine-scented shaving cream dotting his jawline. Hiraoka had never seen the man before, judging by the pure shock on his face. A thick feeling of dread and tension enveloped me, the ominous feeling of unknowing and lies. I mouthed to Binnya, "Stay here," as I summoned the courage to go to my mother's side, both of us watching the scene unfold from the living room window.

Hiraoka was pointing his gun at the man's head, the soldier smiling and revealing yellowed, rotten teeth. The would-be assassin retrieved a revolver from a hidden ankle holster, setting it on the cold ground between them. When Hiraoka asked the sentries to come forward for questioning, the young men whimpered that they were to report to their superior and scampered off, afraid of Dr. Ba Maw's wrath. The assassin did not try to run; he kept on smiling as Hiraoka placed handcuffs on his slender wrists, flashing a menacing smile at my father one last time before he was taken away.

Rangoon was rife with rumors and finger pointing. Aung San, Bo Let Ya, U Nu and Bo Yan Naing hurried to our house at dawn, the morning light chasing their backs. U Nu and Bo Let Ya were fearful, concerned for my father but also worried about the possibility of being assassinated themselves. Aung San, with his entire being draped in melancholy, revealed to my father that the assassin had approached him about a half hour before he came to our house and divulged his plans to deal with Dr. Ba Maw. "I had brushed him off, thinking he was just some manic Japanese soldier. I run into so many of them nowadays," he said in a sorrowful tone. "If I had thought that he was serious, the gravity of the situation, I would have stopped him right then and there. It was all so fast, I didn't even think to phone you as I did not take him seriously."

Bo Yan Naing uncovered further details of the plot after questioning our sentries. The Japanese soldier was named Captain Asahi, one of Isamura's contacts from Shonan and known for being a sociopath even among the lunatics of the Kempetai. Asahi and a Burmese accomplice by the name of Po Tok, a local charlatan, had evaded the sentries by telling them that they detected an American spy at Dr. Ba Maw's house and were sent there to investigate. The naïve young men were only so willing to let them in, trusting men in impressive uniforms. Asahi and Po Tok were to kill our entire family in the bomb shelter, raid sirens the perfect cover to mask muffled gunshots twelve feet underground. No one would have thought to look for us until dawn, more than enough time for the assassins to escape from Rangoon.

Fate had been on our side that evening, the false alarm permitting us to return to the house earlier than usual. We were alive, for now. Asahi and Po Tok were sentenced to fifteen years' imprisonment and Isamura shipped off to Shonan, but it was not long before another suspicious Japanese officer approached Aung San and teased him with the knowledge that he knew that Dr. and Mrs. Ba Maw took long walks at night to clear their heads, an ideal setting for another assassination. Aung San notified my father, who stopped leaving the house altogether unless he was surrounded by guards and on official business. The rest of us did not leave our home at all. The circle of people that we could trust dwindled to a handful of loyal friends, the end nearing for our family.

CHAPTER SEVEN

The assassination attempt cruelly snatched any vestige of freedom left in my young life. My father forbade us from leaving the house and the Imperial Army enforced this by stationing dozens of soldiers at our property. We were prisoners in our beloved home, watched by the very people who had the power, and perhaps the desire, to kill us if the right orders came in. My siblings and I walked around in a daze, no longer chasing each other around the house, the absence of our heavy school shoes scuffing the wood floors. I spent my waking hours huddled over old books, steadying my eyes as the lights flickered like Morse code messages.

I mourned the loss of my brief freedom but was also conflicted with my strong sense of duty towards my parents, family and country. Phay Phay and May May did not ask anything of me except for strength, to keep going as a pillar for my siblings and peers who could not afford to see the leader's daughter fail. Yet my thoughts always wandered to my students at the monastic schools, who kept me feeling alive for the past year, the tiny fragments of personal independence that I had grasped and clung to. Asahi's gun had not gone off, but he made sure that a very important part of my life, my happiness, had been taken from me.

When we grew tired of our books, Mala and I perched ourselves by the living room window, staring into the green beyond of Rangoon. It was the spring of 1944 and the monsoon had come early, the palm trees in our front lawn swaying and rocking under the force of whiplash rain. I didn't think about much during those days, preferring to listen to the drops of water tapping on our stone walkway, meditating to their repetition. Mala, who was fifteen, chose to think about love, a subject that I had not even considered at seventeen. "Someday, my love is going to take me away from this mess," she declared.

"You don't have a love," I snorted at her.

"No, but he's out there and he'll find me," my sister countered without missing a beat. She was looking into the eye of the rain like a heroine in romance novel. I threw a pillow at her head, hearing the pleasing thud of its contact with her face. I wondered when and how love even entered her mind, since it had not crossed mine at all. We had very little interaction with the opposite sex having attended a convent school, and most of our free time was spent in the company of family and close friends. No one had discussed the topic with me as the eldest daughter and there was no outside context where I would even begin to think about myself as a girlfriend, a wife, or otherwise in relation to a man.

I studied Mala, who was not shy about people staring at her in her teen years. Her once-gangly limbs had evolved into a gazelle-like figure. Her eyes and hair shone like black lacquer, her silvery skin dewy and smooth like our mother's. Mala's posture was always straight, never slouching but effortlessly upright and fluid like a dancer's. She was beautiful and preternaturally regal, a crystal figurine hidden behind the mildewing walls of our cordoned home.

I was not as beautiful as Mala. No one was. My sister and I were of the same height and slender form, but my lips were not as full as hers and my eyelashes curled inwards, unlike her elegant crescents. My gums were a little too big when I smiled, but I liked my toothy grin because every ounce of my happiness was conveyed in a single expression. I wasn't envious of Mala's beauty; hers was ethereal, almost unreal for a mere human, and our physical differences were never compared in the entirety of our childhoods. They were simply differences.

We continued to look out the window, watching the gutters heave and flood with each smattering of raindrops. My focus turned to the soldier stationed adjacent to the front door, partially covered by a wilting hydrangea bush. We were forbidden from speaking to the soldiers and I made a game of guessing who they were, where they were from, and if they had families waiting for them somewhere in Japan. This particular soldier's curved jaw swayed back and forth as he chewed rough tobacco, perhaps an ingrained habit from a life spent in the mountainous countryside of Japan's sprawling islands. He was the shade of dark almonds unlike the officers with their ivory skin. The soldier suddenly caught my gaze, baring his muck-stained teeth in a disturbing smile and his beady eyes glanced between Mala and me. There was something about the way in which he looked at us that made me feel uneasy. He was drinking us in and I had never felt so naked though I was covered from head to toe in a long-sleeved cotton shirt and *longyi*. The soldier put his fingers to his lips and whistled to his comrades, three of whom came to his side. He pointed at us through the windowpane, all four of them smiling menacingly at us.

"Tinsa, Mala, keep away from the window," my father's voice boomed from the entryway. I jolted at his command and shut the curtain immediately, the soft fabric grazing Mala's hair. After all of those years of teasing Aunt Kinmimi for her anxieties over something bad happening to my sisters and me, I finally understood what she was fearing. I was naïve and had brushed her worries aside until that very moment, when I was confronted with the darker elements of men's natures.

Our only visitors were the Thakins and Imperial Army officers, floating in and out of our driveway like bees. I made the decision not to contact my school friends as I did not want to put them in any danger by association. Our house arrest felt like a contagion and I was afraid to let anyone whom I cared for get caught in the dragnet. The teachers at the monastic schools wrote to me on several occasions, but I did not reply because I did not want the Kempetai questioning them over me. Their notes remained locked in my nightstand drawer, hidden but not forgotten. I breathed with relief when Thakin Than Tun, U Nu and Bo Let Ya came to visit our home, for they too were monitored, tracked and stalked, and their empathy knew no bounds. The three of them always said hello and cracked jokes to my siblings and me, and I am eternally grateful to them for thinking of us in those small but significant ways, for providing some lightness in the bogs of our suffocation.

In March 1944, days before my seventeenth birthday, a young man dressed in his full Burmese National Army uniform sauntered through the gates. The sleeves and chest of his olive green jacket were encrusted with every imaginable pin, pennant and medal. It was strange for a highly decorated officer to travel without guards, yet the young man seemed not to have a care in the world as he marched along our driveway. I was in the living room reading the day's paper when I heard soft footsteps approaching the front door. Knowing better than to answer his knocks, I glanced at the window to my right, temporarily blinded when the sun hit his left shoulder and his medals reflected in my eye. He let himself in after several unanswered knocks, entering the foyer and looking around to see if anyone would address him. I tried to blend into the sofa, holding my breath and hoping that he wouldn't see me. He was handsome in the way that men who are born from rich earth and live by it are. There was a bruised cut on his cheek, a cruel blemish to his oval visage. The young man smiled as he looked around him, showing crooked but perfectly white teeth. He had taken off his hat and I could see a thick mass of black hair tamed by slicks of coconut oil, which I could smell from fifteen feet away. I was staring shamelessly until he turned to face me, a girl clutching a wrinkled newspaper and bashful in his presence.

The officer's smile did not wane when he looked at me, as if he were looking at an old friend. At that moment, my mother, father and aunt descended the staircase and the young man was escorted to my father's study, vanishing like a ghost. Mala, who had been in the dining room on the opposite end of the foyer, sashayed to where I was sitting and announced nonchalantly, "That's him."

"Who?" Was I supposed to know him?

"Bo Yan Naing," she snapped at my naiveté.

I racked my brain and realized that I had seen Bo Yan Naing days after the assassination attempt when he interrogated our sentries, yet I had no recollection of him as an individual. The events following the assassination attempt were a blur to me, faces and uniforms indistinguishable from one another. Gathering my thoughts, I now knew exactly who he was, recounting the first time that he visited our home in 1941, our first glimpses of each other. He had come to deliver a message from Aung San requesting five hundred rupees from my father. Aung San and Yan Naing were plotting for armed resistance, begging for alms from backers. Yan Naing, a student leader and close confidante of my father's, was sent as the most diplomatic choice. I was fourteen at the time and hadn't the slightest inclination for romance and even if I did, I wouldn't have known what to do with a handsome, well-spoken, twenty-one-year-old man in my vicinity. He was confident, assured of his mission, holding a postcard-sized letter in his hand that carried the weight of his political ambitions.

Bo Yan Naing became the Secretary for National Security and Head of the Executive Guard and was one of the youngest members of the Thirty Comrades. While I did not know of him as a man, I knew of him as a myth. He was at Hainan Island with the Comrades under the name of *Yamashita Teruo* and emerged as Bo Yan Naing, *he who conquers his enemies*. Yan Naing commanded the main BIA regiment through Victoria Point, marching to the north from Tenasserim. The road was so thick with jungle brush that he was forced to sail ahead of his ground troops on an old fishing boat, searching for hidden remnants of British-Indian troops in retreat. It was rumored that fishermen swam after his boat and begged to fight under him, sleepy coastal villages emptied of their young men in his wake. Another rumor spread that Yan Naing was in fact a sea dacoit sent by *nats*[26] to snatch young men from their homes as punishment for their family's sins. Tales of his invincibility swept lower Burma, pro-Freedom Bloc families sitting in their bamboo huts at night and sharing stories about the mighty Yan Naing, how he placed a live gun in his mouth and dared anyone who did not believe in the BIA to pull the trigger. According to the legend, the gun did not go off once.

On March 29, 1942, Bo Yan Naing's regiment prepared for an offensive attack at Shwedaung near Prome. He had attended high school in Prome and spent the latter part of his youth there before embarking to Rangoon for university. He later recounted seeing his hometown of Prome littered with bodies, monks shot by retreating troops, villagers mutilated and their bodies dumped in wells to poison the water supply. There was no one better suited from the Comrades to lead the charge against a detachment from the British 7th Armoured Brigade, which was in retreat from Paungde under the command of John Henry Anstice. British-Indian troops were in the process of clearing Shwedaung when the Japanese 15th Regiment, led by Misao Sato and Bo Yan Naing's 1200 BIA fighters, descended on Anstice's men.

In the words of Edward Law-Yone[27], Bo Yan Naing became the first hero of the war. The BIA seemed destined to lose the battle, sandwiched between two enemy regiments. Sixty of Yan Naing's men perished, three hundred were wounded and four hundred captured or missing. The young boys were too inexperienced and their outdated equipment stalled against Anstice's artillery. Those left on the battlefield prayed to the gods, who responded in the form of a lucky shot from a wayward Japanese tank gun. The shot hit a British tank

---

[26] Burmese spiritual deities.
[27] Founded *The Nation* in 1948, Burma's most influential English language newspaper. Chief Editor until he was detained in 1962. Joined Yan Naing's insurgency in late 1960s.

sitting on a vital bridge, causing Anstice to retreat into open fields where Yan Naing attacked with his remaining men. When the bullets cleared, he saw his troops' lifeless bodies next to him and rushed to check the pulses on their warm corpses, his uniform steeped in his friends' blood. The BIA troops, believing Yan Naing, their leader, to be mortally wounded, ran towards the enemy troops to avenge him. The British troops retreated with heavy losses, several tanks destroyed and nearly four hundred men killed or wounded. Despite the BIA's heavy losses, it was the first major victory for the independence army.

Women flocked after Bo Yan Naing as one of the remaining eligible Comrades, yet he did not have a reputation for being a man-about-town. Without a wife or family of his own, Burma was his only love. He was thought to be even more bullheaded than Aung San, his entire life and being centered on Burmese independence. He had flirted with Communism during his school days but he did not ascribe to an ideology other than pure nationalism, something that I realized that we had in common. When a reporter once asked him about his political leanings, he replied, "I'm simply Burmese. I just want what's best for my country."

I saw more of Bo Yan Naing and members of the administration in the following months. The Imperial Army was rapidly expanding its field operations by May 1944, an impenetrable mass unraveling outward from Rangoon. I sensed their urgency, panic and desperation, though I was not privy to their closed-door discussions. I only caught glimpses of Yan Naing when he scurried through the door and straight to the meetings, and sometimes he would look back and smile. Aunt Kinmimi must have guessed that I was forming a crush because she started to hover around me anytime that I was in the sitting room, shutting the doors when she heard bootsteps approaching our entryway.

Then, in mid-May, my parents sat me down and asked me to make the most important decision of my life. They looked so calm and composed as their world was crumbling around them, Burma collapsing as the tide of war turned against the

Imperial Army and its allies. My mother gave a small smile, glancing upward at my father. His black oval eyes bore into me, a serious gaze normally reserved for lectures or scoldings.

"Tinsa, do you remember how I've always said that I wanted you to finish your schooling before marriage?" he asked in a subdued tone.

"Yes, I do, Phay Phay." With their blessing and my high marks, I still dreamed of attending university for my bachelors and masters degrees, nostalgic about my brief days at the monastic schools. It was not a matter of if, but when I would return to a classroom, both as a student and as a teacher.

Phay Phay looked at May May with a soft gaze. "With the war in our country, a lot of things have changed. Things have become quite dangerous for us and especially for young women. The universities are closed and we don't know when you'll be able to attend school again." A hesitant pause. "Your mother and I think that the best thing for you would be to get married. We don't know how much worse things are going to get, but should anything happen to me, we would like to see another man in this family who will protect you." His words were drenched in hopeful sadness, unspoken implications heavy in the air.

"Who is it?" I asked.

"Bo Yan Naing. I trust him with everything, especially your life," Phay Phay confided. "The Japanese will retreat soon and it would be naïve to assume that they would leave you, my daughter, out of the fray. You're very aware that the officers have been looking at you in an uncomfortable way, yes?"

May May, who had been too quiet during the discussion, cut in. "Let's not go into those details, because you will not be hauled off to a foreign land like some war trophy. School is your priority and you will return one day, but right now we have to be brutally honest about the current situation. Any one of the Japanese officers can ask for your hand in marriage and they may not take too kindly to the word no. Yet there is Yan Naing, who is a good and decent young man, and you are so similar and you don't even realize it. There aren't a lot of people like him who have lived through the same things that you have and importantly, understand them."

I was shocked in so many ways. The thought of marriage alone was a bewildering concept, and to Bo Yan Naing, out of all people. Was I ready? Would I be a good wife and Yan Naing a good husband? How did my parents make it seem so effortless? I was apprehensive, but I was also surprised to feel giddy. I would be lying if I said that the prospect of marrying a handsome war hero wasn't somewhat thrilling.

"I can't say yes right now, but can you bring him to the house tomorrow?"

My mother exhaled with great relief and my father simply nodded. I couldn't help but blush a bit.

*****

Yan Naing came to see me the next day where, naturally, my mother and Aunt Kinmimi chaperoned his visit, my aunt's owlish eyes scanning for wayward hands. Well-raised girls were not to be alone with young men, even if they were potentially betrothed. Yan Naing was a good sport about it, taking it in stride and being the utmost gentleman about our customs and propriety. He sat across the coffee table from me, his hands folded in his lap like a schoolboy. He was shy, glancing nervously to look at me and then looking away. I had never conversed with a man in a romantic sense and even with all of the books that I had read, none had prepared me for this very real situation.

"Are you well, Tinsa?" he smiled sheepishly.

"I'm well, I'm well. Tell me about yourself." It came out like a directive, too harsh for my first words to him. I wanted to crawl under the table and never come out.

My bluntness made him laugh. "Yes, Commanderess!" Yan Naing cracked and we fell into a fit of giggles. He shared that he was born of modest means to U Khant and Daw Thant on November 2, 1918 in Kanmalay village, about 300 miles south of Rangoon. His birth name was Tun Shein, though I would only know him as Yan Naing, his *nom de guerre*. After attending elementary and middle school in Aung Lan, a humid outpost on the west coast of the Ayeyarwaddy, he finished his secondary education in Prome. Yan Naing described the first time that he was arrested in Prome, charged as a leader of the student boycott in 1936 and how his father, U Khant, sensed an unusual brightness and uncontrollable madness in his son and sent him to the Rangoon Arts and Science University. He became immersed in politics there, becoming the Secretary of the Rangoon University Students' Union and the All-Burma Students' Union, the first and only time in history that one person occupied dual posts. He was arrested yet again in another student boycott, forming the All-Burma Students' Steel Force, where he was known as Thanmani Tun Shein (Steel Tun Shein).

Tinsa and Bo Yan Naing on their wedding day, June 23 1944

He regaled me with stories of his travels to India - the land of the Maharajas, the birthplace of Siddhartha, a country alight with nationalist sentiments not unlike Burma – where he attended the Indian National Congress at Ramga as a student representative on March 29, 1940. Fiercely intelligent, he grilled me on my thoughts on philosophy, politics, literature, the latter of which was my forte. He was speechless when I recited verbatim Hamlet's most important soliloquy, always beginning with, "To be, or not to be…"

"You really are your father's daughter, aren't you?" Yan Naing said with great astonishment, perhaps assuming that I would be a willowy socialite. I noticed that he had inched forward, his entire being focused on me and me alone. Aunt Kinmimi was hovering right behind him in case he dared to take another inch.

"I like reading," I blushed, "both in Burmese and in English. But do you know what the strange thing about our language is?"

"What's that?"

"We feel and express so much, yet there are no exact phrases for the two most important feelings in the world."

"And they are?"

"Well, there's no way to say, 'I hate you,' in Burmese, is there? Your enemy could be standing right in front of you and you'd be paralyzed to express just how much you loathed them."

My comment made Yan Naing holler with laughter, the teak chair legs rocking beneath his weight. "No, I suppose not. And what's the other one?"

I smiled. "On the opposite end, there's no way to say, 'I love you,' either."

Yan Naing looked away as I said this, flushing with shyness at my words. "Sometimes love and hate can be one in the same, so perhaps we Burmese were wise to avoid a direct answer, so as to prevent the question in the first place," he mused.

One week later, I said yes. Just like there isn't a phrase for *I love you* in Burmese, there is also no formal way of marriage proposal. I told my parents, who then called Yan Naing to tell him the news. He came to our home every day after I said yes, staying at my side as we called on brothers, sisters, cousins, friends and colleagues who were to be in the ceremony. We had more time to speak and my favorite times were when he would tell me bawdy jokes, the opposite of my father's acerbic wit. Sometimes I would take just one look at him and burst into laughter, remembering some dirty joke that he had told me.

The months flew with wedding preparations and in those days, no one told me what to expect of marriage except for the usual homemaking expectations and the arrival of children. Forget the carnal aspects of love and marriage – neither my mother nor aunt prepared me for the wedding kiss, let alone the racy bits! "There's nothing to tell, she'll learn soon enough!" Aunt Kinmimi declared, banishing all forms of intimate discussion regarding the more vulgar things in life, according to her.

I would have liked an intimate gathering of friends and family, in good taste but private, but my father had other plans for me. Over one thousand guests attended the two-day wedding on June 23, 1944 at the State House on Ahlone Road, a teak colonial building that was formerly the British Governor-General's residence and had been spared during the air raids. Following protocol, we reserved the first day for government and military leaders, followed by a second day for family and friends. I had asked guests not to bring gifts, shocking the sensitivities of polite society accustomed to displaying wealth through extravagance. Any further attempts at austerity were unfortunately quashed. As Dr. Ba Maw's daughter and Bo Yan Naing's betrothed, the wedding was more for the guests than for our personal enjoyment. My wedding became famous when the foreign war press concocted a strange rumor that there were acrobats, elephants and dwarves greeting guests, but there was none of that.

A war, however, did erupt between the Japanese, INA and BDA over who would sit to the right of my father, the simple wooden chair now a politically charged throne. My father wanted Bose to sit next to him according to their rank as leaders, but the Japanese Ambassador and Commander-in-Chief Iida attempted to seize the coveted seat. Their assistants lobbied their case to anyone who would listen, until U Nu and Bo Let Ya surreptitiously ushered Bose to the seat, too late for the Ambassador to pitch a fit. The latter slumped into the second row right behind my father, eyes glowering at Bose for the entirety of the ceremony.

At 10:00 AM, over 200 dignitaries and officers were called to the garden in the back of the house, aflame with blood-red and orange hibiscus trees and bougainvillea, an unusually sunny and dry day during monsoon. In keeping with our spiritual beliefs, my mother and aunt had consulted a holy man said to possess powers to control the weather. The gods must have been in my favor that day because there was not a drop of rain as I descended on the emerald lawn, all eyes turning on the bride-to-be. I was trembling beneath my gold brocade blouse and *longyi*, the silver bolero shaking atop my beating chest. My mother had kept the gold and silver silk hidden in a locked wardrobe, a relic acquired years ago from a passing Jaipur trader, a souvenir from an era that would never return to Rangoon. Yan Naing wore his full military uniform as the Head of the Executive Guard, handsome in his understated manner.

The ceremony followed the ancient traditions of our kings and queens by fluke. During the monarchy, high-ranking Buddhist monks (or Brahmins) officiated all royal ceremonies and weddings. My mother came into contact with these Brahmins during one of her Women's League runs in Mandalay, visiting the three ancient monks who had been taking refuge in a decaying monastery in the outskirts of the city after their centuries-old teak monastery was destroyed in a bombing. They were the Three Wise Men of Mandalay, vessels of centuries of Buddhist doctrine and ancient sacraments.

"Are you Mrs. Maw?" asked the eldest and most senior monk. She nodded and bowed before them, her hands and forehead touching the dirt floor beneath their feet.

"We have heard that your eldest daughter is getting married

and we would like to officiate her wedding."

"Sayardaw[28], it is a great honor, but don't you think it would be a little...politically charged?" my mother inquired self-consciously.

The three laughed at each other with their eyes, a private joke. "Well, it's about time we show the Japanese and British who shall truly inherit this country," they chuckled in unison, their bodies collectively shaking beneath yards of faded maroon robes.

The three Brahmins escorted me towards an elevated stage where an empty silver ewer and a golden bowl awaited me. My fiancé and I clasped each others' right hands, the first time we had actually touched each other. Yan Naing's palms were calloused, rough, a small boil on the left side of his index finger where I imagined him to grasp pens while writing long letters, or possibly the trigger of his gun. His grip was warm, his heartbeat racing through his veins.

The senior Brahmin tied a white silk scarf around our enclosed hands while a second Brahmin poured water from the golden bowl, the cool wetness trickling between my fingers and falling into the silver ewer. A horn sounded to announce our marriage, the crowd bursting into loud cheering and clapping. My seven bridesmaids walked through the aisles flinging gold and silver bundles into the air, a symbol of sharing the couple's good fortunes with their beloved friends and families. Mala, who was one of my bridesmaids, glided up the aisle and held my hand gently. "You're a queen now, Tinsa," she teased, and I beamed and squeezed her hand.

The guests practically ran to the opposite end of the lawn where large banquet tables overflowed with fragrant dishes and cold drinks. The stuffy, formal atmosphere gave way to loosened neckties and raucous chatter. My father's introductory toast congratulated me and his new son-in-law, unable to contain the enormous grin on his face. It had been a long time since I had seen my father with such a genuine smile,

---

[28] The honorific title for a high-ranking monk.

his warmth radiating through the room.

Out of all of the important dignitaries, generals, socialites and hangers-on who attended my wedding, none made so much of an impression on me as one man in particular. Netaji Bose flitted through the crowd, effortlessly charming all who came in contact with him. He smiled and mingled, his warm grip putting the beneficiary of his attention at ease. *This is what it takes to command the INA*, I thought to myself. At last, he made his way towards Yan Naing and me, sitting stiffly on overstuffed, baroque-style matrimonial cushions, where we remained for five hours straight in order to greet all of the guests. Bose's two aides, fresh-faced young men with standard military posture, placed several gifts in front of us. Two diamond-studded bracelets and a ring for me. A classic pocket watch for Yan Naing engraved with *Congratulations from Subhas Chandra Bose*. A signed, silver serving tray gleaming atop the table. 500,000 lakhs in a nondescript cloth bag, an enormous sum that my mother discreetly appropriated and reappeared later in the form of a new wing at the military hospital.

There was an intense lassitude about Bose, thinly veiled behind caffeinated eyes. He spoke in the measured tone of a man accustomed to giving away more of himself to others than he ever received in return. "A hearty congratulations to the newlyweds," he blessed us. "Diamonds, gold, silver, elements created to withstand the test of time. As I hope your marriage will, too."

"We are not worthy of these gifts, Netaji, but thank you for your enormous generosity," I sputtered, in awe of the figure standing before me. Bose's eyes coasted over us, studying our visages, our unlined countenances, the vigors of youth.

"Take care of each other. People always forget that time is the rarest commodity of all, something that we might be in short supply of nowadays," he philosophized, before disappearing into a sea of pastel silk scarves and plumes of cigar smoke.

CHAPTER EIGHT

Yan Naing moved into my family's home following the wedding. My husband did not have many things, just a couple of dented iron trunks, one of which was filled with his books and the other containing the four sets of clothing that he owned. He had been appointed rector of the Mingaladon Military Academy and did not need much other than his uniform, slipping into his faded cotton shirt and frayed *longyi* when he returned home every evening. Even after months of living at our lakeside home, Yan Naing still found himself lost in the tangled network of hallways and bedrooms and dark corridors, never having lived in a house quite like this one. To me, my home was just another like the others on the street, but to him it was an overwhelming maze that he had to memorize by heart. He found safety in the confines of our small room overlooking the back garden, shutting the door quickly behind him and exhaling with relief upon seeing me.

I found out that I was pregnant three months after the wedding. "You see, Tinsa, I told you that you would figure things out on your own," Aunt Kinmimi deadpanned when the doctor confirmed my pregnancy. Yan Naing was elated when I told him the news, grabbing me gently by my shoulders and letting his warm hands rest on my slight shoulders. He did not stop smiling to himself about his child, the prospect of life in the midst of deadly chaos.

Young Tinsa

I inspected my belly obsessively during the first few months of my pregnancy out of fervent anticipation and curiosity. I had always been quite slim and did not show for the first five months. I stood in front of the full-length mirror by my dresser every day and rubbed my abdomen up and down as if my skin would contract at my command, my unborn child answering to my call. A small sliver of a bump finally appeared at exactly five months, my baby revealing himself or herself to the world. Yan Naing, who had been worried about my not showing, relaxed at the sight of my growing belly. I was too tired to read at night before bed, therefore my husband took it upon himself to read to me and our unborn child, his tenor voice lulling me to sleep as crickets stirred in the distance.

I wondered if my child would also be born under Rahu's watch like me, to be given the gift of life in the shadow of death. Would his or her entrance to this world foretell a lifetime of extremes? My marriage and pregnancy coincided with the aftermath of the Imperial Army's disastrous Imphal Campaign that began the previous March, a failed invasion of India through Burma's northwestern border. Imphal, on the India-Burma frontier, was the site of one of the largest Allied bases in Asia and was linked to another large base in Dimapur. Lieutenant-General Masakazu Kawabe believed that he would make history by winning Imphal and crushing the main supply line for British troops, but the campaign was doomed from the start. Neither my father, Bose, or any of the divisional commanders agreed with the proposal but Kawabe was convinced that his plan would succeed. My father and the Burmese cabinet warned Kawabe of the Chindwin River Valley and its jungles, some of the most unforgiving terrain on earth. The likelihood of surviving Allied attacks combined with malaria, dysentery, starvation and cholera was very slim. It was the largest defeat of the war for Japan with nearly 60,000 wounded or dead, most dying of exhaustion, starvation and tropical disease. It was the end for the Imperial Army and consequently the end for my father and the Freedom Bloc. It also meant that we were once again on the defensive from the British, who would reclaim the country and put an end to the Burma Campaign.

During those dark, final days of the war, my father drew increasingly into himself, his great mind trying to find a way out of the situation while his heart told him to keep steady. He could either run and hope that the Japanese would protect him, or he could weasel his way into a truce with the Allied forces. He would be a failure to one and a war criminal to the other.

Yan Naing and I couldn't bear to see him like this, but my father shrugged off our sympathies. "Save your thoughts for your child, for the future," Phay Phay mumbled, as my mother looked on with worry.

I did not know what would happen to us, fearing the worst because we were on the wrong side of history, and for the life of my unborn child. Would the victors be merciful? Would they spare my baby, if not me? These were morbid thoughts but I no longer had the luxury of just thinking about my own survival. The baby kicked each time these questions flooded my mind, a forceful reminder that I had no choice but to keep going.

A second assassination plot against my father followed in the fall of 1944, this time by foreign traders and war profiteers angry with his administration for proposing a series of regulations stipulating that all immoveable property in the country could only be owned by Burmese and that all companies must have at least 60% Burmese ownership. Strangely, it was the Imperial Army that stopped the assassination, needing my father to attend one last meeting in Tokyo. The Emperor invited him as an honored guest in November 1944 as the Allies opened a general offensive to recapture East Asia. Field Marshal Sugiyama requested that Dr. Ba Maw undertake a series of appearances in Tokyo including public speeches declaring his undying support for their cause, a visit to a kamikaze training camp and a nationwide radio address speaking to millions who didn't want to believe that the war was over.

"I will agree to this under certain conditions," he said brusquely to Sugiyama.

"And what would that be, sir?"

"You will spare Burma, spare Rangoon and the Shwedagon. Keep your fighting limited to the jungles, far away from people. You will release all civilian officers and compensate the families of those at greatest risk," my father demanded. Sugiyama shook hands with my father, a crocodile's smile.

When U Nu discovered that my father was going to Tokyo,

he stormed into our house and shouted at my father, "Have you no sense, Sayar? They are losing and you cannot be their lackey!"

Phay Phay had only one thing to say to U Nu. "Have you seen what they did to Manila?" For my father, he viewed it as his last chance to appeal for Rangoon's survival, to avoid the fate and rapes of Manchuria, Seoul and Manila. His exchange with U Nu marked the end of their alliance once and for all. Aung San, Thakin Than Tun, Thakin Soe[29] and U Nu had been meeting secretly to discuss a new resistance movement against the Japanese. The Anti-Fascist People's Freedom League (AFPFL) formed in August 1944 in Pegu, with Thakin Soe proclaimed as the leader. This tenuous coalition of Communists, factions of the Burmese National Army and Socialists had one goal in mind: to push the Imperial Army out of Burma.

My father knew that the Thakins would be leaving, what they had desired for a long time. U Nu informed him of their plans to join the Allies, documented in his war memoirs:

> We discussed whether or not it would be a good thing to consult him [Dr. Ba Maw] about the insurrection against the Japanese and decided that, if he approved it, he would give us all the help he could and, if he did not approve, we were confident that he would not hand us over to the Japanese.[30]

The others followed U Nu's lead. Thakin Than Tun knocked on our front door as gusts of late autumn wind blew behind him, the normally spirited young man in a state of deep contemplation, coated in melancholy. Yan Naing and I were in the dining room listening to a scratchy broadcast of traditional folk music and I hummed to the tune of a lone, despondent

---

[29] The co-leader of the Communist faction alongside Thakin Than Tun.

[30] U Nu. *Burma Under the Japanese: Pictures and Portraits*. London: Macmillan & Co Ltd, 1954. Print.

harp. Yan Naing greeted Thakin Than Tun at the door, who asked to speak with my father. Than Tun could barely look at either of us in the eye, shuffling his feet and looking at everything else in the room except for our faces. I could smell the guilt in his perspiration, souring his usually composed and upbeat persona.

Phay Phay rose from his bed to see his guest in the living room. Since U Nu had informed my father of the AFPFL's plans, he already knew what Thakin Than Tun was going to say, that the Thakins were going to leave his side and that this would be the day. The younger man had not come for a confession but a goodbye. Yan Naing and I pretended to listen to the music broadcast as Than Tun revealed everything in one breath in the next room, not even taking a break for tea. Aung San and Thakin Soe had combined the remaining Burmese forces with the Communists and were to negotiate with the Allies in what would be their last chance to speak with the British on the issue of independence. The AFPFL would help to drive the Imperial Army out of Burma and significantly decrease the Allies' losses in exchange for self-rule. "It's also a way to save our own heads," he joked. "What do you think we should do, Sayar?"

My father thought long and hard and I could hear the silence eating away at Than Tun. When he finally spoke, he encouraged the younger man to do whatever it took to seal independence, whether it was from the Japanese or the British. "It was all I ever wanted," he lamented. "And if you are to achieve this, you'd best keep things quiet from me from now on." He suggested that Than Tun go to Toungoo to avoid arousing suspicion in Rangoon. Than Tun thanked my father before leaving, the last time that they would speak to each other during the war as allies.

My father excused himself to retire to bed and my mother came downstairs to bid goodbye to Than Tun. Yan Naing and I joined her in the living room and I think we all shared the same sentiment about Thakin Than Tun: that he was a good and honorable man and as close to family as we could get despite our differences in politics. It was only fitting for him to be the one to break the news to us. There was nothing that he could say to us to alleviate the situation with the Japanese defeat so final. Before he left, he begged my mother to convince my father to join them. She smiled sadly. "You know that's not possible, but don't worry about us. We were prepared for this from the beginning. They will want his head no matter which side he is on." Than Tun gave a very deep bow to my mother, the greatest respect that can be paid, before disappearing to the north.

Aung San came the following evening, daring not to speak first. There was only one forewarning that my father had for Aung San. "Maung Aung San, you will win this war alongside the British. But it does not stop there. The ghosts of what we have done will come back to haunt us when we least expect them to and those who remained loyal to the British will not forget the specter of the past. Many will come after you and I just want to make sure that you are prepared for what awaits after independence."

"And why do you bring this up now, Sayar? To demonstrate how much of a traitor I am?" asked Aung San petulantly, his temper flaring.

My father sighed, the young man missing the point.

Aung San stayed silent for several minutes, contemplating an outburst and how to process what the Adipadi had just told him. "Sayar, thank you for everything that you've done for us. I...I do mean it. And we will meet again. I look forward to seeing you once this is all over. I do miss the days of sipping a hot coffee with you and arguing over our favorite philosophers."

"Then I shall owe you a coffee sometime soon, Maung Aung San. Now be on your way. It's a long journey ahead."

*****

On March 27, 1945, Aung San and the AFPFL led an uprising against the Japanese Imperial Army while the British prepared to take Mandalay, making their descent towards Rangoon to recapture the capital and the country. The resistance day was supposed to have taken place several weeks earlier but was interrupted by a series of fateful misses. In January, the heir to one of America's largest confectionary fortunes went missing after his plane crashed near Pegu, the base of the AFPFL's operations. The Japanese deployed their best intelligence officers to search the countryside, the young Allied soldier an invaluable bargaining tool in prisoner exchange. He was recovered by his own forces after having been protected by a local ranch owner and his family, but not before the Imperial Army had ransacked Pegu and unwittingly uprooted the AFPFL's base.

The Kempetai confirmed an underground movement due to the Thakins' oversight. They caught several rebels with incriminating papers in hand, including Than Tun's personal secretary[31]. When a local District Officer ran to tell Dr. Ba Maw about Than Tun's secret plot, my father urged him to keep quiet and scolded Than Tun and U Nu for their indiscretion.

Luckily for the AFPFL, the majority of the Imperial Army command left long before their official evacuation in April. There were no more Tokyo boys in uniform patrolling the streets, no raucous laughter erupting from their watering holes. They abandoned the city in its most shell-shocked state, a skeleton of its former glittering self. The Shwedagon was covered in soot but intact. The remaining Imperial Army officers and Colonel Hiraoka advised us to leave at once, fearing that our family would not survive as prisoners of war if we were captured, especially me. I had mere weeks before going into labor, barely able to walk.

May May and Phay Phay thanked the commanders and said their goodbyes to these men, unsure if any of them would make it to see the end. My parents informed the entire family

---

[31] U Nyo Mya. "Flight to Nirvana: From an Ordinary Human Existence to the Nirvana Path". Rangoon: Sar Mawgun, 1985.

that we would be evacuating Rangoon before it fell, instructing us to bring an extra set of clothes and nothing more. The next day, my father gathered the remaining ministers and Thakins in Rangoon in a final session. U Tun Aung, Bandoola U Sein[32] and U Hla Pe[33] agreed to accompany our family on the retreat, praying that the Japanese had enough fire in them to guard us until we reached safe haven. Thakin Mya and U Nu also agreed to join our convoy despite having joined the anti-Japanese resistance movement. Phay Phay advised U Nu not to come with us as his allegiance was clear, but U Nu insisted on joining us until we reached the border, his cheeks a stubborn tomato red.

Our convoy set off from the Kempetai Headquarters on April 23, 1945, carrying Phay Phay, May May, Aunt Kinmimi, my three sisters, two brothers, Yan Naing and me, and a young midwife name Ma Phone who had recently obtained her nursing certificate. I called on Ma Phone after learning that my assigned military doctor, having spent several years on the front lines and awarded with the highest civilian honors, actually had no childbirth experience. The midwife was a petite Bamar girl who looked as if she would fall over if the wind blew against her, and she agreed to accompany me on the treacherous trip as the sole caretaker of my pending labor. My life and the life of my unborn child were completely in her hands.

May May, Ma Phone and I left Rangoon in a separate saloon car covered in a thick film of pollution and debris. The others rode in the back of poultry trucks. Yan Naing insisted on accompanying me in the car but I had asked him to stay at my father's side, since my mother could not be with him. I rested my hands on my stomach, the spring heat unbearable on my tender skin as the car lurched atop cracked concrete. Prickly sweat trickled down my brow and I wondered if my

---

[32] Cabinet Minister in the wartime government.
[33] News broadcaster, translator and commentator for the BBC Burmese from 1942 to 1946. Linguist and contributor to the Burmese–English Dictionary.

child was discomforted by the physical and emotional trauma that I was experiencing. "Where are we going?" I hacked, choking on exhaust fumes and packed dust. May May, immaculate with her black hair in a neat bun and not a drop of sweat anywhere, showed no signs of worry. Was she as calm on the inside as on the surface? What would she do if our convoy were to be intercepted and Phay Phay taken away?

She wore a placid smile, her eyes drifting on the horizon. "We're going to Mudon and hopefully to Bangkok from there. Who knows, perhaps this little one might even be born across the border." She placed her warm hand on my stomach, soothing electrodes calming my tight nerves. Our convoy pushed through winding back roads, abandoned villages and dark huts. The entire countryside had vanished with nothing left but open fields and ghostly emptiness. I had heard stories that many had taken shelter in old pagodas and monasteries knowing that they were less likely to be bombed. People took refuge in the ancient temples of Bagan, cooking by firelight beneath thousand-year-old Buddhist murals, paint cracking against the flames.

Fighter planes dove from the skies sending showers of bullets over our convoy, gunning down soldiers who had no choice but to walk from Rangoon to Mudon. Some tried to climb on to the trucks, the Japanese officers pistol-whipping their heads then pushing their limp bodies onto the hot pavement. Those running from a hailstorm of bullets scratched at our car windows. The lucky ones received a quick bullet to the temple and the unlucky ones were left to die on the side of the road. I instinctively reached for the car door several times to let a suffering soldier in, to save at least one, only for my mother to brush my hand away, shaking her head in despair and resignation.

As we neared a village called Kyaikhto near Kyaiktiyo, the great golden rock staring at us like the eye of God, I felt a sharp pain in my lower abdomen. Then another. Then so quickly in succession that every breath was a knife to my lungs. What was happening to my unborn child? Was he or she hurting? May May knew precisely what was happening after seeing the contorted looks on my face. "Where does it hurt?"

I touched the base of my stomach, pain crashing in increasing, unbearable waves. The air became thinner with each inhale, my only solace to stare at the golden pagoda miles away and pray that God would reach from the sky and pull us to safety. Bombs sounded in the horizon, keeping tempo with my contractions. "Your baby is coming," May May announced, rolling the window down and flagging the other trucks. "We need to find a safe place for Tinsa to deliver her baby," she instructed the driver.

We drove several miles before spotting an intact ranch house on the roadside. My water had broken and the pain was so severe that I was delirious. Hallucinations, my life flashing before my eyes, our home in Rangoon by the lake, my husband's face, my childhood dreams, everything worth remembering. Sweat burst from my forehead in steady streams, my body unable to cope with the pain.

Thankfully the homeowners had kept the house in immaculate condition. Ma Phone produced an abundance of clean towels and linens for my labor. She boiled tap water while my mother helped me to lie down on a child's bed, my feet bracing against the rickety wooden beams. I studied the living room, distracting myself by picturing where the owners were at the moment. Were they safe? Did they have many children like our family? Why did they leave and where did they go? I wondered if they would come back, asking the universe to shelter us so that I could return to this small house in Kyaikhto someday and thank them for their unintended hospitality. Perhaps they had even kept their home in such a state knowing that troubled passersby might take refuge.

A searing pain ripped through my body, splitting my chest open and shooting between my legs. I gripped my mother's cool hands, tears and sweat pouring down my cheeks. I was only eighteen years old and no one had warned me about the extraordinary pain of childbirth, to experience the closest thing to death before giving life. I passed out several times from exhaustion, awakened each time by the stench of smelling salts and my pungent perspiration.

My husband and father waited outside in the garden for the entirety of my labor, Yan Naing pacing the lawn and carving deep pockets into the soil with his boots. When our daughter, Yema Maw-Naing, was born on April 28, 1945, my husband ran to my bedside to hold her in his arms. A plump, grumpy newborn, she had Yan Naing's strong features, his deep-set eyes, and little did we know, his legendary tenacity. My father melted at the sight of his granddaughter, a seven-pound miracle who opened her eyes every time her grandfather walked into the room. He chose her name, a combination of *ye* (brave) and *ma* (resilient), to honor our country and as a promise that we would return one day.

Some would have believed her birth to be inauspicious, to have been born on the run during the last days of the failed independence war, amid unparalleled destruction and instability. Yema would have many uphill battles to fight, the hardships of human life compounded with the legacy of her grandparents and parents. But as I looked at my daughter, I knew that she would be blessed and not cursed. She would follow a different fable, that of the beautiful lotus blossom so honored in the Buddhist canons, a flower so resilient that it grows from the deepest depths of mud.

After resting for several days in Kyaikhto, our fatigued family arrived in Mudon on May 1, 1945. Yema was bundled in warm and clean blankets and was sleeping next to my heartbeat. We did not expect to stay in Mudon for long; we would take the Thai-Burma Railway to Bangkok, continuing overland to Cambodia. A car was waiting for us on the Cambodian border where we could live freely until the surrender orders came, or so we hoped. The paradox of us seeking safe haven via the Death Railway did not occur to me until years later when the Tokyo Trials unveiled the true extent of the crimes committed on our soil. The perfectly perpendicular tracks, the symmetry of the planks, the simple engineering of cruelty.

My father, Yan Naing, U Nu and the remaining cabinet members announced that they would remain in Mudon to wait for surrender. All of the women screeched at once, arguing with the men to come with us as we were so close to safe haven. My father, U Nu and the others stood firm, stubborn in the face of imminent death, a characteristic Burmese trait. They argued that it would endanger the women and children if they were to join us. There was a presumed manhunt for the leaders of the fallen government and a firefight would follow them wherever they went. "This is not a discussion. Cambodia is safe as long as we are not there. You will go and that is my wish if it is to be the final one," Phay Phay directed to the crowd of screaming wives, daughters, mothers and young sons. "Colonel Hiraoka will accompany you and he will make sure that nothing happens." Hiraoka, who had been standing erect and still in the middle of our fracas, tipped his head at my father and stared ahead with a steely, dutiful gaze.

There were no tearful or sentimental goodbyes with most of the women and children storming off into the waiting cars without looking back at their husbands and fathers. I lingered as the crowd thinned around me, holding Yema in my arms as she grabbed at my sore breast, pawing at the holes in my sweat-soaked shirt. She was my only beacon and though I was afraid to embark on the next and final leg of our journey without my husband or father, I knew she could not afford to lose her mother as Burma fell. The car engines started, sputtering clouds of exhaust and struggling to hold on for one more voyage.

Yan Naing looked at me through the crooked columns of smoke, maybe expecting me to yell or kick at him like the other wives. I didn't, because as much as I wanted my husband to be by my side on the way to safe haven, I couldn't bear the thought of my father waiting out the end of this war on his own. Phay Phay was surrounded by his cabinet, Imperial Army officers and loyalists, but Yan Naing was his only family. They were blood now, bonded by me and the fidgeting bundle in my arms. He searched my eyes for an answer and I told him what he needed to hear.

"Don't leave Phay Phay's side for a second. And both of you, come back to us."

CHAPTER NINE

On May 6, we took the last train from Thanbyuzayat Station in Mudon and left for Cambodia via Thailand. My mother, siblings, aunt, baby Yema and I arrived in Chup city in Cambodia, housed in a large plantation hidden under a grove of banyan trees. Notes of lemongrass hung in the humid air, a bittersweet reminder that we were breathing fresh air and no longer bomb exhaust in Rangoon.

Colonel Hiraoka escorted us to Chup. Stoic, silent and loyal as ever, he never told us how he secured such fine surroundings. The plantation belonged to a wealthy French trader who went missing after the Kempetai uncovered his Allied sympathies. I suspected that the higher-ups in Tokyo gave us this mansion as a conciliatory gesture, but its history was a reminder that we were still at their mercy. Perhaps Tokyo hoped that we would be distracted by our surroundings, trapped within the twisting limbs of the banyan trees, our mouths sweetened with mangoes from the orchard. The younger ones spent their days lost in the forest and I eventually succumbed to the Frenchman's vast library. The Cambodian estate manager, a man no bigger than my miniscule mother, stayed on the property and remained perpetually terrified of the day when Japanese troops would come to take him away too. He welcomed our arrival as a cure for his loneliness and also because our presence meant that he was safe from the Kempetai for the time being. He lived in a caretaker's cottage sitting on the edge of the forest, emerging every few days to check if we had enough supplies and to say hello to Yema, who cooed and grabbed at his hardened hands. A month passed, turning into two, three, four. No word from Burma. We hoped for the best knowing that Phay Phay and Yan Naing would do everything in their power to find us one day.

The other families lived not too far from us in the surrounding area and we shared whatever little information we scavenged from the official news. Rumors surfaced that Dr. Ba Maw and his government had perished in a massive fire in Mudon and that a monarchy would return. Apparently the rumors were so convincing that the entire countryside believed them, men and women waiting for the fall of Rangoon in anticipation of a return to the old ways. "Lies," Hiraoka spat in disgust. "You must not believe such horrid things. These rumors are designed to scare people into submission. If Dr. Ba Maw were dead, the whole world would know about it."

Thunderstorms drenched our hideaway as the wet season approached, rain and lightning thrashing hundreds of acres of orchard. On the day of the worst storm, the wind blowing so violently that it shook the pillars of the plantation home, Hiraoka's small red transistor radio announced that two bombs had obliterated Hiroshima and Nagasaki, killing 100,000 civilians on impact. It was the first time that I had ever seen him cry, sleeves soaked as he wiped his ruddy cheeks in suffocating despair, hoping that his sobs would be muffled by the gales outside. Women, children, the elderly had been burned alive by the atomic bomb, a new weapon that we had never even heard about. A wave of panic struck me. If this could be done to innocent civilians, then what was in store for us? Would the Allies be merciful?

While we waited in Cambodia, the men remained in Mudon waiting for Japan's surrender. On August 11, 1945, my father observed five RAF planes flying low above his residence, believing that they were surveying the area for Japanese tanks and what was left of the Imperial Army. Yan Naing approached his father-in-law after the planes disappeared, describing an eerie dream that he had several nights prior. "I dreamt that the Allies had finally come for us. Their planes flew so close to our heads that I could see the chambers of their guns. I know it was just a dream, but we need to be careful." My father disregarded Yan Naing's warnings, choosing to believe in his own infallibility. The RAF planes did not fire on them until the next afternoon, the remainders of his fallen government dashing from their collapsed hideout under a torrent of gunfire.

My father found himself huddled in a shallow ditch, lucky to have run from the house seconds before it caved in. He glanced at his son-in-law, who threw a woman's sarong to him that had been in the wreckage. Yan Naing sprinted towards the thick of the jungle, my father sure that they would find each other again. Phay Phay wrapped himself with the cloth, too frightened to breathe in case the RAF planes could detect his movements. How foolish he had been to ignore the planes the day before, his hubris and fatigue preventing him from thinking clearly. He turned his ear up to the sky, listening for the familiar voices of his companions in the midst of gunfire. The only sound was of the house splintering in two, shards of wood falling on the soft grass. He ran as fast as he could when he felt that it was safe, hoping that the dense forest canopy would stretch far enough to reach Yan Naing and the others.

He found his way to Yan Naing and the remaining fragments of the Imperial Army who were holed up in the outskirts of Mudon. The day after their close escape from the RAF, Ambassador Ishii announced that Japan had formally surrendered according to the terms of the Potsdam Agreement and that Burma was to be occupied by the British again. Phay Phay now had to decide what his next move would be: surrender to the British authorities, an option that did not seem too appealing as they had just tried to assassinate him, or to soldier on with the Japanese. Ishii and his officers implored him to make his way to Japan where he would be safe in exile. *Your chances of survival are much less here*, they argued. *We will protect you in Japan, loyal friend.*

My father did not want to go to Japan. If he were to be tried as a war criminal, then he wanted to face his judge and jury on his own soil, his homeland. He was tired of running, tired of war, wanting to stay in Burma regardless of the outcome. Phay Phay only relented when Yan Naing joined the chorus, arguing that Japan was the safest place for him to be, where he still had friends and most importantly, could trust them, or at least he hoped. My father told Ishii that he would go to Japan on the condition that he make a stop in Cambodia first.

On August 15, 1945, the most destructive war in modern history ended. While soldiers kissed their loved ones on streets all around the world, confetti dousing the streets of New York City, my father and Yan Naing slipped on a train to Bangkok the following day. Yan Naing later recalled seeing his father-in-law turn to smile towards the direction of the Shwedagon, praying under his breath and promising that he would return someday.

* * * * *

An unnerving calm had settled over the plantation. The war was over but we were not at peace without knowing what had happened to Phay Phay and Yan Naing. I was tending to Yema when I saw several cars zigzagging towards the house, presuming that it was a Japanese envoy sent to update us on the political situation. When the cars stopped and the doors opened, my gaunt father and husband stepped out into the quiet of the forest.

I rushed to greet them, giving my father a kiss and turning to my husband, who gave me the biggest grin that I have ever seen to this day. Little Yema was curled up and kicking in my arms, rudely awakened by the loud commotion. "Yema has missed you," I said as I handed our daughter to him. He cradled her in his sinewy arms, her little fingers grabbing at his long, unkempt vines of hair.

My mother, aunt and siblings shouted in unison, a million

unanswered questions. Where had they been? Were they in danger? Were we to return to Burma finally? Their questions were cut down by my father informing us that he was to leave for Tokyo immediately and that he had asked to stop in Cambodia to give us the news in person. My mother wanted to slap him, her right arm twitching. "It's been discussed and the best option for me is to go to Japan for now. I'm so sorry, dear family, that I cannot spend more time with you. We must land in Tokyo before the Americans take full control of the country. It will be safer for all of us that way."

The happiness that I had felt a few moments before crumbled at hearing his brusque words. Wasn't the war over? Why couldn't he stay? Why did we have to continue to endure this war long after the bombs had stopped and the declarations signed? What more could we possibly give them? My father's tone softened at our palpable distress. "Please do not worry for me. I'll be safe and there is no better place for me to go than Japan where I still have good friends and allies."

Good friends. The men who tried to assassinate our family in a bomb shelter not so long ago. The men who watched us at night, monitored our every move. Eyes and ears trained to flip a switch at a moment's notice.

"I cannot risk going back to Burma so soon, but I would like for all of you to go to Bangkok at once. It shouldn't be long before you're home," he murmured. Major Hiraoka nodded, agreeing that we would be just as safe in Bangkok as we were in Cambodia. Better to be close by when the orders came for us to return home, if they would come at all.

"Why can't we go with you?" Mala demanded.

My father winced at Mala's question, shutting his eyes for a brief instant. "I am a wanted man now, Mala and I will not have you hunted down along with me!" Phay Phay shouted, the banyan trees swaying to his echoes.

He shook his head, ridding himself of his temper. "There is one last thing I should mention. I'll be going alone. Yan Naing will stay here and look after you. He has not left my side and I think it's time for him to be with his family," Phay Phay said as he looked at his granddaughter.

Yan Naing's face fell, hurt by his father-in-law's quick dismissal. Most would have rejoiced at being released of their travails but I knew that my husband was not like most men. As a wife and a mother, I felt sadness and a slight pang of hurt at Yan Naing's willingness to go to Tokyo with my father and to leave us behind, but it dawned on me that I was the one who told him to stay by his side in the first place. Even if his soldier's pride was more potent than his loyalty to me at that point, I had given the order in the first place.

My father said nothing more except for his temporary goodbyes and flew via Taipei to the Tachikawa Air Base in Tokyo, an alleged war criminal on the run.

*****

We left the leafy plantation immediately after the surrender orders, our safe haven for months on end. I will never forget those long, serene days on the winding porch, Yema and I listening to grasshoppers singing and nothing else. The plantation caretaker wept as we drove away, wailing for our absence, for the unforeseeable future, his destiny at the mercy of the surrounding countryside. The fallout would be great, opportunists ransacking the hills before the Allies could reach him.

Our boat cruised across the Mekong River, a stunning ride along one of the most verdant deltas in the world. The water was cool and calm, gargantuan buffaloes grazing on the banks and splashing us during their baths. We put on brave smiles for my youngest siblings as we boarded the train for Bangkok in Phnom Penh, telling them that we were going on a long vacation to see the pagodas of Siam. Colonel Hiraoka escorted us to our new dwellings in Bangkok, a dull, leaden block surrounded by fifteen-foot high concrete walls and barbed wire. Had we known that this was to be our final moments with Hiraoka, we would have paid our proper respects, to thank him for everything that he had done for us. He settled us in our new home, reported to the Japanese Embassy in Bangkok and asked the staff to take the utmost care of us, then vanished to Cambodia to return to his other duties. We never saw him again, another ghost adrift in the fog of war.

Several days after our arrival, we heard bootsteps in the hallway followed by a gentle knock on the door. My mother gasped when she saw Netaji Subhas Chandra Bose, resplendent in uniform with his medals gleaming and looking like he had just stepped off the set of a Hollywood film. "I heard that you were in Bangkok. I'm happy to see that you are all looking well and healthy." His words underscored the absence of a central family member. Bose's eyes scanned the room behind my mother; perhaps if he looked long enough and willed it, my father, his ally, would appear from the void.

"I cannot stay for long. I have assigned several of my men to look after you and do let them know of whatever you need; money, medicine, toys for the kids. I am indebted to your family so please do not be shy." My siblings and I greeted him at the door and he gave my younger siblings some sweets from his pocket, turning to look at my mother a final time. "You know, when this is all over, I should like to spend the rest of my life in meditation, perhaps at one of Burma's famed monasteries. Alas, my mind cannot be free until India is." He exuded so much optimism, hope and purpose that it was hard for me to believe that that was to be our last meeting. Netaji Subhas Chandra Bose perished one week later in a plane crash en route to Tokyo on August 18, 1945.

A young British captain named Rhett came to our home the day after Bose's visit, informing us that we were not to move from the premises at all. He handcuffed my husband and placed him under arrest at the nearby British garrison. I feared for Yan Naing because he had been one of the main instigators of the independence movement in Burma, a war hero or a warmonger depending on which side you asked. Two weeks into his arrest, Yan Naing was surprised to see two familiar faces – his old professor from Rangoon University and a friend from university. They chitchatted about the news in Rangoon,

Yan Naing aware that no man ever came to a prison for coffee and small talk. The professor fidgeted and shifted his eyes, his guilty conscience battling his nerves. My husband confirmed his suspicions when they asked where his father-in-law was. *The Adipadi is missing. If the Allies could only locate him, you and your family could go home.*

Yan Naing normally prided himself on his honesty, but this time he prided himself on his quick thinking. "I'm not sure where Dr. Ba Maw is, perhaps near Mudon where we lived for several months." It was half of the truth, none of us knew where my father was, only that he was in the hands of the Japanese. The professor and friend did not press further, evident that that they had been pressured into this mission and wanting to leave immediately after completing their duty. "See you back home, friends," Yan Naing said civilly as they faded into the concrete hallways.

Passing his first test, my husband was allowed by the British authorities to return home during daylight hours, armed escorts appearing at dusk to bring him back to jail. Despite the small comfort of having him back, all we could think about was Phay Phay's safety and our pending return to Rangoon and how this would come about. The one family member who seemed at ease was Yema, whose only concern in the world was getting her fill of milk and then promptly falling asleep in my arms while I paced back and forth in abject frustration.

On a cool December morning nearing Christmas, a clerk from the Burmese Embassy sent a long-awaited message. Governor-General Reginald Dorman-Smith had returned to Burma and had given official notice that we were to return to Rangoon immediately. Two chartered Douglas C-47 Dakotas were waiting for us at the airport, propellers battered and chipped from years of war usage. The planes overflowed with flimsy cardboard boxes containing clothing, cookware, kitchen utensils, toiletries and medicine, an officer informing me that they were for our use back in Burma. "Rangoon is no more than a shell, Mrs. Maw-Naing. Goods are scarce, even in the black market. These things are for you to begin your life in

Burma again." They were just pots and pans but I was touched by the humanity of the gesture, to know that war had not changed some things.

We moved to a small home in Kandawgyi adjacent to our old property. Our family home had been taken over by the British Army with a promise to return it to us as soon as possible. It did not matter where we lived as long we were in Rangoon. The only thing I could have wished for that holiday season was the safe return of my father, my and my family's lives unable to continue without knowing if he was dead or alive.

* * * * *

Dr. Ba Maw had vanished but was very much alive. In his memoirs, my father recounted that after Cambodia, he flew to Tokyo accompanied by Naokichi Kitazawa from the Japanese Embassy and stopped in Taipei for an overnight rest on August 22. As soon as he stepped off the plane, a young Japanese officer sprinted to hand a telegram to Phay Phay. *Bose. Plane Crash. Aug 18. Stop.* He gripped the paper in his hand, not knowing how to process the information. For the first time in a long time, he felt asphyxiated, adrift in a bottomless haze of loneliness and helplessness. One of the few people in the world who understood his quandaries was now just a memory, reduced to a handful of grainy photographs and an excerpt in other men's histories.

My father last saw Netaji Subhas Chandra Bose in Rangoon days before the final retreat. My mother and father asked him to join us on the retreat, to save himself if not his cause. Netaji refused, my father regretting not asking him to come one last time. They did not speak much during that meeting, reflecting on a pact that they had made to continue with things and to push through even if the British recaptured Burma. While my father waited for Rangoon to fall, Bose found himself in a more precarious situation. He and the Azad Hind government would no longer have a base, a dispossessed army that had yet to accept the failures of its mission. Bose never surrendered, never knowing that independence for Burma and India would come just a few short years later in 1947 and 1948.

Kitazawa, wanting to give my father privacy in his moment of despair but also aware of the dangerous mission awaiting them, broke the silence. "Dr. Ba Maw, do you want to go on?"

My father looked dazed as he heard Kitazawa's question, snapping from his shock and shouting defiantly, perhaps madly, "Certainly, let's go at once and end the whole damn show if it has got to end that way!"

He had a fitful sleep in Taipei, his days outnumbered in the aftermath of Bose's death. My father was not a superstitious man but he would never forget his dream that night. His beloved mother, Daw Thein Tin, appeared to him as if time had never passed. She did not speak at all, lips pressed together, eyes piercing him with fear and worry. She drew her hand slowly, her bony fingers pointing at a wall clock that read 12:30. Her apparition vanished, leaving him drenched in cold perspiration, unable to alleviate the prickly goosebumps on his skin for hours. Phay Phay was sure that it was a premonition of his imminent death.

His plane took off in the early morning, carefully navigating Allied airspace along the Chinese coastline. It was a dangerous journey to take so soon after defeat, swaths of unsecured airspace and the ocean abyss. When the plane cut through the clouds, an American warplane tailed them and fired at once, continuing its assault until my father's plane grazed the surface of the ocean, droplets of the Pacific splashing the front window. The American plane left believing that they were doomed to crash into the water, upon which the Japanese pilot skillfully brought them back to altitude, flying sideways with one functioning wing until they reached their destination. My father arrived at Tachikawa Airport in Tokyo on August 24. When he looked at his watch, the time read 12:30.

Phay Phay cruised the midnight streets of Tokyo, confounded by the wreckage of the once-beautiful city. He recollected his previous trips to the capital, haunted by labyrinthine opera houses, enigmatic geishas, the careful design and artistry of the metropolis. None of this existed anymore, not the clean lines and perfectly designed avenues, alleyways bursting forth with cherry blossoms, nor the shuffling footsteps of housewives on their way to the morning fish markets. There was no remainder of life or beauty.

Dr. Ba Maw (center) in hiding in Japan as a mute Manchurian professor

He was exhausted but there was no time for rest, rushing to the Military Staff Headquarters where he met with Mamoru Shigemitsu, the Minister for Foreign Affairs and the liaison for high-profile political exiles, of which there were many. Shigemitsu produced crumpled rail tickets to Niigata, my father to be accompanied by Kitazawa and Fumihiko Kai, the Head of the Political Section Ministry. Their train traversed the mountains of central Honshu, the tranquil countryside a stark contrast to the destruction of Tokyo. When they arrived in the town of Ishiuchi in Niigata, his security detail handed him over to a professorial gentleman by the name of Takuzo Imanari. Imanari was the Vice-Chairman of the Niigata Chapter of the

Imperial Rule Assistance Association (*Yokusan Shonendan*), those who pledged undying loyalty to the Emperor. Imanari said few words to my father, but they smiled at each another knowing that my father's life depended on this man's good graces.

Imanari escorted Phay Phay to a small temple in the center of the village, introducing him to Kakujo Tsuchida, the temple's priest, who would be responsible for his safekeeping. The priest told my father that the temple was founded in the eleventh century by Zenju Jonin, a Buddhist saint with purported powers to heal the sick and resurrect the dead. The grounds were covered with enormous katsura trees and cypresses, thousands of years old, there long before the village existed. My father relished the quiet atmosphere and serenity, the luxury of solitude and peace eluding him for years. In exchange for the priest's kindness, Phay Phay agreed to tutor him in English while Tsuchida attempted to teach my father some conversational Japanese.

From that moment on, my father ceased to be Dr. Ba Maw and adopted his new persona as a college professor in exile from Manchuria who had lost his entire family during the war. To protect his identity and spare him from probing conversations so characteristic of small towns, Imanari informed the villagers that the mute professor suffered from post-traumatic speech loss, so they should merely bow in passing and leave him be. Night after night, the Manchurian professor retreated to his tatami-matted room behind the Hondo in the temple, the Ishiuchi villagers praying for the souls of his loved ones by candlelight.

My father's mind began to wander in the beautiful mountainside sanctuary. Solitude skirted dangerously on confinement; he did not speak Japanese and the entire village would unravel his identity if he attempted to speak English. My father broke down six months into his exile, confessing to Fumihiko Kai that he had reached his limit. He missed us, his family, he missed Burma and he wanted to at least try to come home if that meant he would have to go to trial and die trying.

The two men spent the entire night discussing his options and by the time dawn crept from behind the mountains, my father agreed to turn himself in to the Occupation Forces in Tokyo.

Phay Phay took the first train to Tokyo with Imanari, brisk wind flying through the rail cars, the two men holding on to their wool hats for the duration of the journey. When they reached Tokyo on January 17, 1946, he surrendered to Lieutenant-Colonel Figges, the sitting officer for the British Commonwealth Occupation Force. Expecting the worst - a death sentence - he was surprised when Figges welcomed him cordially. "Ah, Dr. Ba Maw, we've been expecting you," Figges greeted him like an old friend. Phay Phay relaxed his composure, relieved that he would not be needing the small glass bottle in his pocket. Imanari had slipped it into his breast pocket on the train, a small dose of clear, viscous liquid no bigger than several raindrops. He tried to open the lid to sniff at its contents, Imanari immediately placing the cap back on and shaking his head at my father.

"Dr. Ba Maw, as Japan is currently under American occupation, I am under orders to transfer you to the American Intelligence unit. Please forgive the inconvenience." Only the British would apologize for the tedious bureaucracy involved with arresting one of their most wanted men.

The Americans processed my father's pending incarceration with mundane expediency. The intelligence clerk seemed not to care that the fallen leader of Burma was sitting right in front of him, his typewriter keys clacking in a languorous rhythm. On January 26, 1946, he was transferred to Sugamo Prison to be held alongside the most notorious suspected war criminals of East Asia. They waited for their turns at the Tokyo Tribunals, men trapped in the expanse between life and the hangman's noose.

My family and I had no contact with my father at this point, but thankfully Yan Naing still had reliable military and political contacts through which we received continuous news about Phay Phay's detention. Aung San, U Nu and Thakin Than Tun were working with the British authorities in Rangoon and all of the former Freedom Bloc members lobbied for my father's release. When I wasn't busy nursing Yema, I kept an eye on the short driveway in anticipation of a messenger with the latest news from Tokyo.

I was thankful to hear that the British and American authorities operated Sugamo humanely. The cellblocks were spartan but clean, communal hygiene emphasized to prevent the outbreak of disease. The running joke amongst the prisoners was that everyone was to have a clean bill of health on their way to meet the executioner. My father stayed in solitary confinement for over a month in a six-by-nine foot cell at the edge of the prison, afforded privileges such as rations on par with the officers, movie nights and a library full of novels. The darker side of solitary confinement was designed to break men's minds before the Tribunals. American intelligence officers visited my father's room several times a week and showed him grisly photos of executed war criminals. Shot. Hanged. The executioner a nameless, faceless blur in the corner of the photo. *What plots do you know of in Burma? Who else is hiding out? What happened to your Jap buddies, the higher-ups that are missing?* He didn't know a thing, having left all of that behind in Mudon.

On February 27, 1946, the prison command finally allowed my father to mix with the general population during mealtimes. The prisoners were divided into two categories: the Japanese wearing red jackets and everyone else in blue uniforms. Glancing about the room, my father did not see any other Burmese and ascertained that he must have been the only one in there. Recognizing Jose Laurel in the sea of faces, his unmistakable tortoise-framed spectacles and rollicking laugh, he sat down at the Filipino table and chattered nonstop, happy to be among familiar company.

"Say, Laurel, do you know of any other Burmese in here?"

"I only know of Dr. Thein Maung, the former Ambassador [to Japan]. He is not well," Laurel shook his head in sadness. My father was distraught to hear that Dr. Thein Maung, who had been a loyal member of his cabinet, was now on his deathbed in a prison cell so far away from home. Phay Phay was not the praying type but he said a small Buddhist prayer for his friend before beginning his meal, a small tradition carried from home.

I knew that it wouldn't take long before my father would cause some sort of political protest within the prison walls, but even I was surprised by his gall. All of the prisoners were assigned communal tasks ranging from reshelving library books to mopping the floors, the most unfortunate duty that of Kitchen Patrol. When the rotation fell on my father to do KP, he vehemently refused to do kitchen work. This caused great commotion amongst the other prisoners, including Laurel, who collectively refused to take their turns in the rotation in a union of stubborn ex-leaders and politicians. These men were naturally inclined towards politics even as they awaited the executioner's chair. The prison authorities had little patience for a gang of hard-nosed ex-politicos, placing my father into an even smaller solitary confinement cell. He remained resolute even as he was shuffled between the Blue and Red zones. The impasse only broke when Colonel Figges heard about the infamous KP standoff and the British authorities sent orders to release my father back into the regular population.

My father began to receive a steady stream of encouraging news from his friends and the authorities. In May 1946, the British announced that all Indian National Army officers and soldiers would be pardoned, a promising sign for collaborationist governments. At the end of that month, the authorities in Burma sent a letter stating that no one was to be tried back home and that many of his former colleagues were actually working with the British in the new government. Furthermore, every political faction and organization was petitioning for the release of Dr. Ba Maw, his most vocal proponents Aung San and U Nu from the AFPFL.

U Thein Maung was released at the end of May, his body so deteriorated by disease and exhaustion that he was unable to sign his own discharge papers. He passed away at sea en route to Rangoon absolved of all crimes, but his final punishment was to never see Burma again. My father grieved for him and to an undeserved bittersweet ending.

Colonel Figges paid an impromptu visit towards the end of July. "Colonel, how well you look," my father greeted cordially. Figges did not mince his words, asking my father to accompany him at once. It was the first time that Phay Phay had stepped outside of the prison since his internment. Tokyo had been completely transformed, cleared of rubble and dust, cars and people on the streets as if nothing had transpired. There were no mortar shells or remnants of bombed buildings to be seen, the complete sanitization of a recent past that the world wanted to forget. The car stopped in front of the British Embassy, my father's breath coming to a sharp halt at the reflection of the royal coat of arms in the window. *Dieu et mon droit.* The divine right to sentence an execution order, or to send him home.

The British Ambassador greeted him warmly, asking the two men to have a seat. "Dr. Ba Maw, you have been keeping abreast of the trials, correct?"

"Yes, from the bits and pieces I've heard in prison."

The Ambassador sat back in his chair, fingertips pressed against his temples. "Upon much discussion, it has been decided that your crimes were no more severe than that of Aung San and U Nu, both of whom are currently working with the British government in Burma."

"Ambassador, what does that mean for me?"

The Ambassador pulled a small letter from the top of a pile on his desk, clearing his throat before reading an official directive. *His Majesty's Government hereby absolves Dr. Ba Maw of all crimes committed during wartime.*

"Dr. Ba Maw, it means that you can go home."

* * * * *

My father arrived in Rangoon on a Dakota plane on August 1, 1946, the last of its kind to be used for war purposes before the fleet was grounded. Over twenty cars full of dignitaries, colleagues and family welcomed him at the airport, our small vehicles shaking against the violent wind from the plane's propellers. My mother opened the car door before the engine stopped, racing against the journalists who had been waiting since dawn. I rushed to the bottom of the airplane stairs with Yema sleeping on my shoulder and with Yan Naing at my side, waiting for the doors to fling open against the drizzling rain.

A haggard, pale man stepped off the plane, a tired silk suit hanging off of his skeletal frame. If it were not for his signature black cap, I would not have recognized my father at all, quite literally half the man he used to be. The reporters jumped to the front of the queue, pushing me aside and barraging my father with questions. Yema awoke and began to cry over the commotion, frightened by their flashbulbs and the reporters' aggressive shouts.

Dr. Ba Maw, look over here for a photo!
How does it feel to be back home?
How did you survive?
What are your thoughts on Aung San and the AFPFL? Do you feel betrayed?

My father raised his hands to his face, shielding himself from the bright glare of the photographers' lenses. Flashbulbs cut out as they lowered their cameras in deference to his wishes. Perhaps he felt ashamed or was simply tired, making it clear that he did not want to be photographed on that day, a rare occurrence for my father. He would only speak to family and select friends including Bandoola U Sein, Henzada U Mya[34], Pyaw-bwe U Mya[35], U Ba Win[36] and other loyal party members.

I waited for my turn to greet him, watching those around me clamoring for my father's attention. Phay Phay's eyes were immediately drawn to Yema and me, asking the reporters to

---

[34] Member of the House of Parliament.
[35] Agriculture and acting Home Minister.
[36] Minister of Trade in pre-independence government, Aung San's brother, assassinated July 19 1947.

clear a path for him and walking straight towards us. I didn't know what to say to him, because there were no words to express the feeling of an era coming to an end with his return. My stillness spoke volumes, ages since I could indulge myself in the present moment and observe life as it was happening around me. My father, who instinctively read my thoughts, said nothing to disturb me. He took Yema from my arms and showered her face with kisses, my daughter gurgling and giggling at her grandfather's wealth of affection.

My family and I followed my father to the Shwedagon Pagoda, where he bowed before the great golden dome and touched his forehead to the stone path. In following Buddhist tradition, he paid his highest respects and gratitude to the country for bringing him back, followed by a *soon-kway*[37] at noon. May May and Phay Phay offered alms to dozens of monks in our living room, donating new robes, slippers and fans. He did not touch the rich food splayed across several tables the length of the room, unable to digest the peppery curries, heavy spices and thick coconut paste so typical of Burmese fare.

For a brief moment, it seemed as if life had begun to resemble something normal again, or so I had foolishly convinced myself.

---

[37] A *soon-kway* is ceremony offering alms to monks.

Part II

The Invisible War

CHAPTER TEN

Rangoon was nothing but a shell, yet I was blissfully content to live in its wreckage. My family and I were able to return to our home at Kandawgyi Lake, left in immaculate condition by the occupying British officers. Yan Naing and I raced upstairs to our bedroom and stretched ourselves across our old mattress with Yema in between us, saying nothing for hours, careful not to disturb the other's solitude. We had nothing left of our worldly possessions, therefore it was not a matter of moving back in, but daydreaming about filling the room with treasured pieces and memories again.

My family flitted about like ghosts for the first few weeks of our return, living inside of our own heads as we learned to readjust to civilian life. We had returned to the physical familiarities of our lives but it was as if we were strangers in a new land, foreigners in our own home. I had forgotten so many things about my house, surprised by the cracks in the wooden floors that had been there for decades, forgetting to turn the kitchen doorknob left instead of right due to the manufacturer's faulty spring, and waking to the loud chanting of novice monks collecting alms at dawn every morning.

My father buried his head in his yellowed books, retracing the very prose and ideas that had helped to build him into the man that he became, his cheeks slowly returning to their normal plumpness as he reabsorbed each page. May May and Aunt Kinmimi cleaned the house obsessively, their old brooms and rags waiting for them like old friends as the two sisters attacked and expelled every legion of dust mite and mold that had accumulated in our absence. Yan Naing kept his mind and fighting arm busy by helping my mother and aunt with home repairs and baby Yema had an army of nannies tending to her every need.

My own thoughts turned to the future, a long forgotten luxury during war. As I was reading a termite-eaten copy of Burmese folktales one evening, I realized how much I missed being in a classroom, both as a student and as a teacher. I did not have the chance to attend university, a rite of passage that had been lost in the rubble. I still flirted with the idea of attending medical college but it was impossible as the course ran seven years and I could not balance schoolwork while tending to Yema at home. My sister Mala was also of university age and it was to be her destiny to become the doctor in the family.

I approached my father for advice, who wholeheartedly encouraged me to finish my tertiary education and pushed for me to attend courses immediately. "Your mind is your greatest weapon. Never pass up an opportunity to nourish it," he preached as he read Seneca and Sophocles out loud from his study.

My mother and Yan Naing also agreed that I should attend university at once. My husband had no issue with staying at home and looking after our baby, especially as he was in a state of transition himself and his time would be best spent with Yema as he pondered his next steps. The sole dissenting voice came from my uncle, U Ba Han, who was concerned about the state of my mind, immersing myself in work so soon after trauma. "Tinsa, you have a husband, a daughter and more children to come. Why do you need to be away from home?" He tried his best to dissuade me from my studies but to no avail. I did not need to further my education for financial reasons or otherwise; I simply wanted to learn.

I decided to pursue a degree in English Literature, which should have been the obvious choice from the beginning. I was a bookish student at St. John's and reading novels was my favorite pastime, as evidenced by the trail of worn books that I left everywhere.

I entered Rangoon University in September 1945 as a dual Bachelors and Masters student in English Literature. Zali, Mala and I were some of the first students to step inside the soot-covered halls of the legendary school, one of the most prestigious institutions in postwar Asia. The campus had been largely destroyed during air raids but the convocation halls and main lecture theaters were intact, albeit standing in the midst of debris and shattered columns. My younger siblings Theda, Binnya and Onma were attending middle and primary schools. My mother and father were happy to see us off to school in the mornings with five chrome tiffin lunchboxes in varying sizes (according to age).

I slowly dipped myself into the routine of parenthood and my studies, both causes providing me with a long-lost sense of structure to my life. Every morning, I would feed Yema and place her in her crib, to be doted on by her father, grandparents, nannies and aunts and uncles until I returned in the afternoon. Yan Naing drove me to the university but not before stopping at a ramshackle teashop at the corner of University Avenue and Inya Road, where it seemed like the whole of Rangoon gathered before beginning their days. The teahouse was quite literally a shack without walls, with salvaged wooden beams propping up a precarious thatched roof. Eventually some merciful patron donated a proper wooden roof, shielding customers from the burning morning sun. I never saw the shop's owners, nor did the teashop have a name. It was simply referred to as "the shop on the corner," further adding to its aura of decrepit mystery. The food was unhygienic and tasteless, the coffee and tea weak, yet this little unassuming teashop had the distinction of serving as Rangoon's first postwar salon, attracting politicians, intellectuals and business leaders.

The teashop owed its success to its location next to Inya Lake. Most of the key political actors such as Aung San,

Thakin Than Tun and U Saw had moved into lakeside properties shortly before or during the war. The surrounding area was a forgotten forest before the new arrivals, considered a suburb though it was no more than five miles from the affluent downtown area. The shop was also a short walk from the main university grounds, a cheap and convenient gathering spot for students and young activists. Every day, I saw the usual characters in their corners. Yan Naing and I sat with Aung San and U Nu in the far left side of the rectangular seating area. My mother and father sometimes joined us but May May was pregnant with her seventh and final child and preferred to stay at home as a precaution for giving birth in her early forties. Thakin Than Tun and the Communists were to our left within arm's reach, their shirt pockets always flashing a hint of text from the *Communist Manifesto*. The students sat behind the cash register next to the businessmen with their leather portfolios. Members of the Thirty Comrades floated from table to table carrying cracked cups of jasmine tea and gossip. In the process of rebuilding our lives, old and new faces had found an unlikely home in that little rundown hut.

I was perpetually engaged in some sort of debate about literature with U Nu and Thakin Than Tun. I never won the debates but I'm proud to say that I never lost, either, with these two intellectual giants. They encouraged friendly banter to prepare me for academic life, as they did with all of the young students who summoned the courage to approach them and provoke them into mental sparring. My husband and Aung San inevitably spoke of politics, a topic that once broached, spread to the other tables like wildfire.

It was difficult to avoid politics with the teashop audience, who knew that the country was in glorious ruins at Aung San's feet. The AFPFL was now the single most powerful political entity in Burma with him, Thakin Than Tun and U Nu at the helm. After overthrowing the Imperial Army, the AFPFL forged ahead in governing Burma in accordance with its own distinct vision of the future. Governor-General Reginald Dorman-Smith had returned to Burma on October 16, 1945, eager to deal with the Burma issue once and for all.

Bo Yan Naing and Tinsa

Victory had its price. Dorman-Smith and Aung San fought over the main issue of independence, quite evident in a UK Cabinet Report published in December 1945. The British sensed so-called totalitarian inclinations in the AFPFL, representing itself as the voice of the country when there had not been elections to justify their authority in a postwar setting. They submitted a set of demands to King George VI and his cabinet, such that they should have the power to nominate the

Legislative Council and to allocate portfolios, and demanded that the Governor accept seven out of eleven of their appointments to the Council. Dorman-Smith vetoed their demands.[38] The Governor turned to other political leaders as a buffer against Aung San and the AFPFL's ambitions, including U Saw who had been my father's co-counsel during the Sayar San trial and was the former leader of the Myochit Party. U Saw remained unconvincingly independent, wearing his self-interest on his sleeve for all to see. In fairness to him, he had always made it clear that he would align with those willing to cede the most power to him, which Aung San would not do.

Dorman-Smith also courted U Nu, fracturing the AFPFL's governing members. U Nu's politics remained complicated, having switched sides with the AFPFL at the end of the war but never quite immersing himself in their ranks. He remained independent out of discomfort with the entirety of the political system, disillusioned with power plays and things plotted behind closed doors.

Sir Hubert Rance, who was to be the last Governor-General of Burma, was handpicked by Clement Attlee to deal with Burma's inevitable independence following Dorman-Smith's departure. Whilst Dorman-Smith was notorious for his stubbornness and clashed with the Burmese nationalist leaders, Rance had a more refined, appeasing approach. Rance and his cabinet believed that out of all of the major political factions, Aung San and his AFPFL were more likely to cooperate with British interests if granted full independence. The Communists were not a viable option in the postwar context with Russia and China breathing down everyone's necks. It was recognized that Aung San, though an ardent nationalist who wanted nothing more than self-rule for Burma, was enough of a centrist to allay fears of a red transformation. The Americans were pushing the British to isolate Than Tun from the

---

[38] December 4, 1945 UK Cabinet Report for the Month of October 1945 for the Dominions of India, Burma, and the Colonies and Mandated Territories.

bargaining table and Aung San eventually expelled Than Tun and the Communists from the AFPFL in October 1946.

Before the Communists' expulsion, whatever transgressions there were between Aung San and Than Tun were not apparent to Yan Naing or me at the teashop. I was nineteen and exactly one year into my undergraduate studies, fully immersed in my course. I was also pregnant with my second child and struggling to balance my personal and professional challenges. Nothing could have prepared me for the day when I walked into the teashop as usual and Thakin Than Tun, a mentor and my adopted uncle of sorts, was no longer there.

My husband was devastated by the Communists' expulsion, not because of shared ideology but because of the erosion of a once great partnership and friendship. Aung San and Than Tun had been inseparable during the war years, not least because they were brothers-in-law. The former had the ambition, charm and magnetism to ignite a movement. Than Tun had the intellect and managerial expertise to turn any movement into a reality. When the Communist Part of Burma (CPB) was shunted for British interests, Than Tun was visibly shaken by his old friend's betrayal. They would never make amends after that, Than Tun hatching an underground rebellion against the AFPFL and disappearing into the jungle, not to reappear until long after Aung San's death.

Aung San continued to campaign for his last major act before his death. Clement Attlee had invited him to London in January 1946, resulting in the Aung San-Attlee Agreement in which the Crown promised total independence for Burma and not just dominion status as was previously discussed. Aung San, armed with this agreement, returned to Burma and campaigned ethnic groups to discuss lasting unification. The most famous of these visits happened in Panglong, located in the rugged mountains of Shan State, where he organized a conference in which he dreamt that all ethnic groups would be united under his command. Only three major ethnic groups – the Chin, Kachin and Shan – attended the conference and signed the Panglong Agreement. The Kayah and Karen attended as observers, dubious of the upstart leader's hasty attempts to gloss over issues that had plagued their people for centuries. The Mon, Arakan and other populous groups were either not invited or did not bother to send representation at all. The document was doomed to fail with its constitutional flaws and lack of universal support, but his ideas were a watershed moment for the country, in which the people had never discussed unification on their own terms before. I could feel the wheels of our nascent democracy turning, albeit squeaky and hastily engineered.

On the other side of Rangoon, one man yearned to undermine Aung San and claim the title of Burma's savior for himself. U Saw had gained fame as Sayar San's co-counsel along with my father. In the intervening years, the goodwill he accumulated as Galon U Saw was eroded by his nefarious political dealings. When my father resigned as Prime Minister in 1939, U Pu came to power and appointed U Saw as the Minister of Agriculture. When U Pu himself was brought to a no confidence motion at the end of his term, U Saw cast a duplicitous vote against the very man who promoted him from a minor politician to ministerial rank. It was a betrayal of the highest order, especially amongst Burmese politicians who preferred to hold a gentleman's code of conduct in which the matter of debt to another man is of utmost regard. U Saw finally sat atop the golden throne, becoming the third and last Prime Minister of Burma in 1940 under the British. Seemingly loyal to the colonial government, his name evoked vitriol among his peers and simultaneous admiration for his cunning, a snake outwitting the tigers to seize a prized meal.

As his first gift to the nation, Prime Minister U Saw arrested two thousand members of the Freedom Bloc and anyone influential suspected of harboring anti-colonial feelings. My father and others were hauled off to jail on the pretense that their actions violated the Burma Defense Act. Having proved his muscle to the British through this obsequious play, U Saw sailed to London in October 1941 to see Prime Minister Churchill to demand autonomy for Burma. Consumed with the war in Europe, Churchill gave U Saw an icy reception and dismissed his request. Great Britain neither had the time nor patience for an upstart politician's demands for his homeland when its own territory was being bombed by Hitler's war machine.

Undeterred, U Saw sailed to the United States to meet with President Franklin Delano Roosevelt and Secretary of State Cordell Hull. His amateur planning thwarted him yet again: Churchill had already warned the Americans of U Saw's ambitions and they turned him away. He then flew across the world for a last plea to Australia and New Zealand. U Saw's plane happened to stop in Honolulu on December 7, the day the Japanese bombed Pearl Harbor. He stared in awe at the sheer power of the Imperial Navy, watching the American Pacific Fleet blown to smithereens. U Saw had an epiphany as kamikaze pilots exploded around him. Why was he wasting his time on the British and Americans when he could align with the Japanese?

He rerouted his flight to Portugal, a neutral nation, and negotiated an alliance with Japanese government officials. He sent a proposal for Burmese independence to Tokyo, installing himself as the head of state. American intelligence intercepted his message and alerted Churchill, who was in no mood to tolerate U Saw's whims. The British authorities arrested him on January 12, 1942, en route to Burma and he was sent to Jerusalem for detention. The man who had climbed to such high ranks was formally removed as Prime Minister in absentia and shipped to British Uganda where he was incarcerated until January 1946, missing the independence struggle entirely. He was enraged to see the young Aung San at the nexus of Burmese politics and brokering independence, a prize that eluded him in previous years. The elder statesmen resented the wunderkind's smooth transition in the role that he felt was rightfully his.

In spite of U Saw's previous dalliances with both Allied and Axis Powers, the British government needed a counterweight against Aung San's rising power, inviting him to sit at the Aung

San-Attlee talks. U Saw refused to sign the final terms during voting, claiming that independence was not stated clearly enough in the document. Undeterred by U Saw's rejection, Aung San and Attlee negotiated that independence would be given to Burma within one year. And so in 1947, the two politicians – one of the old guard and one of new blood – waged a political battle on the Burma stage. Truthfully, I do not think Aung San viewed U Saw as a legitimate threat, a fly buzzing around his head rather than a hornet. The elder had burned all of his bridges with existing factions and his only option was to ally with those who were similarly jealous of Aung San's feats.

I could not have predicted how far things would go between Aung San and U Saw. Though U Saw viewed my father as a rival and treated him with disdain on numerous occasions, I had no real love or feeling of hatred towards him. He wore his crocodile smile proudly like a military star, his intentions so obvious that I almost came to respect his blunt honesty, if not his values.

On July 19, 1947, Aung San called his Executive Council[39] to edit a draft constitution. Aung San, U Ba Cho[40], Abdul Razak[41], Thakin Mya, Mahn Ba Khaing[42], U Ba Win, U Ohn[43] Maung and Sao Sarm Htun[44] gathered in the Secretariat chambers shortly after 10:00 AM. Four gunmen burst into the hall and opened fire, a massacre on a scale not seen since the time of the kings. All of the men except for Sao Sarm Htun (who died later at the hospital) were killed instantly. U Ohn Maung had only stopped at the Secretariat due to an

---

[39] The interim administration before the transition to independence.
[40] Minister of Information 1946 to 1947.
[41] Muslim politician and cabinet minister in pre-independence interim government.
[42] Ethnic Karen; Minister of Industry in the pre-independence government AFPFL.
[43] Deputy Minister of Transport in pre-independence government
[44] Chief of Mongpawng in Shan State, Minister of Hill Regions in Myanmar's pre-independence government

unexpected emergency, perishing with his eighteen-year-old bodyguard Maung Htwe. The future of our country was reduced to a heap of corpses on the cold stone floor, the constitution stained with the blood of martyrs.

Yan Naing turned as white as marble when he heard the news, choking on his next words. "Ko Aung San...he knew that he was about to die," he sputtered before collapsing on a chair in our living room. I motioned for our maids to fetch fans while I ran to the kitchen for a glass of ice water. My husband's eyes were opaque, marred with the memory of his most recent and final encounter with Aung San. They met at our usual teahouse to discuss bitter politics in the wake of Thakin Than Tun's disappearance. Aung San was aware of Yan Naing's severe criticisms of the independence process, especially involving the CPB and Than Tun's forced exit, but the elder Comrade valued my husband's brutal honesty and sharp opinions, his integrity unchanged since his days as a student leader.

Aung San's demeanor had switched abruptly in the middle of conversation, going completely silent. Yan Naing dismissed it as one of his characteristic mood swings. He remained pensive, eyebrows furrowed in deep discomfort, confiding that nearly two hundred guns and spare barrels were missing from the main armaments depot near the wharf, Bren light machine guns that were the weapon of choice for infantrymen in the Burma theater. The thieves were clever enough to take additional barrels with them in preparation for what might have been an extended firefight. "Do you think it was the Communists?" my husband asked, not believing Than Tun to be capable of such a malicious theft and, frankly, a shambolic execution.

Aung San shook his head no in consternation. "The British are saying that the guns are lost. But..." he stopped. "I think my end is nearing."

Burma was in mourning. What was there to say? Notwithstanding their differences, Phay Phay and Yan Naing had enormous respect for Aung San, unwavering until the end.

They could disagree with his politics but they could never hate the man, an honor code that remained unbroken between them. My husband could not hold any grievances against an old school chum; they were, after all, united by blood through the Comrades. The culprit had stolen the closest thing we had to national unity since the monarchy, flawed but foundational.

My family and I attended the funeral with thousands of others who had come to pay their respects. My mother and I, both heavily pregnant, stood shoulder-to-shoulder with weeping soldiers and women sobbing with yellow flowers in their hair. I couldn't bear to look at the casket, to see the cold and still body of the man who had entered my childhood home as a starving young revolutionary and emerged from the war as a leader. Instead, I concentrated on the mound of flowers next to his body, trying to count the infinite number of petals to keep myself from crying. I had reached four digits when I saw a mass of black hair and a pair of small black eyes peering at me from behind a bushel of peonies, and two more sets joined them momentarily. The three little heads belonged to Aung San's children: Aung San Lin, Aung San Oo and Aung San Suu Kyi.

An irreversible somberness fell upon the little teahouse after Aung San's assassination and the disappearance of Thakin Than Tun. The muted talks eventually turned to the topic of who would lead the nation in the aftermath of the massacre. The general consensus seemed to be that Governor Rance was deciding between U Nu and U Saw as the next Prime Minister. It seems ludicrous now to think that the Governor was considering U Saw to lead the nation, but at the time none of us could have guessed that he was capable of such a massacre given the strong sense of decorum in the small circle of politicians.

It was to be U Nu. Sao Shwe Taik, the diminutive, bespectacled Saopha[45] of Yawnghwe (who would be the last of

---

[45] Saopha (Chaofa, or Sawbwa) was a royal title for rulers of the Shan States.

his royal line), became the first President. The Governor then ordered the arrest of over a thousand politicians, intellectuals and men thought to have been at odds with Aung San politically or personally. The Comrades, Communists, Thakin U Ba Sein and U Saw were taken in. One morning after breakfast, several policemen came to our door and demanded to see my father and husband. My father knew that they were coming for him and gave a reassuring smile before perching himself in the last row of the police van, holding his head high lest anyone doubt his innocence. Yan Naing, less composed than his father-in-law, scowled at the armed uniforms before kissing Yema and me and following behind, staring intensely at any of the officers who dared to look him in the eye. A few days after my father's latest incarceration, my mother gave birth to their last child, Neta, named after my father's fallen comrade and friend, Netaji Subhas Chandra Bose.

It did not take long to uncover U Saw as a culprit. Upon searching his compound and surrounding areas, investigators found several of the missing Bren machine guns submerged in the lake behind his home. The police then raided the Myochit Party headquarters where more guns and barrels turned up. Rangoon was awash in conspiracy theories and rumors, recalling U Saw's longstanding rancor for Aung San, his jealousy visceral in the halls of the Secretariat. He made no secret of his resentment of the young politician, his delusions leading him to believe that Aung San had stolen his rightful place in history. But was this really enough reason for him to murder nine men in cold blood?

Derek Curtis-Bennett flew in from London to defend U Saw, a man accustomed to sitting on the other side of the bench. The Governor assigned a Special Tribunal to handle the case. His guilt was established from the beginning but a tribunal at least gave the appearance of a fair hearing, as opposed to U Saw being publicly vilified in front of an angry mob. Several British army officers were also implicated in the assassination plot, found guilty of selling weapons to U Saw and his accomplices. The judge handed them lenient prison terms in exchange for their testifying against U Saw, their real motives unknown to this day.

On May 8, 1948, U Saw was convicted of murder and hanged, refusing a hood when the executioner extended the courtesy. I could not fault him for holding on to his dignity in his final moments, death the clearest mirror of a man's character. He was forty-eight years old, beginning his life as a landowner's son and ending in a greater spectacle than he could have ever dreamed. Buddhists should not have been surprised to find that his life ended the way that it did: he wished for fame his entire life, the universe and his karmic deeds granting him precisely that.

With two national figures dead and many more still locked up, I wondered why the innocent, such as my father and husband, were treated like criminals if the culprit had been duly punished. The reason was simple. Independence had been hastily arranged under the Nu-Attlee Agreement on October 1, 1947. Burma became the Union of Burma, (*Pyidaungsu Myanma Ngaingngandaw* in Burmese) on January 4, 1948. Attlee and Rance could not risk anything happening during those precious few months in between, the power vacuum an enticing draw for activists and troublemakers. The Crown kept anyone capable of staging a revolt behind iron bars with no evidence, trial, or jury.

My father and husband were finally released one year later on the condition of constant surveillance. They came for my husband a second time a few months later, citing Article V of the Civil Society Code that gave the government the authority to preemptively detain anyone thought capable of civil unrest. Our family was restricted from leaving Rangoon in case my young children or I were plotting a coup in our spare time. Three months turned into a year, then a year and a half. I had been containing my anger until that point, when I forced my father to take Yan Naing's case to court under the *Habeas Corpus Act*. Miraculously, Yan Naing was released in 1950 before the case could be tried.

My husband had very little to say upon his return, the

resentment of incarceration leaving an acrid taste on his tongue. He could only reflect and remark, "Upon what meat doth these vermin feed that they are grown so great?"[46]

---

[46] Law-Yone, Edward. "Dr. Ba Maw of Burma: An Appreciation." *Essays on Burma*. Ed. John P. Ferguson and E.J. Brill. Leiden: Contributions to Asian Studies, No. 16, 1981. 1-18.

CHAPTER ELEVEN

It is funny how life turns out sometimes. I had known only chaos for a very long time and wished for nothing but peace during those turbulent years. Peace did come, but not without the sacrifice of two men's lives, two lions of the past. Another, Thakin Than Tun, had gone missing. We all knew where he was and what he was planning, though we did not want to admit that his spirit, if not his body, was gone for good this time. I had often heard the superstition that in order to make way for the future, the past must be cleared. How cruel it was of the universe to follow its creed with such savagery.

For my family and me, life began to resemble something normal by 1951, right after my husband's release. Memories of air raids and fire sirens gave way to sounds of children playing and household commotion. My father decided to give politics one last go. He disagreed with the existing factions and ran for an independent seat in Parliament, then for the position of Home Minister. He was soundly defeated in every election, a crushing blow to a man who once stood at the helm of Burmese politics, his political career coming to a sputtering end. It was clear that politics was a specter of his past but my father did not dwell on his defeats. He opened a new law practice at No. 50 Barr Street with his brother, collecting an impressive clientele and filling our family coffers with much needed funds.

Tinsa (back row; second from left) at her graduation, University of Rangoon

My mother established a new business called *Maw Taik* importing fine china from Japan. Her business acumen was correct yet again; postwar Burma, booming through agriculture and manufacturing, had an insatiable appetite for luxuries. The society set could not get enough of *Maw Taik*'s fashionable, handcrafted tea services, while their husbands hired the illustrious Dr. Ba Maw to draw up legal contracts for Burma's burgeoning economy.

My siblings had finished their studies at Rangoon University and were in the process of continuing their education at some of the most prestigious institutions in the world. Zali graduated with a law degree from the University of Cambridge followed by his postgraduate studies at Yale; Mala received her postgraduate radiology degree in England; Theda had also gone to Yale where she met her future husband, William Sturtevant. Binnya and Onma were in middle and high schools and baby Neta went to work with my mother everyday.

I worked feverishly on my studies, which had been interrupted again with my husband's incarceration. I resumed courses in the spring of 1951 and struggled to balance schoolwork and my family duties after having given birth to a daughter Kalya in 1947, twin sons Yan Myo and Yan Lin in April 1951 and was expecting another daughter Amaya in July

1952. My daily routine consisted of Dickens and diapers, Thoreau and feedings, and Mary Shelley and first steps.

I was preparing for my master's exams in 1953. The morning of my final tests was just like any other day. My daughter Kalya looked weak but I brushed it off as a brief illness, a frequent occurrence with my children who liked to roughhouse and were always catching colds from one another. An uneasy feeling crept into the pit of my stomach when I left the house that morning, but I blamed it on my nerves before my exams.

Kalya became feverish and collapsed while I sat in an exam room with fifty other students, a muted chamber. My mother and aunt did not fetch me, not wanting to frighten me. They did not know what was happening to my daughter, believing her sudden fever to be a flu. A healthy, normal five-year-old would surely recover from this. By dusk, Kalya was in a comatose state, her eyes dull and gray, death already claiming my daughter. I held her small hands in mine, hoping that there was a way for me to transfer some of my life to her. She was dead within twenty-four hours.

Kalya was the only thing in my mind when my long-awaited dream of becoming a university lecturer came true in 1953. Just as the universe granted me my wishes, it took something precious away from me in exchange. I graduated second in my class and the prestigious medical college offered a full-time lectureship, teaching the brightest minds in our country. The victory was bittersweet, a long-fought battle derailed by war, my father and husband's detentions, and my daughter's death. As I signed the offer, I wondered how she would have looked as one of the many university students who were to pass through my lecture hall had she lived. I prayed for her spirit, that a divine power would guide her to her next lifetime, one that would be rich and long-lived and free of pain.

* * * * *

And so I became one of the first female English lecturers in the Rangoon university system in 1953. Women were forbidden from serving in government posts during the colonial era, including that of academic and research positions in the higher education realm. The best that women could hope for in those days was to serve as someone's secretary, hammering away at stubborn typewriters in stuffy back offices and printing others' words. I promised myself that I would do everything in my power to honor this opportunity, to set a high standard for my students' sake and for those who would come after us.

My parents were thrilled for me, especially my father who had been a lecturer at Rangoon College four decades earlier. "How lucky you are, Tinsa, to be serving in the noblest profession of all and to have a happy, healthy family supporting you at home," Phay Phay ruminated. "These are the best years of your life and make sure to appreciate them every day."

Yan Naing framed my degrees and hung them above our headboard, smiling at them each time he walked into our bedroom. He took to caring for our young children as I went to work in the mornings, happy that I was happy, I suppose.

Before the first day of classes, I decided to visit the orphanages where I used to volunteer with the Women's League. Since the volunteer teachers that I met there partly inspired me to pursue a career in teaching, I wanted to reconnect with them and share the good news in person. Two of the orphanages no longer existed when I arrived, boarded up and abandoned, and the other two might as well have been closed. There were no more than a handful of children left and the jovial head monks had been replaced by novice monks. The younger monks had no knowledge of the teachers or previous tenants and preached to me about the dangers of one's attachment to the past. "Send loving kindness to wherever your friends may be," one of them chanted, as I grieved the loss of yet more people from my past.

Thirty pairs of eyes gawked at me during my first day as an assistant lecturer at the medical college. I walked to the podium and forced myself to stifle a laugh when I realized that my old dreams of attending medical school had come true, albeit in a different form than I had originally imagined. I cleared my throat several times, hoping that the noise would wake them from their trance. They stared at me like a specimen, like an exotic animal in a zoo. Did I somehow break protocol? Was it something that I was wearing, or did I have something on my face or in my hair? I brushed my fingers through my hair, confident that a wayward sparrow had not dropped its business on my head as I walked through the campus.

A tall, impossibly lanky young man raised his hand and stood up. He stuttered, "Are you Tinsa Maw-Naing?"

"Yes, I am," I responded cautiously.

"The daughter of Dr. Ba Maw?"

I nodded.

"The wife of Bo Yan Naing of the Thirty Comrades?"

I nodded again.

Seemingly satisfied with my answer, he whispered, "I told you it was her," to his immediate seatmates. They turned their heads to stare at me again, but this time with big smiles on their faces. Their hands shot up one by one, my students disregarding the curriculum and asking a series of questions about my life.

Do you know the Comrades personally?
Did you know Aung San? And U Saw?
Where is your father? And your husband? Can they visit?
Can we talk about the war?

I did not answer their questions on the first day, nor many days after that because I wanted to follow the curriculum and teach them about the beauty of English literature. My students persisted in asking me until we reached an agreement one day. I agreed to tell them stories bit by bit if they promised to memorize the texts and connect them with modern Burmese history. It proved to be a fair and stimulating arrangement because our modern history was largely a Shakespearean play, with the hopeful pacts and complex heroes and heartbreaking betrayals. It was an unorthodox teaching method but all of my students from that first class passed their exams with flying colors.

Those were the best years of my life, like my father had said. I gave birth to another daughter, Kinsa, and was expecting another baby by 1955. "Teacher Tinsa, always with a little belly," one of my students playfully remarked as I waddled to the podium one morning, my pregnant stomach sagging as if I were carrying a ripe summer melon.

With my five children and one more on the way, my parents decided that the Kandawgyi house was too small and began building a new home at 81 University Avenue. The property encompassed two acres of prime land across the street from a small lake, more than enough space for the children and grandchildren. The neighborhood of Inyamyaing was considered a suburban area of Rangoon at the time unlike its mansions, luxury cars and high-end restaurants of today. The Ambassador to Pakistan lived next door and the Korean Embassy was on the other side. The Japanese ambassador lived down the road on University Avenue and across the way from Daw Khin Kyi (Aung San's widow).

We did need a larger home but I wondered if my father was searching for the final piece of his catharsis, a new physical beginning to wash away the memories of the past. I could only guess at what he was thinking or feeling. He was drafting his war memoirs, *Breakthrough in Burma: Memoirs of a Revolution*, occasionally peeking his head from his study to ask me to proofread the chapters before slinking back. He listened to recordings of the Buddhawin Zat, Kyar-Ni-Kan Head Monk's sermons and U Hla Thein's lectures, popular in religious circles in those days. A new home was within his control, to remove us from the physical ties to a painful era. And who was I to judge him for it?

May May and Phay Phay designed a Western-style villa standing prominently in view from University Avenue. As for Yan Naing and me, my parents gave us a small plot of land in the back bordering Supuong Lane. Thakin Than Tun was right about me, that I was not one for glitz or glamour, choosing the less showy but more peaceful plot for its tranquility. We opted for a simple, wooden ranch with an open plan, nestled under the shade of palm trees. It was quiet, private and an ideal atmosphere for our first real home together. There was a small lake in our yard where I envisioned Yan Naing to spend long days fishing.

I thought about how life had settled so quietly in the intervening years, as if it had never been broken. My father's law practice flourished as did my mother's import-export business. I loved working at the university, content to be in a classroom full of bright students and becoming close with them, often inviting them to my home to picnic by our pond. These casual gatherings evolved into an annual tradition in which my students would celebrate their yearly exams with a lakeside picnic with my family. Phay Phay loved to regale them with stories from the war, his life and historical anecdotes. They were utterly charmed by him, my father never losing his ability to win hearts and minds.

81 University Avenue became a gathering place for my young children who invited their friends to fish and swim in the pond. My twin sons Yan Myo and Yan Lin were soccer fanatics and played whenever they could, their imaginations and limbs flying everywhere. They played drenched in rain when the monsoon inevitably came, their knees splattered with dark coffee mud. I was a strict disciplinarian and routinist, coming home from work every day at the same time and lining up my children's designated chairs around our dining table in order to help them with their schoolwork. Yan Naing staged table tennis matches in the front yard to celebrate good marks, the winner receiving a coveted trip to the ice cream parlor for a double scoop of their flavor of choice.

Yan Naing and I made a small group of friends from the neighborhood. Our closest friends were Mr. and Mrs. Nemoto, a young Japanese diplomat and his wife posted in Rangoon. The Chesser family lived across the street, an American couple and their two sons (Roger and Michael) who attended Methodist High School with our children. The Beldens were another American family to whom we grew close, going to their home in the evenings to watch American films and drink California wine. In our free time, Yan Naing and I never stopped debating about politics, literature and philosophy, and I suppose our conversations were a great aphrodisiac of sorts since we managed to have eleven children in the end.

I knew that my husband was struggling to ease into civilian life though he tried his best not to show it. He was a wonderful father and loyal husband but domestic tranquility proved to be a greater challenge to him than guerrilla warfare. He was a son of war and did not know anything else until now. An activist at heart and a soldier by training, he tried his hand at many things after his retirement from the army. Yan Naing had been a promising law student at Rangoon University before running off to Hainan with the Comrades and finally completed his Bachelor of Arts in Law in 1955. He continued to self-study at my father's office but could not focus on civil law as his heart was always in politics, yet he also refused to run for office. My husband was ardently critical of our so-called independence and the new administration. There were still political prisoners and he could not believe that a government relying so heavily on martial law could be called democratic. He did not believe in the Communist or Socialist ideologies either but empathized with their attempts to provide a new world order for the downtrodden. By not voicing his support publicly for the incumbent regime, he earned himself a coveted spot on the Communist watch list by default, thus invalidating him from public office.

Yan Naing never had a mind for business and was terrible with handling money, and he did not pretend to be good at either. My husband briefly worked with my mother on her *Maw Taik* import-export business in addition to continuing to help my father at his legal practice. Finding that fine china was not his preferred industry, he then bred chickens imported from the United States and sold eggs for a short period before settling on the bamboo business after discovering a niche market in delivering fresh shoots to Japan. He and an old friend, U Kin Choon, established a canning factory in Mudon to which they would travel frequently. The family got used to him being gone for days, weeks at a time. Bamboo trading was not a terribly exciting venture but at least he found comfort in financial stability and a chance to roam free in the forests surrounding Mudon.

Progressing in my career as a university lecturer, I was happy that my husband found independent work and I no longer had to worry about his mental state. It was my fault for not searching deeper into his soul to find not a tamed man but a soldier at his core. What was most dangerous was that he was a soldier without a war, left to wander until another cause would inevitably snatch him away. My life was simply too idyllic, serene and routinized for me to force myself to peer down from the clouds and touch the earth. I should have known that in a Rahu-born's life, the calm will always be followed by a storm so great that it shakes their lives, a natural balance to their destiny.

CHAPTER TWELVE

Rangoon was preposterously wealthy in the age of democracy. Under U Nu's leadership, Burma was Southeast Asia's greatest success story, rich and stable against the backdrop of upheaval in neighboring countries. British-steered development had served the country well and our impressive agricultural output earned us the nickname as the 'rice bowl of the world'. The reputation was only half true. Rangoon, and not Burma as a whole, was wealthy beyond belief. Chauffeured Rolls-Royces gleamed in the driveways of homes in the Golden Valley and Kandawgyi neighborhoods. Friends and neighbors skied in the Alps and sunbathed in the French Riviera, tales of rubbing shoulders with Elizabeth Taylor and Marlene Dietrich. The Rangoon tycoons owned thousands of acres of land across the country, stretching from the powder sand beaches of Ngapali to the snowy caps of Kachin state.

Beyond Rangoon, the majority of the population lived in abject poverty and in the same conditions that their ancestors lived in generations ago. If one were to drive an hour outside of the capital, the country fell into pitch-black darkness, electricity an unimaginable luxury for the masses. Estates and plantations owned by the Golden Valley residents housed thousands of workers living in bamboo huts and picking rice with their bare hands. The rice bowl of the world was cultivated with their sweat and enduring.

Bo Yan Naing (center) at the little teashop around the corner

My family was still considered upper class by virtue of name, if not by our assets. We were by no means poor but the halcyon days of silk wardrobes and trunks overflowing with priceless jewels were gone. I had never been to St. Moritz or Acapulco, but the fact that I even knew about these exotic locales and the people who frequented them spoke volumes about my perceived standing in the class hierarchy. Despite having a famous family name, my parents, husband and I still had to work and there was no such thing as a vacation for us. This is not an indictment but rather a reflection of the class system that permeated Burma during those boom years.

My students were some of the most vociferous critics of the growing inequality in the age of democracy, identifying with Communist teachings like so many young people at the time. It was the height of the Cold War and it was difficult not to be drawn in by the various manifestos and slogans that came from China and the Soviet Union. Many of them dreamed of becoming revolutionaries and fighting for equality but few were serious enough to take up arms. I tried to steer them back to the curriculum, to draw them in with fictional battles and heroes, but they could not help but circle back to their romanticized notions of a real and pending class struggle.

I could no longer ignore the class struggle when infighting erupted within U Nu's party, the AFPFL, which was the single most powerful political entity in Burma. A growing majority of AFPFL members identified with a socialist platform while U Nu favored capitalism and free market ideology in practice, if not completely in ideology. The Socialists had had enough of his policies and broke away to form the National Unity Front (NUF). U Nu underestimated the NUF's base and was shocked when the opposing faction nearly defeated him in the 1956 general elections. The Prime Minister was paralyzed, unable to stop his party from splintering into further groups, his political base eroded by the encroachment of Socialist and Communist voices and voters.

Groups outside of the main political arena began to revolt against U Nu. Along the eastern border of Burma, deep in the hills of Shan State, breakaway factions of Chiang Kai-Shek's forces prepared for renewed conflict against Mao Tse-Tung's Communist People's Republic of China. They posed the greatest threat to U Nu's regime, not only because there was already a large Communist base in Burma ready to fight for their brethren, but also because the CIA was allegedly supporting Chiang Kai-Shek's forces. A pending war would be more devastating than World War II for the country, this time Burmese fighting Burmese in a civil war. It was only a matter of time before Burma's internal divisions were ignited by the outer conflict.

I had not heard Thakin Than Tun's name in years. Though he had not contacted my family during his absence, I still considered him a great friend and never forgot his kindnesses towards me. It wounded me to hear that he and the Communist Party of Burma (CPB) had intensified their armed struggle against U Nu and his government. Than Tun and the Communists' aspirations had been muted during the independence war, secondary to the greater goal of national independence. Now that independence had been achieved, it was time for them to resume their original purpose, which was to dismantle the class and economic divide in the country. Though they were an underground movement, having been unceremoniously thrown out of the AFPFL by Aung San and Governor Rance, it did not deter the Communists from establishing their headquarters in Pyinmana and several other guerrilla bases along the Chinese border. Than Tun sent hundreds of his best fighters across the border to China to be trained by revolutionaries and they demanded a series of agrarian reforms for poor farmers right after the 1956 elections, a direct attack on the capitalist system that made Burma so wealthy in the postwar years.

When U Nu refused to capitulate to their demands, the CPB found an unlikely ally in the Karen militia who were fighting for an autonomous state. The Karen armed forces, led by the dominant Christian faction, had previously staged an uprising in 1949 coinciding with the Communist struggle. The Karen National Union (KNU) and the more radical Karen National Defense Organization (KNDO) demanded a fully autonomous state, which the government denied. They commenced armed struggle in retaliation, joining forces with the CPB when they realized a common enemy. The joint CPB-Karen coalition captured several army strongholds moving outwards from Toungoo, skirmishes inching closer to Rangoon as the years went by.

Since we were and continue to be a nation comprised of hundreds of different ethnic groups, the civil conflict between the Communists, Karen and the central government stoked the embers of centuries of ethnic and sectarian grudges and inspired others to take up arms. Dozens of other groups declared war, and their struggles are not mentioned here not because I was not aware of what was happening, but because I cannot do justice to their stories. I can only speak of what I know firsthand, which is how the Communist and Karen efforts shaped the remainder of my life.

Despite their military successes, the CPB-Karen coalition was doomed from the start. Whereas the Communists were mainly of Bamar ethnic origin and sought to reinvent society, the Karen wanted nothing more to do with Burmanized society. Their enmity with the Bamar reached back to when Burma was a series of warring kingdoms, each ethnic group ruled under warlord kings. The Karen, a proud and gentle people, resented the cruelty of Bamar kings who defiled their traditions and enslaved their people. The Karen and other minority ethnic groups had partnered with the British as a safeguard against the Bamar. The British welcomed these advantageous allies into a sub-class of civil service that excluded the Bamar. The colonial government gave them elite military training, reserved the highest posts in local civil service for them and made life peaceful again in Karen state. There was also no doubt that the Crown had ulterior motives, seeking to maintain ethnic divisions. Divide and conquer, as always.

World War II intensified hostilities between the Karen and Bamar. The Karens refused to ally with the BIA and the Comrades since the British were favorable allies and the BIA had yet to earn their respect or trust in national matters. Many Karens clashed with BIA soldiers, particularly those hell-bent on a mission to promote Bamar supremacy. If I had to pinpoint the precise moment in our modern history that altered Karen-Bamar relations, it was the death of Colonel Ijima in 1942. A close friend of Colonel Suzuki's, Ijima was patrolling the area near Myaung Mya, the site of one of the largest Bamar refugee areas, when a band of Karen guerrillas attacked and killed him. When he heard of his friend's death, Suzuki made one remark: *Burn them all.* He selected two villages at random, Kanazogon and Thayagon, and ordered the BIA to destroy the villages as a lesson to the Karens. Families were burned alive, men, women and children cut down by machine gun fire if they tried to escape.

A minor Karen leader by the name of San Po Thin planned an attack on Myaung Mya where thousands of Bamar refugees lived in cramped conditions. The BIA uncovered the plot and subdued the Karen forces before they could reach the camp, arresting all but one man, Saw Pe Tha. Saw Pe Tha was a

Karen parliamentarian before the war, held in high regard by many across ethnic lines. One of the Thakins, whose identity remains in shrouded secrecy, harbored a profound resentment for the elder man and took matters into his own hands. The Thakin and his men went to Saw Pe Tha's house later that evening and set his house on fire, murdering him and his entire family. The Karen have never forgotten these massacres, the blood of innocents and martyrs stained indelibly in their collective memory.

While the Communists and the Karen forces were fighting over their alliance, it was a prime opportunity for the Commander-in-Chief of the Army, General Ne Win, to crush the opposing armies in their weakened state. General Ne Win was a member of the Thirty Comrades but remained curiously apolitical after the war, choosing to work his way up the army ladder. He took thousands of soldiers deep into the eastern lowlands and firebombed the rebels' strongholds until the CPB and Karens were contained in just three remaining holdout areas. After the success of the army's campaign, U Nu called on General Ne Win in 1958 to act as interim Prime Minister in the months leading up to the 1960 elections, unable to contain ethnic fighting. Smaller conflicts arose, ethnic groups inspired by the Karens to take up arms. At the time of General Ne Win's appointment, U Nu's remaining supporters had split into even smaller groups and the minority faction called U Nu to a no-confidence vote, accusing him of having little power beyond the capital gates and earning him the nickname of the *Prime Minister of Rangoon*.

Ne Win's caretaker government lasted for a year and a half beginning with a nationwide sweep of high-profile Communist leaders, including young activists from the Rangoon University Student Union and many of my students. Outside of Rangoon, he quelled private militias and also coerced the Shan and Kayah royal families into exchanging their monarchial seats for lifelong government pensions, similar to what the British did with the Indian maharajas. Burma paid a heavy price for U Nu's re-election in the spring of 1960. General Ne Win relinquished his post without great fanfare and U Nu was reelected, but it was too late. The latter's alliance with the army had alienated any potential reconciliation with the Communists who were still in open rebellion. His agenda was hopelessly confused, suffering from the political descent from which he would never recover. It was a great shame. U Nu was a good and fair man, and there was never a doubt in my mind that he loved Burma to his core and had always intended to do his best for his country.

On March 2, 1962, General Ne Win declared a state of emergency and staged a coup d'état, forming the Revolutionary Council and appointing himself as Chairman. The Council boasted of its bloodless coup although this was far from the truth. Several of our close friends, neighbors and peers disappeared, never to be heard from again. Sao Shwe Taik, who had been the first President of Burma under U Nu's government, lost his son, a mere teenager who had been watching tanks roll into central Rangoon from the roof of his house when he was shot and killed by an unknown gunman. He was the only recorded victim of that day. Sao Shwe Taik did not know about his son's death, the former President arrested during the coup and dying in prison in November 1962.

The Burmese Socialist Program Party (BSPP) was founded on July 4, 1962, to be the only political party in Burma. On July 7, dozens of students gathered at Rangoon University to protest the military takeover, the same bravery displayed by young student leaders generation after generation. Some of my students, the brightest medical and academic minds in Rangoon, marched at the front of the protest. Their cries met machine gun fire and in a final spectacle, a moment of shock and awe in honor of the new party, the Rangoon University Student Union was dynamited on July 8, its history and feats turned to ashes. RUSU had been the birthplace of the modern Burmese army where Aung San, my husband and countless others had gathered to ponder a better future for their beloved Burma. Students remained trapped inside, their screams echoing down University Avenue.

Some of the first people to go to prison were familiar names from my childhood and the country's collective memory – U Kyaw Nyein[47], Edward Law-Yone and Bo Let Ya. A new set of reforms called the *Burmese Way to Socialism* expelled foreign influences in Burma and all industries and private enterprises were nationalized in October 1963. The most successful and well-known business minds of the boom years – CEOs, industrialists, entrepreneurs, among others – were arrested and their assets seized. Since the colonial government had discriminated against the Burmese in commerce, many of those who were arrested had climbed their way to success through hard work and industry. They were my neighbors and friends, and putting aside political matters, they had done nothing wrong. The Revolutionary Council blamed Burma's unrest on British-influenced economic policies, also targeting Indian and Chinese-owned businesses that flourished. My father was troubled and saddened upon hearing of the mass expulsion of innocent people. "Who is truly Burmese, anyhow?" he thought out loud, none of us able to give him an answer. "Burma will never recover this exodus of skilled labor and knowledge," he predicted, and he was right.

Yan Naing said very little in those days, but he did say one thing that encapsulated the changes going on around us and foreshadowed Burma's economic decline for the next few decades. "Soldiers are not equipped to be businessmen, and vice versa. A gun and a pen are two very different things."

The Council extended a general amnesty to the Communist Party because some of the CPB leaders were still respected as independence heroes and Comrades. Bo Ye Htut[48], Bo Ye Maung and Bo Sein Tin took the amnesty and returned to Rangoon to be reunited with their families. The remaining CPB leaders organized a delegation to Rangoon. Thakin Than

---

[47] Deputy Prime Minister under the AFPFL.
[48] A member of the Thirty Comrades, student leader, Communist leader of the 1948 Army rebellion, arrested after 88 Revolution.

Tun was noticeably absent, choosing to remain in the jungle until the smoke had cleared. Thakin Soe, Bo Zeya[49], Thakin Zin[50] and others flew from as far as Peking to attend a meeting together in over fifteen years.

In November, the Council presented a series of immutable demands: the CPB would be contained in certain zones, members were not to leave cities without permission and growth and funding would be cut off from that point forward. Calling their bluff, the Communists staged a march to the capital amassing thousands of supporters in a spectacular display of manpower. When they arrived in Rangoon, they realized that the puppet masters had been pulling the strings all along. The BSPP and Council had offered an opportunity for a ceasefire, but in the event that peace talks failed, they were now in army territory. The Communists made the grave mistake of revealing themselves and their supporters in the process, many of whom had kept their sympathies a secret but had been foolish enough to follow their lead now. In the aftermath of the march, thousands of CPB supporters were arrested, left to languish in newly constructed, clinical detention centers with the paint still drying on the walls.

---

[49] A member of the Thirty Comrades; became a Communist leader of the Army rebellion in 1948, returned from China for the 1963 peace parley, killed in action on April 16 1968.
[50] Became leader of the Communist Party after Thakin Than Tun's death in 1968.

CHAPTER THIRTEEN

I was thirty-seven years old in 1964 and had come to realize that my life had largely been defined by silences and disappearances. When I was a child, my classmates from St. John's left without a trace, and this time, it was my own students who began to vanish. My students had always been political with their Socialist and Communist leanings, but they quickly abandoned their old rhetoric and adopted a purely anti-government stance. They began to speak of armed uprising similar to what was happening in Latin America, particularly in the wake of the May 1964 currency devaluation that marked the beginning of the end of Burma's modern economy. Intended to curb black market trading, the Council believed that ridding certain high value notes would quash smugglers and underground businesses. The initial devaluation was ruthless, the government announcing that 100 kyat notes would no longer be accepted at a time in which one kyat equaled one dollar, enormous purchasing power. We were given two days to exchange currency at the central bank and tellers ran out of smaller notes within two hours, fortunes vanishing into thin air. The government did end up bankrupting the black market but also wiped out half of Rangoon's cash flow. The black market that had all but disappeared under the currency devaluation scheme simply reappeared under new ownership, the regime and its followers owning both the formal and informal economies.

In tandem with economic domination, there was a systematic campaign to culturally isolate Burma by expelling all foreign elements, for good this time. The single most devastating xenophobic policy affected our educational system, an issue dear to my heart. The Burmese educational system was the crown jewel of Southeast Asia. We managed to thrive in the postwar climate primarily because of our education, a combination of Burmese and Western teaching. The regime loathed that English was still taught as a primary language, viewing it as a tool for the West to control us. It was the opposite: by learning English from a young age, the Burmese had a competitive advantage over other nations without bilingual facilities. Even the most flagrant nationalists saw that English instruction was a necessary tool in getting ahead in the twentieth century, as long as we did not forsake our native language.

My older children were attending Methodist High School and their beloved teachers were given short notice to leave, some having been there since my school days. Universities were ordered to discard English-language textbooks and to begin teaching in our mother tongue with propaganda texts. The nuns at St. John's protested, continuing to teach a new generation of girls English prose, poetry and culture, until one day a government official placed them in the back of a police van and escorted them to the airport, handing them one-way tickets to Bangkok and nothing more. Private estates in Golden Valley and Kandawgyi emptied their magnificent libraries of foreign texts, the words of Twain, Bronte and Byron wrapped in rough brown paper and stored beneath creaky wooden floorboards.

As for me, I became a relic of the past with my specialized knowledge of English literature. My skills were no longer needed in the current era yet I was still employed on paper and had a classroom. I found a clever way of circumventing the authorities by ripping the covers off of old Burmese novels and taping them to my English-language books, but my subversive techniques went to waste as the number of students dwindled in my class. Some of my students disappeared on their own accord, and some did not. Whatever their reasons were, most were never heard from again. Yan Naing and I tried to visit the families of some of my students, only for their parents to smile politely and request that we never ask about the whereabouts of their sons and daughters again.

Only one of my students managed to say goodbye to me before he vanished. I shall call him Thant and he was one of the brightest students to grace my classroom in over a decade of teaching. Thant was a card-carrying member of the Communist Party and unafraid to show it. On the morning of our winter exams, I noticed that he was sitting in his chair and not writing in his exam booklet. He waited and waited for the other students to hand in their tests before approaching me with his empty pages. "Thant, I know times are tough but you must not forget about your studies," I began to scold him.

"I'm leaving, Teacher Tinsa," he interrupted me. "I just wanted to thank you and my teachers for the knowledge that you have given me," Thant said mournfully.

"What do you mean leaving?"

"I'm going to fight. I don't know where exactly, but a car is waiting for me outside. Either I stay and they throw me in prison, or I make a go of it." Thant smiled sadly at the pile of exam booklets on my desk, letting his gaze trail across my desk and then into my eyes. "I'll be okay, Teacher Tinsa. Please don't tell anyone what I've just told you." He inhaled deeply before giving me an unexpected warning. "But just know that they'll be coming for you, too."

The Revolutionary Council was systematically ridding itself of its political foes, real and imagined. I thought back to 1959 when my family and I were asked to leave Burma, though I did not realize that we were being coerced at the time. The caretaker government had offered the coveted Ambassadorship to Japan to my husband. It was a brilliant move: placate political rivals by sending them to far-flung postings, ensuring that they would not partake in any political activity in Burma in anticipation of a systemic overhaul.

Back row: Yema, Onma wth baby Kinthi, Mala, Tinsa, Kinsa
Front row: Amaya, Yan Myo, Yan Lin, Neta

Yan Naing and I said no to Japan, yet I could not help but reflect on what could have been had we settled for a comfortable existence as an ambassador and ambassadress. I cleared these thoughts from my mind and asked myself if I really would have been happy as a powdered housewife in a foreign land. The answer was no. I wanted to live in my homeland as did my husband, no matter the consequence.

I fought the instinct to grieve for my country yet again. By 1964, I had eight children and a daughter, Tinthi, on the way. They could not afford to see me falter. My husband, on the other hand, fell into a deep depression over the state of affairs, a bottomless pit of rage against his former comrades. Yan Naing despaired over the army and Communists' betrayal of the integrity of the independence movement. They were bound under an oath to protect Burma from her enemies, but what was to happen when they became the enemy? Who would guard the guardians? I foolishly chose not worry about my husband during this initial emotional phase, thinking it normal for him to feel angry. How wrong I was.

My worries came true when Yan Naing's sulking turned into something revolutionary: a planning phase. He began to speak of overthrowing the regime, that there was no other way to save the country's dire situation but to launch a rebellion with the most influential pro-democracy activists and leaders. I later found out from my father that my husband sought to contact U Nu, who was imprisoned after the 1962 coup. Though they disagreed on some political sore points, my husband maintained the utmost respect for U Nu, believing that he was the last man left who had never betrayed Burma. Using his bamboo shoot business in Mudon as a cover, Yan Naing began to build a secret training camp near the Three Pagodas Pass on the Thai border, receiving funding from anonymous backers.

Yan Naing first approached my father for his blessing, fearful of what the elder would say, that he was about to leave his young wife and nine children to fight an invisible war. To his great relief, my father gave his enthusiastic approval to Yan Naing, encouraging him and likeminded activists such as Edward Law-Yone and Bo Let Ya (recently released from prison) on the condition that all activity must take place away from our family home. Phay Phay, from the moment that he introduced Yan Naing to me, knew that his son-in-law shared his undying loyalty for his country and was proud to have him fight for democracy when he himself could not. Burma was their queen, the timeless monarch whom they all served and would never stop serving.

My husband approached my mother and me with great anxiety, saving us for last. As soon as I heard his confession of an underground rebel camp, the air was sucked from my lungs and everything went black before me. I couldn't breathe, couldn't process what this man, like a stranger, was telling me. I felt angry with him and selfish at the same time. I knew that what was happening to our country was worth fighting for, but it infuriated me to be kept in the dark until this very last moment. I was not angry with him for wanting to fight, but it was shattering to know that my husband had been keeping things from me that would alter my life and our children's lives and that we were not consulted from the beginning.

My mother's face was ashen. Yan Naing exited the room for a brief respite, allowing us to collect our shock and thoughts but also protecting himself from a caning. Gracefully, my mother turned to me and said words that broke my heart. "Men must be allowed, within reason, to achieve their political ambitions," she reasoned. What other choice did I have?

I looked straight into my husband's eyes with as much confidence as I could. Nothing needed to be said; he understood everything. "You know that I must leave," he said to me.

"Then go," I replied.

* * * * *

The monsoon rains came just as Yan Naing left. On May 29, 1965, I awoke in the middle of the night to see my husband gathering his things, a silhouette darting in between shadows. He heard me stirring, glancing at me from across the room, his dark eyes locking with mine. Yan Naing could not tell us the location, route, or any details regarding his mission. He dared not reveal the name of his new political initiative, which I later found out to be the Union of Burma Party. This knowledge, the slight utterance of these names to the wrong people, would have dire implications for all of us, especially my elderly parents and children. My husband and I stayed silent for lifetimes, the understanding that there would be a price to pay for a traitor's family.

Yan Naing and I woke our children and lined them up one by one in the kitchen so that he could say goodbye to them. They believed that he was leaving on one of his business trips and did not realize that he would be gone for the next fifteen years. Half asleep, minds straddling their dreams and reality, their father kissed them on their foreheads. The younger ones went back to sleep oblivious to the significance of that farewell, the elder children sensing something amiss but too polite to ask questions.

Yan Naing had said his farewells to my parents the previous night and we decided not to wake them on that morning for fear of arousing suspicion. When we were sure that the children were asleep, he took his old army rucksack and slung it over his shoulder, the canvas scratching against his cotton jacket. I handed him a three-tiered steel container with rice, chicken curry and a side of vegetables.

There were no kisses or grand hugs. I have never been sentimental about goodbyes, nor is it customary in our culture to act in that manner. I chose to believe that if karma wills it, then we would meet again soon.

"Do you remember when we first spoke, when you said that there is no way to say *I love you* or *I hate you* in Burmese?" Yan Naing whispered as he leaned against the front doorway.

"How could I forget?" my voice croaked.

"There are so many times when I wish for the former, and then there are the times when I'm thankful that you cannot say the latter to me."

"There is also no word for goodbye."

"This isn't a goodbye. That, I promise."

I watched his obscure figure grow smaller and smaller in the driveway, until at last he turned the corner and disappeared into the horizon, and out of our lives.

* * * * *

I did not expect contact from Yan Naing in the weeks following his disappearance. My father, mother, aunt and I did not speak of his leaving and thankfully the children did not question where their father had gone. They were accustomed to his frequent trips, assuming that he was on an extended mission and would be back any day now. My heart broke whenever we sat down for meals and their father was not there at the head of the table. More and more families became like us, the great men of our society leaving to fight for what they thought was the moral thing to do. There was a stinging irony in so many of our children growing up fatherless so that the next generation would not have to.

I was no fool. I knew that I would be punished for my husband's insurrection but I was not sure how. Would I be fined? Would I be demoted from my position at the university? My worst fear was that there would a lengthy trial in which my name and my children's names would be dragged through the mud. Since I was the main breadwinner for my family, Yan Naing's absence did not affect our finances but I still worried about my career prospects. I had not heard of other women in our circle being questioned therefore my concern was mainly financial. The only war that I had lived through lasted about four years, so I assumed that my husband's war would be over by then, if not before. I had no idea that his was a guerrilla war, its tactics often times more brutal and protracted than a clash of empires.

Resentment enveloped me in a slow, dense, sour haze. When Edward Law-Yone visited my father to tell him that he was leaving to join my husband on the border, he offered to carry messages for Yan Naing. "What should I tell him?" He looked at me with such hope.

"Tell him this," I pointed bitterly to my belly, pregnant with the son that Yan Naing might never meet. Edward Law-Yone gave a weak, faint smile, his eyes searching mine for understanding before he too disappeared.

Three weeks after his departure, six policemen dressed in identical, starched blue uniforms came to my home and inquired about Yan Naing's whereabouts. "We have been informed that your husband has been away for a few weeks now. Where did he go, Daw Tinsa?" they asked me politely, sternly.

"My husband is always in and out of Rangoon due to business. I have no knowledge of his exact whereabouts but he should be home soon." It was the truth; I actually had no idea of his exact location. The police realized that they were not going to get any information from me and left. The questioning persisted with weekly home visits from the special forces, a benign knock on the door by a clean-cut officer each time. Where was Bo Yan Naing? Why hadn't he returned from his business trip? Why hadn't I, his wife, reported his absence to the police?

Several months pregnant with my last child, a boy conceived weeks before Yan Naing's exit, I struggled to support my nine children on a lecturer's salary. One October day, the rector of the medical college, a fair man by all accounts, released me of my teaching duties. He held his head down as I gathered my belongings, ashamed of what he was being made to do, a betrayal that he could not refuse. And how could I blame him? Did he not have a family to protect over mine? The financial setback was lessened by my mother's support but my pride prevented me from asking for more charity. Though my mother and father offered help, I refused their offers and took only what was necessary. The rest I would have to make up for on my own, no matter how difficult it was.

A family friend alerted me of the recent opening of a rather prestigious intergovernmental organization's office in Rangoon, an organization known for its peace, conflict and human rights efforts, or so they claimed. They advertised a position for a Liaison Officer, someone who was fluent in both Burmese and English and had high-level contacts. I was naïve in assuming that I was qualified for the post, appearing at the nondescript gray office in a simple lilac shirt and *longyi*, grasping my resume in my hand. I was called into the Director's office, a man who greeted me with great friendliness until he saw my last name. "Maw-Naing?" he asked nervously. "What an interesting name. Are you related to Dr. Ba Maw?"

"I am his daughter."

"Ah yes, I see. Where does the Naing come from?"

"From my husband, Bo Yan Naing."

The Director pulled a thin booklet from his desk drawer and studied it thoroughly, going up and down the rows of finely typed letters. He was trying to be discreet but I could see that it was a list of names including Bo Let Ya, Thakin Than Tun, Bo Ye Htut and other politically resonant names. He stopped when he reached the last page, presumably the Y section. "Mrs. Maw-Naing, I'm sorry but we cannot process your application further."

"Please have a look at my qualifications. I feel that I possess all of the skills that you are looking for," I pleaded him.

He waved his hands in front of his face, as if I were some petulant saleswoman offering him a useless product. *I'm sorry, I'm sorry. We cannot help you further.*

CHAPTER FOURTEEN

Almost a year to the day after Yan Naing took off, I awoke at 5:00 AM as usual to begin the morning's routine. The household help was on their annual leave, the house at a standstill without the children's nannies, our corridors steeped in light from the morning sun. Zarni, born on January 10, 1966, was four months old and required feeding every few hours. I saw flickering figures in the front yard from the corner of my eye, quick to dismiss it as my imagination, my mind weary from nursing and anxiety. I went to open the gate for the milkman like any other day and continued errands when my daughter Kinsa, an unerringly bright and observant child, stood in the hallway shaking with fear.

"May May, there are soldiers outside," she quivered. Her lips trembled with every word. "I was in the bathroom and when I looked out the window, there were soldiers in our yard. They're hiding so that we won't see them." Blood rushed through my head, temples, burned my eyes, pricking every nerve in my body. I crept against the side of the window, slowly sticking my head out so that I could get a glimpse of the yard. I was not sure of how many soldiers I saw - maybe five, a dozen - positioned in strategic positions and hidden from plain sight. They had finally come to take me away.

Suppressing a gasp, tears, whatever my body was screaming at me to do, Kinsa and I ran to the other children's beds. We roused everyone making sure the young ones kept quiet as they woke from their deep slumber. While the older children calmed their younger siblings, I scurried through the house pulling as many suspicious documents as I could, ordering my children to hide irreplaceable documents in their underwear. They did as they were told, pairs of eyes searching for answers from their mother. Furiously shredding all of the other sheets and flushing them down the toilet, I watched as the tiny scraps floated clockwise in the water. All of Yan Naing's letters to and from his friends, my private letters to family and friends, and even the little note that Thakin Than Tun had left in my book when I was spying on my father and the Freedom Bloc as a child. They were mere memories, fragments of my sentimentality, but it only occurred to me now that they could be somehow used against me. I felt so stupid for not getting rid of the documents earlier but I had no idea that the authorities would search my home in this manner, with my children present.

A terse knock came at the front door. Every particle of oxygen was sucked from the room, my children's fearful eyes on me, wondering what their mother would do next. I answered the door with shaking hands, with as much bravery as I could muster. A boyish officer in a freshly ironed uniform introduced himself, but he didn't need to say anything. The only possible reason they had not appeared sooner at my doorstep was because of my pregnancy. "Daw Tinsa, I have orders to search the house." Efficient. Professional. Banal.

We sat on the porch while the men went through our belongings, hours passing before they ended their search. The boyish officer asked me to accompany him to meet his superior who had a few more questions for me, not a request in the least. I asked for a little time to collect essentials for the baby and to call my parents who lived in the same compound on the other side of the pond. No, I was not allowed to call nor could I bring the baby. I insisted that Zarni was still breastfeeding and there was no household help with whom I could leave him. He finally gave in and let me collect the bare necessities for my son and we left.

I glanced across the yard to my parents' home as I entered an unmarked black sedan, hoping to catch a glimpse of my mother, father, or aunt. A wall of guns surrounded my father and he, such a mythic and large hero in my eyes, looked so small at that moment. My heart sank, my father to be punished for his son-in-law's disappearance. Phay Phay caught my eye to wink at me before entering the police car, sitting erectly and proudly as one of the soldiers cloaked his head in a black hood. When his car drove off, my escorts nudged me into the backseat of my car. My sole reaction was to crane my neck out of the open door and look at my children, all nine of them staring at me in horror from the porch. "Go to your grandmother's and stay there until I get back!" I yelled at them before the door creaked shut in my face.

Zarni slept on my lap and there were two people on each side of me blocking the view from the windows, a driver and an officer in front. They avoided driving on the conspicuous University Avenue and took the long and winding back roads branching from Inyamyaing to Boundary Road. The car entered the gates of an old colonial home that did not reveal any of the sinister activities going on inside its premises. My escorts took me to a waiting area and told me that a Colonel would be joining me shortly. I waited patiently, feeding the baby and keeping him amused. A platter of cold fried noodles appeared for lunch and I was taken to another room to meet with this elusive Colonel. He rose from a chair behind his desk and introduced himself as Tin Oo from the Special Intelligence Services.

"Do you remember me from university?" he asked as if we were old friends. It was a seemingly innocent but tricky question to answer. He was asking if I, the daughter of Dr. Ba Maw and a member of the upper class, knew who he was. A subtle reminder of how far he had come since his university days, a feat not achieved by academic merit.

I had indeed known him in passing during my university years but he did not leave any impression on me, good or bad. "Yes, I remember you. Since I had children at home, there was not much time for me to get to know the other students." It was the truth; with several children, pregnancies and a husband recently released from political detention, there was barely enough time for me to attend my classes let alone partake in the university social scene with students much younger than myself.

Back row: Yan Myo, Tinsa, Minshin, Yan Naing, Yema, Yan Lin
Front row: Amaya, Kethi, Nanda, Kinsa

There was no indication back then of the man that he would become. He was a slight and bookish young man, completely unremarkable in appearance with the exception of his dark-rimmed glasses, earning him the nickname *Myit-hmanh* (Glasses) Tin Oo. The Colonel was taken under General Ne Win's wing during the postwar years, his mentor so impressed with his loyalty that he gave him the coveted role of interrogating VIP detainees.

His niceties stopped there, releasing a barrage of questions intended to intimidate me. But he underestimated me. Having experienced so much in my short life in addition to drawing on the anger of my husband's departure, my skin was as thick as steel.

Where did your husband disappear to?
He went away on business and has not returned.
Have you received any news or information of his whereabouts?
No.
Has he tried to contact you?
No.
Let's talk about your students. Many of them were openly Communist. Did you encourage this?
No.
Do you know a young man named Thant?
Yes, he was my student.
And did you know that he was caught on the way to join your husband's insurgency?
No.
Don't you think it odd that your husband has started a war against our country, one of your students was caught and you are somehow the link in between?
No.
If I were to tell you that you could walk out as a free woman right now, if only you were to denounce your husband and students, would that be an acceptable understanding?
Never.

Droplets of sweat collected on his forehead, his eyes squinting behind his trademark glasses. Tin Oo decided to take a softer approach with me, revealing tidbits about his family. I had lost focus of the conversation at this point, not bothering to listen to his tedious stories, until he mentioned something that I still remember so clearly to this day. *I have a son, who was born blind*, Tin Oo said, his singular human sentiment of that meeting.

I'm not sure why he shared such an intimate detail about himself, perhaps to evoke sympathy from me. It did, but not for him. Buddhists believe greatly in superstition and karma and we believe that one's deeds determine the outcome of our present and future lifetimes. Normally, these acts are repaid in the next lifetime, but great misdeeds can impact the current lifetime. Colonel Tin Oo's reputation and his deeds had actually caught up with him in this life, so damning that the sins of the father were inflicted on the son. It is often said that you reap what you sow, and for a parent to endure his child's lifelong suffering is one of the greatest punishments that can be given. I prayed that his son would grow up to be a much better man than his father.

Reflecting on my own karma, what sorts of deeds did I commit in my past lifetimes to deserve this, for my own family to suffer? My mother and children were strong but I worried for my aunt. She was in ill health and dying at that very moment. Aunt Kinmimi had never married and was devoted to my mother and us children. My mother was very close to her sister and only living relative; they had never been separated at any time. When my mother married, Aunt Kinmimi accompanied my parents to wherever they settled and helped my mother to raise us with a firm hand. I loved her like a second mother; would I ever see her again?

Colonel Tin Oo grew tired of questioning me but it did not mean that he was satisfied with my answers. "Daw Tinsa, we need more time to clear up the reasons for your husband and brother leaving the country so abruptly and for so long. We will be taking you to another location to continue the interview." I braced myself, rifling through the few things I had gathered at my home for Zarni, keeping my hands and mind busy. He was oblivious to our bleak surroundings and unaware of the enormity of our situation. Taking some milk powder and a thermos filled with hot water, I made a small amount of formula in his bottle and put it to his pursed lips. "May I please have some more hot water for my son?" I asked the guard standing closest to me. The young man looked surprised at my sangfroid, taking the thermos and returning several minutes later, the bottle burning my palm.

They came for us at dusk. Cradling my four-month old son in my arms, I was barely able to keep my knees from collapsing beneath me. They covered my head with a dark towel like a common thief and I could not discern anything except for the start of the car engine and men coughing. "Is this necessary?" I asked my captors of my new accessory. I had not done anything wrong and was not ashamed to show my face to anyone passing by.

"Daw Tinsa, perhaps it is the government that does not want people to know that they have taken you into custody," murmured the quiet one to my left. It was the only thing that they said to me for the entirety of the car ride. I could not see anything, relying on my other senses to detect that the car was on asphalted roads for about two hours. Then, the car stopped, the men stepped out, and I was told to step out as well. The towel was yanked from my head and my first sight was of a barn-like structure.

I knew exactly where I was: the notorious Ye Kyi Aing Detention Center just outside of Rangoon, the subject of much speculated political gossip. I had heard of many going in but none so far living to tell their stories. Upon crossing the threshold, I was now officially an anti-government conspirator and about to be labeled as one of the greatest threats to the state.

CHAPTER FIFTEEN

I walked into a sparsely furnished room with a sallow light bulb swinging overhead. I chuckled inadvertently; everything looked just like it did in the movies, the coldness, gray walls and perfectly sharpened corners. The harsh, artificial light stung my eyes after having been blindfolded for several hours. The guards brought a cold steel chair and placed it in front of me, signaling a long wait. Zarni cried, confused, disoriented by his gray surroundings. I rocked him back and forth in my weary arms, his tiny body convulsing with violent sobs.

A half hour passed before they came for me again. Another set of four or five nameless, faceless green uniforms took me from the building, again covering my head with a dark towel. I could only look straight down, tracing the heavy boots of the soldier in front of me. There was no one around to witness me so I wondered whom it was that they didn't want me to see within these walls. Tufts of wet dirt littered the uneven path, colorless concrete columns at equidistant lengths. I could tell that we were under a long and winding roof judging by the shadows on the ground, reminding me of the layouts of monasteries, open tunnels sheltering people from rain and sunshine as one walks to the inner temple, except that there was nothing sacred about this place. Zigzagging for ages, a guard jangled a set of keys and fumbled to open a heavy door. The chain and padlock were of heavy iron, rust screeching like train tracks, designed so that whomever was inside could not get out. We stepped inside and they took the towel away from me.

I was in a barrack. There were eight old, pine beds in total – four on each side – all barren. Two dim fluorescent lights buzzed overhead, barely enough light for me to see a small table at the end of the room. A small door on the side led to a bathroom, a sorry sight with one toilet and washbasin for eight inhabitants. Nevertheless, the room seemed in order and the furniture in a good state, indicating not many previous inhabitants. "Daw Tinsa, this will be your accommodation for the time being," the guard said tersely. I looked at this man, no older than my younger brothers. He did not seem cruel, his bureaucratic manner suggesting a career soldier and someone who did not think too profoundly about his day-to-day responsibilities. They vanished into the night just as quickly as they had come, locking the heavy chains behind them.

I was too exhausted and hungry to sit down and rest my eyes. I had eaten the meal of cold noodles during my initial interrogation and Zarni did not have much more formula left. He clawed at my breast, hungry and frustrated that I was no longer producing milk due to stress. Another young soldier came and delivered the bedding – a thin mattress, a pillow, a mosquito net, a sheet, a pillowcase and a thick blanket for the both of us.

As Zarni slept, I went to the bathroom to wash up before bed, drawing from a large drum in the crude bathroom, water spurting from a tired old tap directly above it. The toilet was a bucket with a wooden seat over it. It was a tiny bathroom lit by a small bulb hanging from the center of the ceiling, and in the dim light I could see that some basic toiletries were provided. *Five-star treatment at a VIP prison*, I couldn't help but laugh to myself. I cleaned myself quickly and laid my weary body next to Zarni's, drained emotionally and physically.

Zarni stirred at dawn, his fat little hands grabbing at my breast demanding his usual meal. The morning light streamed through cracks in the darkened windows, doing its best to illuminate the barrack. To my surprise, I discovered a yard with a mango tree but no grass, flowers or other vegetation. I was grateful for a space where I could see the sun and breathe fresh air. If I was hoping that there was more to see beyond this small patch, I would have been disappointed. A wall of corrugated iron sheets ten feet high surrounded me with barbed wire on top, to keep me in and everything else out.

I heard keys jangling and a soldier brought me a mug of coffee, afraid to look me in the eyes. He left without a word and I gulped the coffee down, the coffee grounds scratching at my throat. It was a weak brew, the acidity barely detected on my tongue, but I was so happy to have something hot to drink. The toiletries, yard, coffee – these human touches, intentional or unintentional, were getting me through the morning. This was followed by a macabre pondering of what the worst could possibly be if these were the finer things in this prison.

The door opened again and I expected to see another green uniform. Surprisingly, two women entered and announced, "We are here to help with the baby." Neither introduced themselves, presumably the wives of soldiers stationed at this post. They chatted with each other but did not speak a word to me, and I also chose to keep my distance and did not strike up a conversation.

Lunch came in the form of three-tiered containers: a portion of yellowed rice, some unidentified meat and a clear broth. This container would become one of my sharpest memories of my imprisonment, always rice, a small entrée and soup that would sometimes be substituted with vegetables. My prisoners gave me meat everyday initially until it was rationed to once a week. The empty containers would be taken away and new ones left at the door in their place.

On the third day, the soldiers came with heavy parcels. I could hear them dragging something of significant weight across the threshold, two loud thuds on the floor when they were set down. It was two medium-sized suitcases from a mystery sender. "These are for you, Daw Tinsa." I rushed to fling the suitcases open, eager for anything that broke the monotony of the passing days. My eyes welled with tears when

I saw what was inside.

My mother, left to cope with my nine children, her dying sister, my father in jail and no men around the house, managed to put together some basic clothes and toiletries that she thought would be of use to Zarni and me without having any notion of where we were and under what conditions. There were fresh cloth diapers and milk powder for Zarni, a godsend as I could no longer rely on my breast milk to feed him. I was unable to produce enough milk to keep him healthy, mere droplets at his lips. My mother had packed three sets of *longyi*s and shirts of heavy and durable cotton for me, the kind that would last me for weeks or years. I inhaled the fresh scent of the newly washed *longyi* in my hands, reminding me of home, my family and the familiar.

There was another surprise a few weeks later. Seven women stood at the threshold of my barrack clutching their belongings in their hands, their eyes scanning the barrack. Seven sets of eyes assessed me and I them, wondering who they were and what purpose we were all here for. "Daw Tinsa, you may already know some of these women. They will be staying here from now on," said the soldier in front, presumably the superior. The two women who had been with me to help take care of Zarni gathered their things. I turned to say something to them, to say thank you, but they disappeared just as quickly as they arrived on that first day. There we were – eight women and one baby – in a barrack in the middle of nowhere.

The women introduced themselves and to my amazement, they had been there before me. Some were placed in detention months ago and some more than a year. What we all had in common was that our family members were vocal dissidents of the regime. Their husbands, fathers, brothers and sons were taken to Insein Prison and I realized that that was where my father was most likely being kept. Uttering the name was enough to send a chill through my body. Ye Kyi Aing was not particularly known for its warmth, but Insein was notorious for its brutal tortures and prisoners disappearing into thin air.

I immediately recognized four of them. Ma Hla Than had

taught English sporadically at the central university when I was at the medical college and I had run into her on campus and at school gatherings. She had been one of the highest-ranking females in the civil administration before being detained for allegedly helping Bo Setkya (one of the Thirty Comrades), who had gone to join my husband at the border. Bo Setkya would die shortly afterwards in the jungles between Burma and Thailand and before my husband had met with U Nu in the late 1960s. Ma Hla Than continued to remain in custody long after the hunt for Bo Setkya ended.

Two of the women were sisters whom I knew socially but had never had time to get to know on an intimate level. Ma Maisie and Ma Marie were women-about-town in Rangoon, flitting within the American social circle. They frequented events sponsored by the United States Embassy, promoted Burmese-American relations, and proudly moved about the Burmese and American circles as socialites. The regime became highly suspicious of their involvement with foreigners and had them arrested on charges of spying for the Americans, but their only crime was having been too popular for their own good.

Daw Khin Kyi (no relation to Aung San's wife), whom I would refer to as Daw Kyi Kyi, had been there the longest out of all of us. She was a high-ranking member of the Women's Group in Rangoon and the wife of Thakin Zin, second-in-command of the CPB and one of the most wanted men in the country. She, her husband and four children fled Rangoon to the Pegu Mountains in central Burma, a lush and unforgiving range, notably the incubator of Sayar San's grassroots rebellion. Moving from one hideout to another, Daw Kyi Kyi and her children had only the clothes on their backs and enough food to sustain them for a few days at a time. When that ran out, they foraged in the hillside, killing whatever animals came their way and cooking over a low light so that the army would not detect smoke and fire from their hiding places.

Thakin Zin left one day to resource supplies and to find a secure location for their next hideout, staying one step ahead of their trackers. Daw Kyi Kyi and her children lived in abject fear of being caught and what the government's forces would do to them if they were to meet. Using trained hunting dogs, the soldiers sniffed out the family's hiding place and dragged them to Rangoon in shackles. Daw Kyi Kyi's four sons and daughters were sent to live with their uncle and she was brought to Ye Kyi Aing.

The other women were Ma Molly and Ma Hlaing, a CPB member and nurse. These introductions were a brief glimpse into our personal stories, everyone keeping a part of themselves private, never truly revealing their inner thoughts. An underlying sadness hung in the air, our constant chatting a desperate attempt to ward off despair and loneliness, the inevitable side effects of imprisonment. Times of melancholy and sadness were interrupted by the women's boisterous joy over Zarni. It was difficult not to be won over by him after long periods in isolation and without the luxury of humanity. I was truly grateful for the women doting on Zarni, who reveled in the extra attention. He was the only one adjusting with ease in his surroundings, not knowing any better.

We chose beds that delineated our own space. As I had had the bathroom to myself for quite some time, it was the most obvious indicator of more people in the barrack. We took equal turns emptying the bucket of excrement and washing down the bathroom after each use, maintaining a sense of cleanliness and order in what would have otherwise been chaos. The bare wooden room had some semblance of comfort with windows filling the room with daylight, shelves for our personal items and a small table where we could fold our clothes. During our baths, we followed the Burmese bathing tradition of wrapping our *longyi*s up to our chests, lathering ourselves and washing our hair as we cupped water from the single drum. The cool and consistent water was a blessing during the monsoon months, the air so hot that it was difficult to breathe.

Every morning at 6 AM, a soldier would materialize carrying a big kettle of hot coffee. Sometimes there would be a second soldier but we could not figure out why he was there. He was always silent, standing still as we assembled our clean mugs on a small table next to the door. The soldier with the coffee pot would fill the mugs with hot, watery coffee and promptly leave, locking the door behind them. We would drink the coffee while it was still hot, our only nourishment until lunch. One time, I caught the silent second soldier smiling at Zarni, making his usual morning giggling sounds and grabbing at the air with his pink fingertips. It was a father's gaze and I wondered if he had a child of a similar age waiting for him at home. When I went to meet his eyes, he had already transformed back to his stern and observant deportment, no trace of his smile.

Lunch and dinner were served with military precision at 11 AM and 5 PM. Sometimes we would have a tough chunk of stewed water buffalo instead of stir-fried vegetables as the entrée for dinner. The nondescript mystery broth became a running joke for us:

I wonder what's for lunch today?

Lucky us, nylon soup...again!

We were anemic and weak from lack of nutrition, deteriorating from within, with heartier meals only served on commemorative days such as Independence Day, Martyrs' Day and Thadingyut. The women and I would eat chicken curry or hilsa on those holidays accompanied by a more flavorful soup. Our stomachs had become so accustomed to our scant meals that it was difficult to digest richer food. We discovered that the best way to preserve what we could not digest was to eat half of our meals and to save the other half to be rationed for the next two days, knowing that meat was served irregularly.

Whenever one of us felt ill, we would inform the soldiers at mealtimes and they would inform the prison authorities, but we had gotten use to the harsh conditions and none of us had any major illnesses. The state of the infirmary was enough to will myself to stay healthy. A single syringe for dozens of detainees. Reused bandages. Homebrewed morphine. Bullets to bite on during amputation, I later heard.

My parcels from home became routine after a period of four or five months when my mother realized that I would not be discharged anytime soon. She continued to send essential toiletries for me and milk powder and clean diapers for Zarni. On the luckiest days, my mother, ever the clever woman, would sneak *nga-pi-kyaw* (fried shrimp balachaung) and *le-pet* (pickled tea leaves) in the linings of clothes and hidden in milk powder cans. May May also stuck small notes from my children behind the labels of Zarni's formula cans, small scribblings of cheerful messages saying that they missed me and that they were doing well at home. I wanted so desperately to write back, to just send one sentence telling them that I loved them and that I missed them, but even the passage of this note would have dire consequences for me and in the worst case, for them. I burned their notes after I read them, memorizing their distinct crooked writing and their messages of encouragement, never leaving a trace of our communication.

Every now and then one of us would find a book in our packages and we would take turns reading it aloud. Since all of the boxes were opened and censored, the books that reached our hands were mainly religious texts. On the most desperate days, we resorted to reading the papers used to pack our parcels, ads depicting scenes of happy families buying cars and trips to the beach, images so remote from our reality. It did not matter to us at all; we were happy to have something to keep our minds off of the daily stresses of detention and uncertainty.

I thought about everything and nothing during my initiation to imprisonment. At first, it was easy to fall prey to the deepest recesses of my mind where anger, regret and pain lurk, desperate for my company. To despair is a drug in itself, intoxicating in its ability to swallow time, a cheap narcotic turning days into nights. I would close my eyes and all I would see were my children's faces. If I've never had the opportunity to say it before, I shall let it be known that I thought about my children every waking moment of my days in prison. I felt like an abject failure for not protecting my children sooner, yet I was at a loss to find a solution when my own choices were so limited. Though my mother was still at home, she was in her sixties and no longer fit to run after nine children and look after her own household, including my aunt who was ailing. Yema, as my eldest child, was in charge of her siblings but I felt an enormous sense of guilt that this burden had been placed on her shoulders. She was twenty-three and had graduated from university with a degree in statistics. Yema had begun her job at the Finance Ministry and had to become the second mother to her siblings at a time in which she should have been exploring the world. I had passed on a legacy of sacrifice and enduring to her, her youth forfeited for the decisions of her grandparents and parents. It was something that I never intended but regretted for the remainder of my life.

My twin sons Yan Myo and Yan Lin were seventeen and I knew that they would take turns being the eldest men in the brood. Amaya and Kinsa, both teenagers, were undoubtedly the most academically gifted and had inherited their grandmother's tenacity and ability to get things done on their own terms. Kethi, the middle child at eleven years old, was sensitive and empathetic, the moral compass of the pack. Nanda was beautiful and confident, while Minshin and Tinthi were the youngest and the most rambunctious, spoiled by their older siblings' attention. I recited their personalities and attributes in my head every day, somehow afraid that I might forget them. Ye Kyi Aing was, after all, the kind of place that wanted you to forget about your life outside, to dehumanize you so that you would begin to lose pieces of yourself and the things that you once loved.

One day, I heard Zarni chortle, awakening me from a trance-like state of misery. Looking at my son, I realized that I had no choice but to will my morbid thoughts away or else we would never survive. From that point on, I thought about nothing except for the routine of prison life, the emptiness of my mind and spirit more tolerable than living in anguish. And so our lives moved on with our mealtime visitors, tidying our beds, sweeping the floor, washing our clothes and hanging them out to dry in the little yard on the clothesline, cleaning and putting away the dishes. I lost track of time as every day was a repetition of the previous day.

I always had religious faith, but what I remembered next had little to do with dogma and everything to do with the strength of my belief in humanity. One of my barrack mates, who was Buddhist but had attended a girls' Catholic school like me, began to hum bits of *Ave Maria* with her cracking soprano voice. I was playing with Zarni in my lap when I began to smile, each note taking me back to the halls of St. John's. I walked through every corridor in my mind, retracing the lines of the classrooms, inhaling the smell of fresh pen ink, remembering every crag and wrinkle in the nuns' expressions. My breath stopped when I revisited the day of the bombing of Pearl Harbor and heard the headmistress's voice as if she were in the barrack with me then and there.

The innocent shall always find salvation in the end.

I don't know why her words, and none of the other memories that I meditated on before, triggered the hope in me that had been smothered by guilt, mourning, anger and nihilism. At that moment, I truly believed in salvation, different than mere survival. I was innocent, we were all innocent in that room, and I knew that justice would be served in the end.

Baby Tinthi, Tinsa and Minshin

CHAPTER SIXTEEN

I used to count the days on my fingers when I first arrived at Ye Kyi Aing. Zarni had turned one right after the new year and several months passed marking almost one year of my detention. When three soldiers came to our door one April morning, I presumed it was for some sort of Thingyan (Burmese New Year) announcement. Instead of addressing all eight of the women, they turned to me in lockstep. "Daw Tinsa, will you come with us briefly?" An order, never a question. I picked Zarni up and left the barrack, going down the same dirt path from a year earlier leading to a bare, concrete room where a high-ranking officer was seated at a cheap plywood table.

"Your aunt, Kinmimi, passed away. You will be taken home to attend her funeral and will be brought back before nightfall." There was no emotion in his voice. The officer signed several forms securing my temporary release and handed them to the men at my side as he left the office. Another blackened sedan. Another head towel.

Zarni slept soundly in my lap, the rocking car his temporary crib, while I digested the news. My aunt had been dying since before I was taken away and I had a growing sense of her deteriorating health from the little notes I received in my packages from my mother. Her time had come but I had hoped in vain, perhaps too optimistically, that I would see her one last time before she passed on to the next life. She had always been there for me, my parents, my siblings, my own children, never asking for a thing in return.

My aunt lived a healthy life until the war when she developed hypertension, bronchial asthma and gastric problems not long after their mother and my grandmother, Daw Sein, passed away in Mogok. Aunt Kinmimi was never the same after independence, a part of her lost with Burma's past. I was bereft with grief that I would no longer see her doing fine needlepoint in the living room, basking in the quiet sunlight. A petite woman with the quiet force of ten men in her spirit, an army unto herself.

The towel was snatched from my head and I blinked twice to adjust my eyes to the outside world. We were at the corner of Prome Road about to turn onto Inya Road, the Rangoon University campus looming on our right with Inya Lake on our left. The roads, normally filled with all sorts of cars, trucks, rickshaws and students piling on every corner, were oddly deserted. My heart beat with every passing scene, taking in as much of the lake, the blue sky, the trees, as I could. Soon, we approached University Avenue, my home. My lungs and my heart beat furiously against my ribs, Zarni's sleeping state the only thing keeping me from opening the car door and running to our front gate.

Over a dozen cars were parked in front of the gates to my parents' house facing University Avenue. I exited the car with baby Zarni in my arms and the two women who were assigned to escort me. No one was told that I would be allowed to attend the funeral, pure shock on everyone's faces when I burst through the front door, the room at a complete standstill. To my amazement, my father was sitting next to my mother, who was tending to my aunt's coffin. Since he had arrived before me, my family must have hoped that I would be let out as well, but knew better than to keep their hopes up.

"Phay Phay? May May?" I called to them in a small and strained voice, fighting back the hot tears welling in my eyes and my throat tight with wrenching pain. A year's worth of words straining to reach my mouth, fighting to be said. Before they could say anything, I knelt to pay my respects to my aunt and to my parents. My daughters Amaya and Kinsa, who were fifteen and fourteen years old at the time and much more grown up than I remembered them to be, appeared at my side and took Zarni into their arms. Arms outstretched, he kicked and played in their arms, a child instinctively knowing whom to trust. My mother gripped my elbow, afraid to let me go though she knew that my father and I would be leaving again. My children rushed to my side as soon as they saw me, taking turns hugging me. I held each of them as tightly as I could. They smelled fresh, clean, the scent of safety.

"She passed away peacefully," my mother said of my aunt. I wondered if the news would reach my husband and Zali in whatever forsaken jungle they were in and I hoped that they would take one brief moment to kneel down and pay their proper respects for my aunt's passing.

"Tinsa," my father called to me as we sat around the round teak table. "You look well." I studied my father, deep lines circling his eyes from extreme fatigue and weariness. He had lost weight and his cheekbones protruded from beneath thinning, sallow skin, not getting enough nutrients from our daily prison specials. His mind was still as sharp as ever, refusing to succumb to the prison officials' attempts to break his spirit. His barrack mates later revealed that he recited Shakespeare, Dante and Thomas More verbatim in his attempts to thwart the sorrow of knowing that his daughter and grandson were suffering too.

"Phay Phay, I'm so happy to see you." There were so many things I wanted to say to him but I could not force the words out of my mouth.

"We don't have a lot of time," my father said tiredly as he glanced at the two women flanking me. He shook his head and his eyes became alert, almost feline. "Do you remember all of those years ago when I told you that I believed in justice, that righteousness and good will always win in the end?"

I nodded.

"I've never stopped believing in it, and I hope you haven't, either."

"I haven't," I whispered, unsure why those two words were so difficult to say at that moment despite my conviction.

My family and I spent the remainder of the time catching up on the children's progress and light neighborhood gossip. We could not delve into intimate topics with my escorts around, such as my father's health and my treatment. My mother looked at the wall clock and announced that the funeral procession would start soon. "How do you feel about accompanying the funeral cortege?" she asked me kindly. My aunt would be cremated at Kyantaw cemetery on Prome Road, a long way from the house. I was not sure that I would get back to the detention center in time and did not want to risk any trouble for the family. I declined, as did my father.

I was overcome with a wild urge to run away at that moment, to grab my parents and children and never look back. Perhaps Yan Naing would be waiting for us at the Thai border with Zali, U Nu, the Comrades and everyone that we knew. I went through a list of friends that I had in foreign countries, a global network that could secure transport and supplies for us. We could even make our way to America where Theda was living with her family. *We would forget all of this, it would be so easy,* said a small voice in the back of my head.

But what good would it have done? It would only mean that more of my loved ones would be detained in my stead, the possibility of greater punishment for my friends and family left behind. Running was not the solution. My husband and brother were gone and I was determined not to lead the family further down this path.

I did the bravest thing that I could have done, the opposite of running away. Looking at little Zarni, his fingers curled around mine, a slate too clean for prison walls, I handed him to my mother. "He needs to be here at home with his family. Where I am is not the place for a one year-old child to be," I said to her. She looked at me with great pride and sorrow. My other children gathered around me, the younger ones clutching my *longyi* and not wanting to let me go. Tears streamed down my face but I refused to let them see me break. One of my escorts scribbled notes in her little black book. Kissing each of my children, I made sure that they knew that this was not a goodbye, that I would be back someday. I stepped inside the waiting vehicle with my escorts, who did not cover my head this time.

The streets remained deserted. We were the only ones on the road and I asked my escorts why Rangoon was at a standstill. The lady with the notebook replied, "There have been some issues with the Chinese. Things are tense and some people are scared to leave their homes." Hundreds of Burmese-Chinese homes and businesses had been torched in Rangoon and beyond, innocent people losing everything they had. Later, I learned from my mother's letter that the funeral procession had arrived without incident and that the family had made it back home safely. Immediately after they returned to University Avenue, thugs appeared from the slums to burn and loot some properties at Kamayut circle, dangerously close to our home and where our friends lived.

The car slithered past the gates of Ye Kyi Aing, my entourage returning to the same interrogation room where an army captain was waiting for me. I was emotionally, mentally and physically exhausted, too tired to care about the questions he asked. I had nothing more to say.

I hope that the journey to your aunt's funeral was suitable, Daw Tinsa.

It was.

What went on at the funeral?

I paid my respects to my aunt and saw my family.

Was there anything of interest that was said?

No.

Was there anything exchanged?

What do you think?

Pitch-black nightfall enveloped me as I walked to my barrack, unable to see the dirt and rocks at my feet underneath. My barrack mates surrounded me, anxious to know what had gone on during that long day. *Why did you leave? Where did they take you? Are you hurt?* They went silent when they noticed that Zarni was not with me.

I finally broke down and told them about my aunt's death, my decision to leave my son behind, meeting with my father again, as waves of hot tears streamed down my cheeks. Sobs racked my body but I was too proud to let them touch me. I told them about the feeling of fear in the city because of the escalating ethnic conflict. Rangoon was a different world than what we remembered it to be. They let me crawl into bed without any more words, Daw Kyi Kyi covering my body with a soft sheet.

The next morning I awoke to the reality that Zarni was no longer next to me, his gummy smile greeting me every morning. The silence in the room was stifling without his cries, his pitter-patter and his little gurgling laugh. Life continued behind closed doors as it always had, monotonous and drawn out, without my little boy.

* * * * *

The other women were taken away one by one, leaving me with Daw Kyi Kyi and Ma Dolly in the following months. We knew better than to ask where the others had gone, the likelihood being that they were reassigned to another barrack or perhaps even freed.

It was our turn next. We moved to the barrack next door, walking a short distance through a tunneled passageway to an identical wooden building. There were four women in there, other inhabitants of this wretched prison. This was our first time seeing other prisoners, often hearing voices in the distance. It was a sad confirmation that there were many more of us out there.

The first to introduce herself was a young Communist Party member, a miniscule woman who looked as if she could not harm a mosquito. To my utter shock, the other three were the mother-in-law and sisters-in-law of Kyi May Thein, a woman whom I knew very well and had not seen since before my arrest. She helped me to look after Zarni when Yan Naing left and when I had few friends to rely on. She was the wife of Captain Kyaw Zwa Myint, the personal assistant to none other than General Ne Win himself, a member of the inner circle. Her mother-in-law recounted that like Yan Naing, her husband was repulsed by what he saw. He resigned and formed an underground resistance group, receiving help from high-level contacts that he had cultivated over the years. The last that they had heard from him, he had resurfaced in Australia and was trying to raise funds for a counter-insurgency.

Happy memories at University Avenue

Very few people can successfully betray a dictator. There was an executive order to arrest Kyi May Thein and the two others for Captain Kyaw Zwa Myint's absence. I did not press for details, the hollowed look in the three women's eyes hinting at something far more ominous than anything I had been through. Looking at their cowered demeanors, I felt such overwhelming sadness that these polite, quiet women who had never been politically active were made to pay such a heavy price, their only "crime" being related to the captain. Since Kyi

May Thein was not in the barrack with us, I hoped that she was safe within the compound and that perhaps I would get to see her again.

Lacking the dynamics of my previous barrack and without Zarni to unite us all, the seven of us kept to ourselves. Our scheduled routine did not change at all from my previous living situation and we found ourselves in a comfortable setup. When I had just begun to feel like I had settled in with the new women, I was moved again a couple of months later. We were never warned beforehand if we were being transferred, always told to come as we were, never enough time to bring our belongings with us. It was a game of dice: moved, freed, or headed to a worse fate. I had instructed Daw Kyi Kyi that should they come for me and only me, that she should keep all of my belongings and not to expect me to retrieve them.

I moved to a new barrack with one other woman. She introduced herself as the daughter of U Ba Swe[51], the former Prime Minister who was my father's contemporary. I did not get to know her very well because the next morning, a new set of soldiers came for me alone and told me to follow them once again. Moving to increasingly smaller barracks, separating me from the only kinships I had, it was all a form of mental preparation for something much worse.

There was little time to unpack my suitcases that had arrived in the night. Judging by their weight, Daw Kyi Kyi decided not to follow my instructions and did not touch any of my belongings. I followed my usual routine of washing myself, having coffee and went to unpack my suitcases when I heard the familiar jangling of keys.

"Daw Tinsa, will you please follow us?" Would it be freedom or death?

Colonel Tin Oo was waiting for me in a small room. I had not seen him in the two years since I was brought in, confirming my suspicions that something big was about to happen to me. I recited as many prayers as I could, hoping that

---

[51] Second Premier of Burma from June 12 1956 to February 28 1957.

they would protect me for whatever I was about to face.

He looked the exact same as when I last saw him, down to the same uniform and glasses. There was nothing about his manner to indicate that he was weighed down by his actions and what went on behind these closed gates. Tin Oo simply acted as a man following orders, content. "How are you, Daw Tinsa?" he asked lightly.

Oh just fine, immensely enjoying imprisonment at the expense of my family and children.

"I am how I usually am," I replied. Beady little eyes scanned my demeanor and looked for signs that I was intimidated by his presence. The truth was, I realized long ago that I was not afraid of him or this prison. If I was being led to my execution then at least there would be closure on some level. If I were to go back to the barracks, then I would continue living as I had for years.

He pushed a set of papers in front of me, a stack of twenty hefty pages. I was afraid to touch them, to be a willing part of his games. "Daw Tinsa, these papers are an agreement that you will denounce all political activities from hereon. You will not partake in any attempts to undermine the government. You will, in short, keep the peace."

This is a joke, I thought to myself. *Don't believe him.*

"What is the purpose of this?" I demanded, growing impatient.

A small, wry smile. "Once you sign these papers, you are free to go home, Daw Tinsa." Was this some sort of prank? After nearly two years at Ye Kyi Aing, all I would have to do to return to my family was to sign some papers?

The colonel surveyed me, predicting how I would react and what I was thinking. "Your brother, Binnya, is in the next room waiting to take you home. I assure you that everything that I am saying is the truth."

I signed the papers. I was released from Ye Kyi Aing in January 1968.

CHAPTER SEVENTEEN

Binnya looked shell-shocked. Out of our seven siblings, he was asked to retrieve me as the eldest male in the household, my mother having gone to Insein Prison for my father. Zali of course was with my husband and the only other brother at home was Neta, too young for this task. *Where is Phay Phay? How is May May doing? How are the children?* I had so many questions I wanted to ask, unable to sputter simple words.

"Everything is fine," he assured me. "Yesterday night, some men showed up at our house and asked to see May May. They weren't there for long, just announcing that you and Phay Phay were to be released immediately and that we should be ready to pick you up at a certain time. You don't know how excited everyone is to see you and Phay Phay again."

Binnya and I were not the closest of the siblings with a ten-year age gap between us, but throughout the years I grew to respect his quiet nature and reserve. He was the youngest child for a long time and spoiled with attention until Neta came along. He had been an introspective child, never mischievous, always obedient and studious. Binnya had gone to Germany for his higher studies and had come back to Burma to settle down, or so we all hoped. His calm demeanor helped me to stay collected, a part of me wanting to jump out of the car and run all the way home, feeling the cool winter air on my skin and to hear leaves rustling, all of this as a free woman.

My children swarmed me, little bees buzzing about, each orbiting in his or her own conversation with me. The elder children had tears streaming down their faces, overjoyed at being reunited. The little ones, too young to understand what had really happened for the past two years, were simply excited to be around their mother again, jumping up and down and pulling me by the wrist. They had all grown – in years, physically and in maturity. I was overjoyed to see their round little faces and baby fat, well fed and nourished. They had moved from our small ranch house to my parents' home in the front yard so that my mother could keep a closer eye on the entire family, and they were spoiled with attention by their aunts and uncles, who took the time to look after my little ones.

Family portrait at University Avenue

My father stood beside my mother having arrived not too long before me. May May, noticing the look of surprise on my face, explained, "I received notice of both your releases yesterday. It was decided that I would go to fetch your father at

Insein while your brother wanted to come and get you." She paused with tears in her eyes. "Welcome home."

It was one of the few times I saw her true emotions, for she was accustomed to masking her thoughts in the most difficult times and showing no fear. May May looked frail, suffering from hypertension as a result of stress, the same fate as her sister. It had been an enormous burden for her though she never complained about life's travails. She took everything in stride, confronting hardships without any grudges and with the generosity that naturally flowed from her heart. She was faced with the seemingly impossible task of keeping the family together, while also preparing care packages and making sure that my children wrote to me regularly. In the midst of this, her sister, her best friend and lifelong ally, passed away, leaving her alone with no one to share her grief with. She would not admit it but she kept all of her sorrow within herself, over a dozen people depending on her for survival. My mother was the thread that ran through all of us, the sum of all of our parts. My father may have been the more publicly recognized face but there should be no doubt that she was the steel in all of our backs. She was universally respected amongst family, friends, the Comrades and political acquaintances, friendly or otherwise, who may have turned on everyone else but dared not to disrespect her.

My father had lost some of his spark, his joie de vivre, partly due to his age but largely due to his incarceration. Anyone could see how weary he looked. We did not touch the subject of our imprisonment, the wounds too fresh. I was careful not to bring up anything sensitive in case of wiretaps in the house or spies listening in on us from beyond the gates. "Phay Phay, what would you like to do in the coming days?" I asked him.

Such heavy eyes, his smile trying to conceal his mental fatigue. "Tinsa, I would like to spend more time with the family. I want to be at home with your mother, in our yard. It's been so long since I've been here."

"I know, Phay Phay. I know."

"I've done a lot of thinking and I think it best to leave the law practice to your uncle. Ba Han, that old chap, is a much more spirited barrister than I am at this point. He'll have a good run with it on his own," Phay Phay grinned, his old self returning. "What about you, Tinsa? What will you do?"

"Well, I certainly can't go back to teaching now," I joked with him. Even if I had wanted to go back to the university, there was no way for the school to accommodate me, nor would I put my former colleagues and friends in danger by trying to return. "No, no, Phay Phay, there's far too much work to be done around here," I said as we were ambushed by my children, eager to play after their tea break.

I stayed at my parents' home for the few first days after my return, doing my best to adjust to a steady home life. It was the second time that I had to rearrange my life, but this time was more difficult. Everyone had moved on while my life remained static. The sights and sounds of everyday Rangoon were too much for my senses, everything brighter, sweeter and fresher. My mother prepared *mohingar* as a welcoming breakfast, its sharp fish taste and cool vermicelli nearly causing my father and me to vomit.

After a brief rest, I decided to move all ten of my children back to our ranch across the pond. My mother's face dropped and she pleaded with me, "Don't you want to stay for a bit longer? It's been so long since we've all been under the same roof. Please think about it."

I did think about it. I thought about the burden I was placing on my elderly parents every waking moment. It was not fair to them to have to take care of my children and me on the account of my husband's politics. May May and Phay Phay were no longer in the best of health and the family's finances had gone from steady to bad in the intervening years. May May discreetly sold off several of her inherited properties, the whole family lucky to be living off of the monthly rent from the Kandawgyi home. Luckily, the government provided free schooling from primary to university level so the children were able to pursue their education unhindered. I still worried about food, clothes, school supplies, transportation and all of the other costs that were slowly strangling us. Gaining mental and physical strength, I was determined to survive on what little savings I had before my incarceration and Yema's income. We began our lives again as a family with these meager resources.

The initial days, weeks and months were a tremendous struggle. On the worst days, I would boil an egg and cut it into eleven pieces, our only nourishment for the next twenty-four hours. The children did not complain once, forced into a situation where they needed to learn to survive. There were no luxuries nor did anyone dare to dream of them. I did my best to find work, attempting to provide private English tuition, searching for odd jobs and reaching out to people whom I thought were safe contacts. Nothing came up. When my savings ran out, I turned to my increasingly frail parents to help us out financially, a bitter pill. I was no longer in prison but I was never to live a normal life again.

I was not the only one afraid during those days. Everywhere people lived in fear, no one knowing whom to trust. Your closest friends could prove to be your enemies and we lived in isolation for that reason. Nobody, friends nor relatives, dared to acknowledge their link to us and I did not encourage them to out of mutual safety, pariahs within society. The only people that I could turn to were the ones who were with me in detention, who faced an identical banishment from society.

Upon leaving Ye Kyi Aing, I was asked by Daw Kyi Kyi to visit her children in Rangoon, exchanging contact information on scraps of paper that we tore from our parcels. I kept my promise and visited her four children. Optimistic and exuberant, they were remarkably entrepreneurial, having set up a home business preparing, packing and selling masala powder. It became a tradition for my family to purchase *Lwin Masala* during every visit and it became a fixture in the homes of all of the women from Ye Kyi Aing. In our family, the masala traveled to the States, Africa and South America where my children in their later years lived and worked.

Daw Kyi Kyi's brood wanted to know everything about their mother.
Is she in good health?
Is she keeping up her spirits?
What does she need? Food? Clothing? Medicine?
Are there any instructions from her?
They were also deeply concerned for their father, whom they had not communicated with in two years. In 1967, Thakin Than Tun systematically cleansed the Communist Party of suspected spies. Paranoid that government operatives had infiltrated their ranks, he purged his party members in the wake of the failed peace talks with the Revolutionary Council. His was a self-fulfilling prophecy: Thakin Than Tun was killed on September 24, 1968 by one of his subordinates, a young man who had supposedly defected from the army just a few years before. Thakin Zin became the de facto leader and took his activities completely underground, cutting off all communication with the outside world including that of his children. I wish that I could have told them some good news about him. My own children also wondered about their father's whereabouts.

Some of the other women were released shortly after me. Ma Hla Than happened to live walking distance from our home in Inyamyaing and she would invite my children to play with her two daughters and son. The others took turns inviting us to their homes for *soon-kways* and family events, making sure that we all stayed in touch. My children were luckier than me in their social surroundings. Though the neighborhood children stopped associating with them a long time ago, they had ten companions amongst themselves. They bickered and had rivalries with one another, nothing lasting long enough to leave scars. I counted my blessings, lucky to have children with a natural instinct to make the best of the worst of situations.

The children went to school early in the morning and came home in the afternoon, the extent of our outside contact. They studied voraciously under the tutelage of my father, teaching the third generation the value of education and a sound mind.

His belief that one's mind is the only thing that matters when all else is lost could not have been more relevant. No matter what happened to the children, whatever humiliations small or large, no one could ever take their education and minds away from them.

I became reacquainted with a long forgotten Singer sewing machine that my husband had brought back from Europe during an economic commission trip to Europe to explore the machinery trade during the U Nu years. The day that he came home, he set down a massive electric sewing machine in the middle of our living room, beaming with pride at his technological find. At the time I could only sigh at his whims, wondering when I would have time to sew when I had a full-time position at the university and children to chase after. Laughing as I dusted off the metal behemoth, I wondered if my husband would be gloating if he could see me with it now. The nuns from St. John's would have been happy to know that the sewing lessons I learned at the convent were finally put to good use three decades later. The younger ones were growing out of their clothes and the older children, though they never asked, wanted more youthful designs to fit in with their peers. Cloth was expensive in those days but I made do with my income and the children understood that the rest of their clothing would come from hand-me-downs or refashioned secondhand pieces.

The older children up through Nanda attended Methodist English High School, regarded as the best school in the country and renowned for its rigorous curriculum and emphasis on discipline. The principal was Mrs. Logie, a formidable educator and disciplinarian. Whilst so many former friends, acquaintances and the general public were afraid to associate with my family, she welcomed my children to the school. The same could not be said for some of the teachers and peers who mocked my children. It broke my heart whenever one of them would come home in tears. They remained stronger than I could have possibly been if I were in their places, wiping their tears and trudging to school every day wearing the Maw-Naing name like a badge of honor.

My children were bright and ambitious, always getting top marks in class and studying feverishly at home in the hopes that someday, they could work their way out of isolation. Kinsa was the most academically gifted, studying obsessively for exams and achieving the highest marks. Yet each year when the honor roll was released, her name would always be excluded from the top class even though every teacher and student knew that she had earned her place there. She believed that if she worked hard enough, that she could shatter our invisible prison through sheer willpower.

General Ne Win's children also went to Methodist and were in the same classes as my children. His daughter Sandar was a classmate of Amaya's, his son Phyo in Kinsa's class, and Kethi became friends with Kyai Hmone, his youngest daughter. Both sets of children put aside political tensions and enmity between the older generations and became friends. They remained close through adulthood, with Sandar and Amaya attending medical college together, Phyo and Kinsa to the Rangoon Institute of Technology and Kyai Hmone and Kethi to the medical school. Neither my parents nor I discouraged the bonds that developed between them. Some have asked how I could have allowed our children to become friends in the political mire. If only it were that simple. Some of the only moments of childhood normalcy came from those friendships: birthday parties, sports and lunches together. What right did I have to take those small happinesses away from children who were not responsible for their parents' politics?

There was no other way for my children to have a normal upbringing, not least when plainclothes detectives trailed us everywhere. Wherever we went, whatever we did, every breath was tracked by a silent force. This extended beyond our immediate family. My siblings and our household help were spied on every waking moment and we were all suffocating living under a microscope. Rain or shine, the surveillance vehicle would perch itself on a neighbor's narrow, hilly driveway. It became a part of the neighborhood scene, like the newspaper boy or milkman.

The only ones who seemed to find amusement in the surveillance were my twin sons, Yan Myo and Yan Lin. When the twins were in their last year of high school, they began to notice that they were being followed everywhere they went, apparently coming of age and requiring constant monitoring. If they went on foot, they would be followed by shadowy men darting in and out of the bushes, failing miserably in their attempts to blend in with the shrubbery. If they went by car, a fleet of black cars would surround them, trailing them on their otherwise uneventful journeys to school or on errands. The boys started a game by giving their companions the slip, separating and finding their own way home and leaving their shadows panting on their trail.

Sometimes being followed had its advantages. Yan Myo and Yan Lin would accompany their aunt Mala to her clinic downtown, quite a distance away and not appropriate for her to go alone as a single woman. One night, their car broke down in a dark alleyway with no means of calling for help. The intelligence vehicle stopped in its tracks and called our house, enabling us to send a second car to retrieve Mala and the boys. As soon as they got into the car, the surveillance car started its engine, business as usual.

*****

In the summer of 1971, I received a bizarre missing persons report regarding my second cousin, U Than Han. An unassuming man of slight build and extreme introversion, he was the Rangoon District Chief of the Inland Waterway Tax Bureau, a position whose lengthy title did not necessarily equate to lengthy amounts of work. We were not close but he struck me as a sensible bureaucrat and family man. One day, he decided to take a ride on a riverboat and fell overboard into the murky waters. The authorities had been unable to find his body in the aftermath. The Rangoon police force searched for him since he was a high-ranking city official, but the investigation ended several days later with many assuming that his remains were trapped in deep water or had been swept out to sea.

The story was so strange that I could hardly believe that it had transpired. Our family shared similar sentiments, scratching our heads in disbelief. How could someone who did not normally visit the riverbank area somehow end up there and mysteriously fall in? Was he pushed? Did others see him? Was it intentional?

Fresh rumors circulated in Golden Valley that U Than Han had faked the accident in order to run off and join Yan Naing's rebel camp. I was stunned. My cousin had occasionally expressed some critical viewpoints about the state of the country, none serious enough to arouse suspicion. Perhaps he hid his true sentiments not to keep his immediate family in the dark, but to protect them. More so, to know of his plans was sufficient cause for arrest.

Speculation gave way to resignation that he would not be returning for a long time, if at all. Faking one's death ensured that he would never be welcomed back to the full extent of the law. All that we could do was pray for him in the meantime, for his safety and for his family. I could have never suspected that another storm was to come.

*****

My twin sons Yan Myo and Yan Lin were in their final years of university, growing restless. They were born on April 24, 1951, Yan Myo beating his brother by minutes. My father nicknamed them Ho Chi (Yan Myo) and Mosie (Yan Lin) after Ho Chi Minh and Mao Tse Tung. Their siblings called them Ho Gyi (Big Ho) and Mo Gyi (Big Mo). Ho Chi and Mosie were charismatic children, the apple of their grandparents' eyes. They used their charms to twist May May and Phay Phay around their fingers and especially my aunt. Before her passing, Aunt Kinmimi had doted on them as if they were her own, her most gentle and tender moments reserved for them. Ho Chi was more serious and intellectual while Mosie was outgoing and extroverted. They did everything together, had the same set of friends, played the same sports and even had the same boisterous laugh. Unless you knew them very well, it was hard to distinguish the two of them physically – handsome, dark complexioned like their father, thick eyebrows joined in the middle with bright white smiles that melted many hearts.

They would come and go freely, disregarding their military shadows. However outgoing they were outside of our home, they were fiercely traditional and protective of their siblings, especially their younger sisters. The girls were not allowed to be around their male friends without a chaperone, following the rules of society at the time. My mother and aunt enforced these customs, Ho Chi and Mosie insisting that it was absolutely forbidden for their sisters to go unaccompanied or to be seen in the company of their friends. To do so would have sullied the girls' reputations and they would not risk that in the line of brotherly duty. They roughhoused with their younger brothers, Minshin and Zarni, the three elder boys usually running amok in the yard with baby Zarni in one of their arms.

They entered university in 1968 and were separated for the first time in their lives. Both achieved high enough scores to attend medical school, but Mosie felt that medicine was something that he was not passionate about. Ho Chi thus went to the Institute of Medicine and Mosie enrolled as a chemistry major at the Rangoon Arts and Science University, his father's alma mater, where he had sown his political seeds. Mosie was a mediocre student at RASU, whereas Ho Chi threw himself into student political life, becoming the secretary of the high school student council, a chip off his father's block. The descendants of the previous generation's political leaders were coming of age and had begun to take an active interest in politics, causing the regime to intensify its surveillance measures. Every millisecond of their lives was monitored, every person we knew a potential informant. The walls, floors, roofs, everything had ears.

Drowning within the confines of their invisible prison, there was nothing that I could do to alleviate the heavy burden on my sons' shoulders. They daydreamed of joining their father on the River Kwai, an idea that I quashed with stolid silence. They were restive, we could all sense that, but I would not allow them to throw away their lives for the bleak existence of war and violence. They had heard stories of the independence war but were too young to understand the realities of battle. How could I possibly describe the utter chaos of daily bombings, hunger, witnessing the surroundings and people around you obliterated by mortar shells and gunfire? One can never aptly describe the true cost of war, its lessons only learned through experience and terror.

Several months after U Than Han's disappearance, my sister Mala met a new patient at her radiology practice at the Worker's Hospital. She had never seen the man before, asking rudimentary questions about his health and the reasons for his visit.

"Daw Mala, I'm actually not here as a patient," the man confessed. She was stunned and fearful of the stranger's presence.

"Then who are you?"

* * * * *

Mala came home, visibly shaken by the day's events. My sister was not stirred easily and I asked her what had happened. "Did you have difficult patients today?" She had a tendency to get into moods after hectic office hours.

She looked at me with a frightened stare, afraid for what she was about to tell me next. "There was a man in my office today, Tinsa," she said quietly. "He gave me this." Mala handed me a small piece of paper with a telephone number scribbled in hasty script.

"What is this?"

"He didn't tell me his name, just that he was sent by U Than Han." She paused. "He is with Yan Naing."

So, our suspicions were finally confirmed: our cousin was alive and had found his way to the rebel camp. "He wanted you to know that your husband sent him as an emissary and that we should call this number if we ever needed anything." Her voice shook as she relayed his words. "This man wants to see you. I don't think you should, but he's very persistent and said that it was urgent."

I went to meet this mysterious messenger at his behest at Mala's office. He assured me that our calls would be heeded should the need arise. We would be needing his help much sooner than I expected.

* * * * *

The new year rains were nearing an end. My children grew anxious from being indoors all day and I too longed to take quiet walks in the garden again. The twins, young men consumed with their studies, no longer played soccer matches in the rain and mud with their friends. They were withdrawn, pensive, and ready for the weather to clear so that they could venture out once again. The two approached me shortly after my meeting with Yan Naing's emissary. "May May, it's time for us to join Phay Phay," Mosie confessed. They were twenty years old, too old for me to threaten them with spankings or send them to their rooms. I should have seen the signs of this coming: their restiveness, political activism at their schools and the fatigue of being trapped in a cage from which they could not escape. Denial is always a mother's most potent poison: I could not and would not see the truth until it slapped me in the face. All I could do was let my boys go and hope that they would return to me someday.

Remembering the messenger's visit days before, I reached into my purse and gripped the one item that would have released them from their troubles and reunited them with their father. I hesitated at the touch of the piece of paper, a mother's worry whether giving them the key to their perceived freedom was the right thing to do. My hands trembled when I handed the vital contact to them. Their expressions were full of relief. "This is all that I can give to you. I love you more than you will ever know, but I cannot stop you from leaving. I can only hope that you will want to stay."

Ho Chi and Mosie left in August, disappearing into their new existences on the River Kwai. I wished that they had been more superstitious, for there were bad omens ahead of their journey. Two weeks before their departure, Ho Chi was walking in the garden and fell into a rat hole, spraining his ankle and immobilizing him. He was still limping as he got into the car on that fateful day. And on the day before they left, Mosie became suddenly ill, vomiting and suffering from diarrhea throughout the night.

The house was in an uproar, their brothers and sisters confused as to where their beloved brothers had gone. My parents were heartbroken, unable to do anything in their ailing conditions. My mother said nothing, staring out the window with a rare look of helplessness.

My boys did not let me know their exact plans, sparing me the details of their escape, to get as far away from their prison at University Avenue as possible. They had asked Khin Myint, Yema's husband, to drive them to the cinema and to lose the plainclothes officers on their way. He did as he was told. The twins bought tickets to a matinee and snuck through the back exit, boarding a train to Moulmein from the central railway station and continuing overland until they reached the camp. My husband was overjoyed to see his boys, his rebel army welcoming the prodigal sons with open arms. I hoped that they would be happy in this next chapter of their lives, that they would finally find what they were looking for in the thick forest of no man's land.

I never saw my sons again.

CHAPTER EIGHTEEN

Our family kept up appearances after Ho Chi and Mosie left. When the boys' university instructors asked of their whereabouts at the beginning of the school term, I sent a note saying that there were family matters that they needed to tend to during this time. No one knew where they were, only guessing that they had somehow ended up in their father's safe company. The regime must have been asking the same questions that puzzled us. *What route did they take? Who was with them? Did they make it?*

We all knew what was coming and this time I was able to prepare my children and parents for it. When would they come for me again? How many of us were going to prison? Would the children be adequately prepared without the adults?

To get my mind off of my worries, my sister Onma and her mother-in-law, Daw Khin Thein, invited me to the Shwedagon Pagoda to offer special prayers for Onma's husband, who had also been arrested. It was a cool, brisk November day with no sign of winter winds. They picked me up in their car, the three of us looking forward to a day at the most sacred site in Burma.

When I saw the great, golden dome looming ahead, I felt a sense of calm wash over me. To the Burmese, the Shwedagon Pagoda is a symbol of the continuity of our country, its constant presence a reminder that no matter what happens in life, we can count on our spirituality to get us through the hard times. I had spent countless hours there, kneeling before the golden mosaics and glittering Buddhas shining down on me, when I had nothing else but my faith to rely on.

Tinsa, Mala, Onma and Daw Kinmama Maw

We climbed the dozens of stairs leading to the Pagoda, stopping to buy flowers, water for donation and gold leaf to place on the statues. We draped traditional jasmine garlands around the holiest statues and poured water over them. Peeling the fragile gold leaf sheets with our hands, we meticulously covered old statues in desperate need of renovation, a sacred act. We returned to the parking lot after finishing our prayers, where Onma's driver was waiting for us. As soon as we reached the car, two men approached us. Onma and her mother-in-law thought nothing of them but I knew who they were and had been waiting for them ever since my boys disappeared. "Daw Tinsa, we are from Military Intelligence," they identified themselves, not wasting any time. "She is to come with us. The two of you, please get in your car and go home," they instructed Onma, terrified and frozen in her spot.

I nodded to the two women, signaling for them to go and that I would be fine. Daw Khin Thein looked at me with sorrow, the elderly lady knowing exactly what was about to happen to me. Onma did not move until her mother-in-law took her by the elbow and forced her into the car. They drove away, Onma's wide eyes looking back at me through the rear window until they were out of sight.

"Please come with us," they ordered. Their car was the same blackened vehicle that had transported me to and from Ye Kyi Aing, a standard issue government car. They took the long route past Boundary Road until reaching University Avenue.

"Daw Tinsa, we would greatly appreciate if you could pack some of your belongings." Such polite manners for such a brutal task. I did not know how long I would be detained but I knew what I would be needing from my previous stay: toilet paper, sanitary towels, toothpaste, toothbrushes, towels, underwear and the three sets of *longyi*s and shirts that my mother had given me during my first imprisonment.

The children gave me long, lingering hugs. They did not cry this time; they knew that this day was coming and were old enough to comprehend the situation. They knelt in unison and paid their respects to me, the Burmese tradition of sending blessings to an elder before a long journey. I chanted my blessing quietly. *May you be healthy, may you be wealthy*, before the two men led me from my home.

I did not have time to say goodbye to my parents, looking across the pond to their house as I had the first time. There did not seem to be any untoward activity on their side of the compound, to my great relief. In retaliation for my boys' daring escape, the regime had come for me and me alone, or so I thought.

* * * * *

"Back so soon?" teased one of the guards who recognized me in the interrogation room. I clenched my jaw and gave a tight smile, though what I really wanted to do was not very ladylike and would have left a sizeable imprint of my hand on his cheek. No one needed to tell me that I was at Ye Kyi Aing again – the same concrete interrogation room, the same stench of sweat and staleness. Memories of my previous imprisonment came flooding back, long suppressed in the intervening years.

Colonel Tin Oo did not welcome me this time. The last that I had heard, Tin Oo became the Council's invaluable right hand and the members could hardly go anywhere without their best man around, earning Tin Oo the moniker of *The Shadow Dictator*. His new responsibilities meant that he was far too important to interrogate political prisoners, at least not personally.

The man who sat across the table from me did not go through the niceties of introductions. He pushed a paper in front of me. "Daw Tinsa, please write down everything you know about your sons' disappearance. How did it happen? Who was involved? Who went with them?"

I pushed the paper back at him. "I don't know anything about their disappearance. I woke up one day and they were just...gone."

Dissatisfied with my response, the officer pummeled me with the same questions for the next hour, hoping that I would slip, psychological warfare at its finest. "I don't know. I don't know," I kept repeating. Finally, he grew tired of questioning me, knowing that he would not get anything more out of the conversation.

"Daw Tinsa, we have reports that Yan Myo and Yan Lin crossed the border into their father's rebel camp. Are you telling me that your sons told you nothing of their plans?"

I shook my head no, defiant.

"Why would they do that? Don't you feel betrayed that your sons would not tell you such important details of their plans, of their lives?"

"Perhaps they did it to protect me," I said quietly, before being led out of the interrogation room and towards my old home, the barracks.

I will never forget the smell of rotting wood, the feeling of damp and stagnant air in the place where I had spent countless hours as a supposed criminal. The daylight illuminated every nook and cranny of the barrack, unchanged since my departure. The mango tree still stood where it had several years ago, growing a foot since the last time that I had last seen it. *Back in familiar surroundings*, I laughed bitterly.

A few days later, I was surprised to find a woman at the door. I did not recognize her as one of my previous barrack mates, so I introduced myself. "My name is Tinsa, I'm Bo Yan Naing's wife and Dr. Ba Maw's daughter." Since so many women were detained because of their husbands' or fathers' actions, introducing oneself through their names explained a lot about why you were there in the first place.

"I'm Ko Htwe Myint's sister. He ran off weeks ago and left us with no notice. We think that he fled the country to join your husband's group." I did not know Ko Htwe Myint, one of many young men who felt that the only way to save Burma was through armed struggle. I did not ask if she had been detained before, but her ease in the surroundings suggested that she had been here long enough to know to make herself at home. She did not offer conversation, too lost in her own anxieties.

Every morning after breakfast (the prison's coffee special), an investigator would blindfold me and lead me back to the interrogation room. "Please sit," the captain would bark, a jumpstart to the interrogation. It went on for hours, the same redundant questions to which I did not have the answers.

Where are your sons, Daw Tinsa?

Did they display any odd behavior in the weeks and months leading up to their disappearance?

What are you hiding from us?

He would point a bright light directly at my face to scrutinize my every movement and tic. At times I felt dizzy and nauseous, the light so strong that I felt like I was going blind. The combination of the light and his repetitive questioning was beginning to drive me mad, on the verge of collapse.

If you don't tell us what you know, we'll have to ask the children at home. Some of them might even be brought here for further questioning.

I drifted in and out of the conversation, staring at a large, full-length mirror in the corner of the room that had not been there during my first detention. It looked totally out of place until I recalled reading about two-way mirrors in magazines and novels. The interrogator would look at the mirror when questioning me, revealing his bluff.

The guards brought my lunch at noon. I laughed when I saw that it included the same *nylon soup* as before, their culinary tastes not changing in the slightest. I could not stomach the contents of this soup and decided to play a small game with the men behind the mirror. Before every meal, I would slowly push the bowl of nylon soup before me. Dipping my hands in the bowl, the *nylon soup* became a finger bowl to wash my hands before eating. The watchmen likely thought me mad, but I would stare directly and intensely at the mirror during this ritual, daring them to come out from behind their cover and ask me what the hell I was doing. They never did, of course.

Back in my room, I heard voices and people moving in the adjacent barrack. The wooden walls were thin enough that the slightest sound – sneezes, coughs, sobs – would carry through. I would intentionally raise my voice when speaking to my barrack mate to signal to my neighbors that we were here and they would do the same. After several hours of doing this I finally discerned that one of the voices belonged to Daw Kyi Kyi, my closest confidante from the previous detention. I was relieved to hear her voice but also saddened to realize that my friend had not left the four walls of the prison at all. If she had been released, I would have certainly seen or heard of her in Rangoon, especially from her children. While I had a chance to see my family again, she languished behind these prison gates as the outside world passed her by.

It was not long before I was unceremoniously asked to gather my things and move barracks, just like in the good old days. The guards moved me to the adjoining barrack where I was reunited with Daw Kyi Kyi. She waited until the guards left to give me a big, sisterly hug. "I knew it was you when I recognized your voice from across the yard," she said in a hushed tone. "After I heard your voice, I went and stood in the yard where I saw a part of your clothesline. When you hung your *longyi* on the line, I knew that it was you. There was no doubt in my mind."

I smiled, grateful to my mother for having sent me that *longyi* during my first detention. It was of Arakan weave, a strong cotton fabric with a distinct tribal zigzag design made for women who endured long days in the fields under the blistering sun. It was a godsend, easy to wash, dry and most of all, comfortable to wear. I kept it all of these years not wanting to toss aside a faithful friend. And now, it had done me yet another great favor.

"How have you been, sister?" I asked, already knowing the answer to the question.

She gave a faint smile, trying to hide her mixed emotions. "It's the same as it's always been, Tinsa. Seeing you today has brought me much joy, but I'm sad that you are back here again, away from your family once more. What happened?"

"Yan Myo and Yan Lin." Not much else could be said. I had not shared this information with my first bunkmate but I told Daw Kyi Kyi everything. She listened attentively, empathizing with every detail. Who better than her to understand my plight? Who else could have understood what it was like to live a life constantly on edge, wondering what might bring us back to prison, or worse?

We caught up until nightfall, oblivious to anyone who may or may not have been listening in. Daw Kyi Kyi wanted to know everything about the outside world – how her children were, what Rangoon was like now, what gossip there was to know. "Your children are doing just fine. They miss you," I told her on behalf of her four kids. "As far as gossip in Rangoon, I really wouldn't know since no one dares to speak to me or my family. I, myself, am a topic of gossip, given my colorful arrest record and my husband being gone for nearly a decade," I joked.

Daw Kyi Kyi also revealed to me some truths about her life that she had not shared before. She told me that she had been married twice and that her first marriage failed because she was far too young to have gotten married and to know better. Her first husband was related to Onma's mother-in-law, making us very distant relatives. Thakin Zin was her second husband but she, in her own words, "was obviously not blessed with domestic tranquility the second time around, either."

Daw Kyi Kyi and I were eventually separated and it was my turn to be left alone, she wishing me a safe journey onwards. "I don't think I will be seeing you here again. You will be out sooner than you think," she bade goodbye. Daw Kyi Kyi was right, we did not see each other inside the walls of Ye Kyi Aing after that. The next and final time that I would see her was on her deathbed in the early 2000s, the authorities releasing her to a general hospital in the last days of a terminal illness. By that time, she had been in prison for nearly four decades without ever seeing the light of the outside world, and I believe her to be Burma's longest-serving political prisoner.

Two or three days of solitary confinement were broken by the guards once again bringing me new company. I was astonished to see Mala, my sister, standing in the doorway. How incredibly happy I was to see her and also heartbroken to know that she had been caught in our politics. I assumed that I would be a natural target for when Ho Chi and Mosie left, but I never would have guessed that they would come for Mala too. "They came for me days after you were taken away," she said in low tone, trying to calm herself after the initial excitement of seeing me. "Khin Myint and Neta are also in jail. I hoped that I would see you in here, just to let you know that we're in this together."

There was a lump in my throat when I heard that my son-in-law and brother were jailed for my sons' actions. "What did Khin Myint and Neta do, exactly? On what grounds are they being detained?" I asked angrily.

"They must have guessed that Khin Myint was the one who drove the boys to the cinema, though he had no knowledge of their exact plans. Neta was accused of looking on at student demonstrations. You know that he was just at the wrong place at the wrong time, Tinsa. He's so innocent, a child, hardly a grand revolutionary."

"And your charges?"

"Oh Tinsa, it was all written down on a stupid piece of paper that they tried to force me to sign. They accused me of providing Ho Chi and Mosie a room at the hospital where they 'plotted against the state.' They must have also figured out that I was the link between you and U Than Han's contact." Her voice was barely audible. "I didn't sign it, which I guess is why I'm still here."

I could tell that it had not been easy for Mala despite her defiant nature. Unlike me, this was her first time in prison. There were dark half-moons under Mala's eyes and she had budding strands of white hair. Yet, she was as beautiful as ever, always the great beauty of Rangoon that men and women alike fawned over. The guards at Ye Kyi Aing stared at her luminescence, unable to look away from her glow. Blessed with good looks and great intelligence, she shunned politics though her blood was destined for it, directly or indirectly. She went to England for her studies, receiving a degree in radiology. The British boys couldn't resist her either, dozens of admirers sending her love letters, flowers and chocolates, all wanting to be a small part of her orbit. She maintained contact with only one suitor, whom I shall call Edward for his privacy. They wrote to each other from across continents and I deduced from her tone that he was the true love that she wished for when we were children.

Nevertheless, she was headstrong and feisty and returned to Rangoon to work at the Women's Hospital. "I don't think the hospital will be calling me back anytime soon," she lamented with stilted laughter. All of those years of her dedicating her life to medicine were reduced to nothing, her former colleagues unable or unwilling to speak out on her behalf.

Imprisonment sealed our already strong bond. We made our barrack as comfortable as possible, pooling the supplies that May May had sent to us: small portions of mutton jerky, dried fish, chicken powder, a little bit of masala to sprinkle over our prison menu. The most difficult thing for me to live without was reading material, the hobby that kept me sane in Yan Naing's absence. This time, I was not even allowed prayer books. Mala, noticing the loneliness that overtook me without my reading material, entertained me with stories of England, Europe and all of the beautiful things she had seen on the other side of the world. She lulled me to sleep with tales of jazz clubs along the Thames, bespectacled suits on Bond Street, the scent of Earl Grey tea against the backdrop of the cold London winters, how everything in the modern world was so polished, new, moving at the speed of light.

"I wish I could have seen all of those things with you."

"You will. You will someday," Mala assured, both of us falling into a deep slumber, dreaming of smoky jazz numbers and the world beyond these thin barrack walls.

CHAPTER NINETEEN

In July 1972, the guards at Ye Kyi Aing dragged Mala and me from our beds and sat us in the interrogation room. Mala was visibly upset and I held myself together for both of our sakes. My mind raced, wondering what would happen to us. *Did they find my boys? Yan Naing? Were my other children involved? What was going on?*

Several minutes, feeling like hours, passed before the main investigator calmly stepped into the room. I tried to read his body language and facial expression but he did not give away a thing. "Daw Tinsa, Dr. Mala Maw," he addressed us, "I have some news regarding your mother." Mala took a sharp inhale. The tension was so thick in the air that I could hardly breathe.

"What happened?" I demanded.

"She's quite ill. You will go to her bedside and pay your respects. She doesn't have much time," he said a matter-of-factly.

Mala and I arrived at May May's bedside to find a frail, immobile woman, unrecognizable. Our mother was unable to speak after a heart attack, years of high blood pressure and stress paralyzing her. It was only her weary, black eyes that alerted us of her awareness, straining to dart between our two forms at her bedside.

I felt the most guilt that I had ever felt in my entire life. Mala and I, so consumed with imprisonment and expecting regular packages from my mother, had failed to keep up with her needs. We had no indication of how rapidly her health was deteriorating, as letters to and from the prison were the most difficult items to send. I knew that she had suffered from hypertension and was on medication, but we did not expect this. To us, she was a godlike entity, incapable of death or the travails of mere mortals. This couldn't be, it wasn't a fitting end for this woman. My mother, a deity.

I knelt in front of her bed, clasping my hands in prayer. "Please forgive me, May May. I wish that I could have done more. You have given us everything."

My father was sitting in the living room, a faraway look in his eyes. He could barely look at me, his grief too overwhelming for anyone to understand. Phay Phay was in the advanced stages of Parkinson's Disease, his hands shaking at his side. I had never seen him look so defeated. This was his single greatest battle, one that he could not win no matter how hard he tried. I knew that he could not fathom a long time in this world without her and I took his hands in mine, warm to the touch. He nodded at me, unable to voice the imminent loss of his wife, his greatest champion, his soulmate. "You'll meet her again in the next lifetime, Phay Phay, and many more after that." His eyes were downcast, slowly taking in my words.

At that moment, Yema and Kinsa walked into the room. "May May, can I speak to you?" Yema asked in a small voice. I followed them to the front hall and the three of us sat in the dining room. "We tried to tell you sooner, but our letters were intercepted." Though Mala and I were able to receive some letters, they were inevitably censored and often confiscated. Anything considered inflammatory was blotted or cut out.

"We should decorate our barracks with these letters because they look so much like paper snowflakes," I joked to Mala. The approved letters had a cheery contrition to them, the children writing about school, that everything was fine and for us not to worry.

"May May," Yema began, "we received a visitor from Thailand not too long ago." I inferred by her tone that it was an emissary sent by Yan Naing. "He came to tell me," her voice cracked, "that Yan Myo passed away. He caught cerebral malaria and by the time they took him to a hospital in Bangkok, it was too late. Yan Myo passed away on January 24, 1972." Yema and Kinsa broke the news as gently as they could, in tears, the wounds still too fresh.

"Thank you for telling me, Yema." I did not recognize my own voice, as if my spirit had left my body and there was nothing but a shell standing before Yema and Kinsa. I suddenly felt lightheaded, all of the lights and sounds of the world muting before me as I entered a state of total shock and detachment. I was trapped in a chamber of numbness for several minutes, not moving at all, until I felt something like a pinprick in the middle of my chest. That sensation woke my nerves and grief began to flower within me, a thousand petals of sadness and anger waiting to be released. What I did next was not healthy, but I could not bear to confront the worst kind of pain in the world, which was to lose a mother and a child at the same time. I pushed down any emergent sense of fragility or pain in that moment, contained in a little ball in the pit of my stomach that I carried with me for years, and forced myself to stay silent and stoic for the remainder of the day.

Yan Myo's death was the fatal strike for my mother's health. She was suffering tremendously and to learn about the loss of her favorite grandson was more than she could bear. Our family physician, Dr. Myint Swe, defied public opinion and scrutiny to treat my mother during her final days and had not given her much time after hearing the news. "When Grandma heard of Yan Myo's death, she did not recover," Kinsa recounted. "The day that she suffered an attack, one of the house girls alerted me and I ran as fast as I could across the pond to reach her." It was too late by the time she arrived.

Back at the barrack, Mala sat on her bed in shock, inconsolable. I crawled into bed, my entire body and mind collapsing, sobbing uncontrollably. That night, I dreamt that I was in my parents' home, my mother sitting by the front window with an unfinished quilt across her lap. She looked happy, the sunlight bouncing off of her lustrous hair, her pale skin luminous, radiant, resplendent. Her eyes met mine, the warmth of her smile penetrating the entire room. On the opposite side of the room, Yan Myo and Yan Lin stood beside a teak coffee table. Yan Myo ran to hug me. It was so vivid that I could smell him, the scent of the jungle, rustic, earthy. "May May," he began to say.

"Shhh," I cut him off, continuing to hold him in my arms.

* * * * *

Dr. Ba Maw and Daw Kinmama Maw

My mother, Kinmama Maw, died ten days later. I knew that she was not likely to recover but the reality of her death was a severe blow nonetheless. The guards brought us the newspaper that day and I showed her obituary to Mala, who covered her mouth with her right hand and stared straight ahead with distress.

"Mala, I don't know if I can bear going to her funeral," I croaked, believing that the sight of my mother's lifeless body would drive me mad.

"Me neither," Mala said almost inaudibly, staring blankly at the wall in front of us.

But when the escorts came to retrieve us, we rose instinctively and changed our clothes into darker hues. We followed the men to the waiting cars, forgetting the conversation we had just minutes ago. We needed to be there for our father even if our hearts were shattered in the process.

My mother was on her bed, her stillness the most unnerving thing of all. Her hair was swept into a neat bun, arranged by Yema as the duty of the eldest grandchild and now the lady of the house. I kissed my mother's forehead for the last time.

I had never seen my father so despondent, a shell of his former self. He had the symptomatic rolling tremors and scuffling gait of someone in the advanced stages of Parkinson's. His mind remained as sharp as ever, noticing every little detail of his wife's funeral preparations. He bit his bottom lip, not wanting to cry in front of us. Mala and I took his hands and held them for what seemed like ages, his palms shaking while enclosed in ours.

Phay Phay, being much older than my mother, had always thought that he would be the first to go. Though she lived a full life, he always wanted to give her the peace and tranquility she so deserved to make up for a life confronted with death, illness, absent children and political woes. "I wanted to go before her," he finally spoke, those few words revealing the magnitude of his sorrow. "I wanted to go first," he kept on repeating like a funeral hymn. He would not and could not accompany my mother's cortege, the first time I had ever witnessed him refuse to perform his duty. Phay Phay did not move from his spot, the same one he sat in all morning long while visitors floated in and out of the house.

My mother's final gift to me did not reveal itself until much later. Mala and I returned to Ye Kyi Aing and spent days in catatonic silence, swimming in thoughts of mortality. I needed to keep my mind and hands busy so I started to refold the few items of clothing that I had. A small set of books dropped to the floor when I reached for my stack of clothes. They were long-forgotten prayer and meditation books from my mother, herself a deeply spiritual Buddhist who had always hoped that her children would share her faith someday. Her death gave me the realization that maybe it was time for me to awaken my mind and for once confront my own consciousness.

I devoted myself to these books, studying the teachings of the Mahasi Sayardaw and practicing meditation on my own. I sat on the floor and concentrated on my breathing, feeling the air going in and out of my nose. An uncontrollable tremor overtook me, running up and down my body, terrifying in its strength. I could not and should not control it, according to basic meditation principles. I could only observe it, every ounce of pain, weakness and discomfort that lived inside of me and was fighting to leave. The tremor subsided after several tense breaths, enough to make me stop meditating, not knowing what to make of this eerie feeling of helplessness. I closed the books and did not press on.

I peered at the books with guilt over the next few days, feeling as if I had failed my mother somehow. I had not given meditation a proper chance and decided to try again. Every session that followed helped me gradually, learning not to fret over the millions of tiny sensations in my body. The more that I trained my mind to stay tranquil, the better my mental health became. I began to sleep through the night, not needlessly worrying about what I was missing in the outside world and had good dreams every night.

One night, I fell into a deep sleep and found myself standing on the porch of our old home at Kandawgyi Lake. I glanced across the lake, past the willow trees and past the buzzing of crows to see people standing on a faraway hill. They were being pushed into the lake, turning into fish as soon as they hit the water. There must have been thousands of small, iridescent minnows wading and circling five bigger fish. It was so vivid that I could feel the breeze from the lake blow through me, specks of pollen against my skin. Before I could make sense of this vision, I awoke covered in a thick film of sweat, the barrack's stale air in my lungs.

CHAPTER TWENTY

On January 5, 1974, I was released for the second time under an amnesty pardoning hundreds of political prisoners from well-known politicians to little-known activists. I wondered if my dream was a premonition of what was to happen, the release of the big fish and all of the little fish in our small pond. Mala and I were overjoyed to see Neta and Khin Myint at home, collectively imprisoned for two years. For once, there was nobody in jail, perhaps a record for our miscreant family. Mala remained skittish about being back out in the open, life in prison leaving her with a strange feeling of uncertainty and mortality. "It will take some time to feel at home again, Mala," I assured her, "but we will resettle and adapt again. We have to."

My children were doing well for themselves, resilient as ever. Kinsa had graduated from the Rangoon Institute of Technology, Amaya and Kethi were at the medical college, Nanda was studying chemistry, and Minshin, Tinthi and Zarni were forging ahead in their elementary and middle school studies.

Khin Myint, Yema's husband who was imprisoned, came home to find a baby girl who was eagerly awaiting his return. Yema had given birth to Haymar, nicknamed Mu Mu, when he was in prison. It was not an easy time to raise a child in Rangoon compounded with our circumstances. Khin Myint used to be a geologist at the Myanmar Oil Corporation and had no hope of being hired by another company. Yema was still at the ministry, receiving her meager salary once a week and struggling to afford the exorbitant prices for baby items in Rangoon.

Mu Mu grew bigger by the day and had a ravenous appetite for milk. Yema found it difficult to feed Mu Mu since she could not come home from work several times a day to breastfeed her daughter. Milk powder prices skyrocketed due to dwindling imports and fresh milk was impossible to buy during the socialist period because of the government's disastrous livestock policies. What was labeled and sold as "fresh milk" had a plastic chemical smell and a suspicious coral tint.

Khin Myint bought a single cow so that Mu Mu could have fresh milk. He came to me for my approval and constructed a cow shed in the corner of our garden, a sturdy wooden structure spacious enough to house more cows should the business take off. What began as selling the surplus of Mu Mu's milk to neighbors transformed into a small business with twenty cows and several employees. Every morning at 5 AM, Khin Myint and anyone with a free hand would make deliveries, our customers families from the American Embassy and the diplomatic circle in the Golden Valley area. This cow business supported our entire family for years on end. There was finally enough food on the table, we had one phone line running and one car for the whole family. It wasn't much but it was enough, more than we had had in nearly a decade.

For my son Minshin, a stable home life was no longer sufficient to keep him within reach. A teenager with a wild streak, he waited five days after my return before running off to join Yan Naing and his older brother. He took off with two of his friends, armed with small rucksacks, and hitchhiked to Thailand to be with his father. Yan Naing, having lost Yan Myo all too recently, thought him too young to make such a drastic decision. Minshin begged his father to let him stay, but Yan Naing would have none of it and contacted my sister Theda, who was in the U.S. My husband dragged Minshin to the train station, handing him a one-way ticket to Bangkok, where Theda was waiting for him. To my great relief, he arrived safely and she whisked him away to America where he remained for the rest of his schooling and adult life.

This time, I marched down to our neighborhood's council office and reported my son as a missing person as a precaution for my family and for myself. He was only thirteen and I did not think that military intelligence would come for me again because it was so apparent that it was a child's hasty decision and not a grand political scheme. I was too numb to reprimand Minshin for his daring escape. I tried my best to play both mother and father to all of my children. For the sons of political enemies, what future could we offer them here? There was no work to be had, nothing for them to aspire to. I could not fault my sons for spending their nights dreaming of fighting alongside their father, in some exotic jungle where they could play heroes, all of the power in the world sitting in their hands.

* * * * *

I never stopped thinking about my prison mates, calling on Daw Kyi Kyi's children from time to time to see how they were faring and if they needed anything. They were well-raised and independent, never wanting to trouble others for help. Their masala business was a success and they lived quietly in the hopes that no further disturbances would rock their mother's case.

Ma Hla Kyi, a small wiry woman who had been with me during my first time in prison, visited me in the aftermath of the Minshin interlude. I told her about Minshin running away and she sympathized with my third son's disappearance. "Tinsa, why don't you join me for a meditation period at the Mahasi Meditation Center? Take your mind off of things?" she asked, as if she were mentioning some sort of luxury vacation. I was skeptical of her offer, remembering the difficulties of attempting to meditate in my barrack, my mind a constant whirlwind of activity, anxiety and despair.

Dr. Ba Maw in his final years

"I don't know, Ma Hla Kyi, perhaps it might be too much at this time. Minshin just ran away and there are far too many things for me to be worrying about right now. I'm afraid that being alone with my mind will drive me crazy," I laughed.

"All the better reason for you to find solace and inner peace, away from home and your daily surroundings. It's only a few days, Ma Tinsa, what's the harm in it?"

I agreed with Ma Hla Kyi and went with her to the Mahasi Center. For the first time in my life, I learned to let go of the things that I could not control, simply by focusing on my emotions and wondering why I felt the way that I did. Yan Myo's death. Minshin's absence. My mother's death. My father's deterioration. The total and complete captivity of my mind.

January 28, 1976. I took a quick shower, meditated, prepared the children's breakfasts and reached for the daily newspaper. When I looked at the front page, I saw the announcement that my son, Yan Lin Naing, had been shot dead. *Yan Lin Naing, Son of Traitor Bo Yan Naing, Shot Dead by Yan Naing Follower.* Both of my twin sons were now dead and gone, their deaths separated by four years and four days. I mourned openly and fully this time, not fighting the tears when they stung my eyes, nor trying to hide any facet of my vulnerability, especially when my children or friends wanted to console me.

The only people who came to pay their respects were some neighbors courageous enough to step inside our gates. My former prison mates were at my side, all too well knowing the feeling of losing a husband, father, brother, son, to politics. The family made a collective decision not to tell my father about Yan Lin's death. My father, at eighty-three years old, was still mentally fit but physically weak in the final stages of Parkinson's Disease. The news of his beloved grandson's death would have destroyed him. He spent the rest of his life unaware that Yan Lin was gone, believing that he was still deep in the jungles of the Thai-Burma border with his father.

My father was slowly drawing into himself. His life had lost its spark, its meaning, without my mother. His words, *I wanted to go first*, echoed in the weeks and months leading up to his death. Phay Phay had given up on life, waiting for death to claim him. Every day, like clockwork, I would take my children to his house to pay him a visit, reading to him, telling jokes and doing everything I could to cheer him up. He would smile tiredly at me, the look of a man who knew that his time was near.

On May 29, 1977, my father, Dr. Ba Maw, passed away in his sleep. He had caught pneumonia during the new year rains and went into a coma for fifty days. My father did not suffer, his breath slowing with the passing days. We sent an obituary notice for family, friends and the public to pay their respects, placed in the classified section of *The Worker's People's Daily*, *Light of Burma (Myanmar's Ah-Lin)*, *The Mirror (Kyai Hmone)* and *The Guardian* for three consecutive days. It vanished on the second day. His obituary was never supposed to have been printed in the first place, an oversight on the editor's part allowing it to slip through the censors. It was suggested the editors were ardent nationalists and wanted to give Dr. Ba Maw the full respect that he deserved, so they went ahead and printed it. Nevertheless, the government's antenna was working again the following day and removed all traces of the notice from their records, fearing that it would attract large crowds of activists.

Most heard of his passing through newspapers, word of mouth, and the BBC radio waves, and came to pay their respects in person. One thousand relatives, friends, acquaintances and admirers came from near and far to see him one last time. The crowd attracted soldiers to our compound, like bees to honey, but they could not do anything to stop the throngs of people who dared to defy the public gathering ban on this day. We ate coconut noodles, vermicelli and semolina cake with snipers pointed at us from nearby rooftops. For seven days (the traditional mourning period), political friends and foes came, people who had been too afraid to associate with us for the past decade and a half. Burma's sleeping giants awoke to pay their last respects to my father, knowing that they would be under scrutiny as sympathizers to an anti-government family. U Ba Swe. U Kyaw Nyein. U Thein Pe

Myint[52]. U Pe Khin[53]. Thakin Chit Maung[54]. We scattered my father's ashes in his hometown of Maubin, all traces of my father swallowed by the jagged currents of the mighty Ayeyarwaddy River and swept to sea.

U Ba Swe eulogized my father, remembering one of his final meetings with Dr. Ba Maw before he lost his ability to speak. He and Edward Law-Yone had come to deliver their monthly round of gossip, unafraid of being seen in the company of a pariah as they had been detainees themselves. My father welcomed them into the living room, shuffling as he called the maids to bring a fresh pot of coffee, eyes blinking erratically, his smile unwavering. Naturally, the conversation fell to politics. The two men teased Phay Phay about his former title, *Anashin Adipadi*, which translates to *he who holds all power and knowledge*, a close but not quite exact synonym for dictator.

"You simply did not terrorize anyone enough to earn the title," U Ba Swe chuckled.

"You assumed the title of Dictator yet you never once jailed, let alone killed, anybody. You must be a bogus dictator,"[55] joked U Law-Yone, the two guests having great fun at the expense of their host.

My father reclined in his chair, unable to contain the widening smile on his face, the ever-present mark of his true nature. There was only one thing that he needed to say.

"A man's best weapon is his eye. The other kind are not dictators; they're thugs."

---

[52] General Secretary of Communist Party of Burma, journalist.
[53] Architect of the Panglong treaty, later to become ambassador to various countries.
[54] Helped established the Red Socialists in 1950. Member of Parliament representing the National United Front.
[55] Law-Yone, Edward. "Dr. Ba Maw of Burma: An Appreciation." *Essays on Burma*. Ed. John P. Ferguson and E.J. Brill. Leiden: Contributions to Asian Studies, No. 16, 1981. 1-18.

CHAPTER TWENTY-ONE

The rainy season was right on schedule at the end of May 1980. The mango trees bloomed, fragrant fruit dangling from crooked branches, their smell beckoning the waiting monsoon. I could hardly believe my eyes when I opened the newspaper to find a long-awaited official notice, checking other papers to see that it was real and not a joke. It was indeed real, an official government notice plastered across newspapers, magazines and bellowed on every radio show in Burma.

The government had declared an amnesty for all insurgents, illegal emigrants, Communist fighters and guerrillas in hiding. All opposition groups and members were allowed to return to Rangoon and present themselves to the authorities, whereby they would be absolved of previously accused "crimes" effective immediately. Those who turned themselves in would not be punished and would be able to return to their old lives. Alternatively, those residing abroad illegally would be given legal passports, able to live in their adopted homelands in peace.

Of course I remained skeptical of the motives behind such a generous amnesty. Not trusting the papers or official notices, I asked friends and acquaintances if they had confirmed the news from other sources. *Are they sincere? Do you know anyone who is making plans to come home?* No one could give me a clear response, scratching their heads in equal confusion.

Bo Yan Naing

Even if I wanted to find Yan Naing, I had no idea of his whereabouts, grasping at small tidbits of information over the years. The last that I had heard, Yan Naing made contact with U Nu, who formed the Parliamentary Democracy Party in August 1969 on the border, the latter appointing himself president of an exiled government. They united with the Chin, Mon and Karen rebel groups to form the National United Front. What began as an idealistic battlefront rapidly dissipated, men of great stature still unable to compromise amidst infighting, with stubbornness as the innate way of the Burmese. Demoralized, U Nu resigned and moved to India in the mid-1970s, the last time I received any confirmed reports of my husband's activities, dead or alive. U Nu returned under the amnesty from his exile that took him to India, England and the United States, the first encouraging sign of change. If U Nu was permitted to return, then Yan Naing would be as well. Other prominent dissidents trickled in, including another Comrade, Bo Hmu Aung, who had been on the Thai border with a different armed faction.

I was still doubtful despite all of the signs before me, not wanting to risk sending a false message only for my husband to arrive in Rangoon and be handcuffed on arrival. My friends tried to convince me to accept the amnesty on his behalf. "You have to accept, Ma Tinsa," they pleaded. "You don't know when the next opportunity like this will appear."

It was far more complicated than just signing a document. I would have loved nothing more than to bring my husband home after fifteen years, to reunite our family though he was a stranger to me at this point. There was no question of me wanting him back in Rangoon, for us to meet again and for him to be able to see his children and to meet his grandchildren. I never judged him for his mission to free Burma and some have asked me if I was angry with him. I was, for a very long time, but I was also ready to forgive him just so long as I could understand the truth of what had happened to him.

My husband was the most stubborn man I knew and my signature and handshake were worthless if he himself did not agree. "It's not my decision to make," I told my friends, who looked at me with such great pity. "Yan Naing alone has to accept and make his amends on his own."

My daughter Amaya came to me with a long-awaited message. Her friend Sandar, General Ne Win's daughter, relayed a message saying that her father was sincere in his offer of amnesty with Yan Naing specifically in mind. Furthermore, he wanted nothing more than his old comrade to be able to return to Burma in his elder years. I decided to write to General Ne Win hoping to unravel the situation. *Thank you for the offer of amnesty. I would be happy if my husband were to accept it, if the spirit in which it is offered is genuine.*

Another message via Sandar. Her father had no ulterior motive, still valuing my husband as one of his brothers from their Thirty Comrades days. Yan Naing was assured safety. As I mulled my next move, an emissary came to me instead. A soldier stood on our porch, calmly stating, "Daw Tinsa, you are to come with me to see Colonel Tin Oo, the Chief of Intelligence. I would appreciate if you could come with me at once." All of the oxygen left my body for a split second, my heart stopping. A morbid stream of thoughts rushed through my head, a million scenarios presenting themselves one by one.

Are they after me again?
Was the amnesty a trick all along?
What could have happened for them to come after me?
How long would I be away this time?

We set out for the military headquarters about ten miles from my home. I entered a damp, dark government building, the walls a subdued, institutional green. The young soldier took me to an office on the furthest side of the building where an old friend sat behind an imposing metal desk. "Please, have a seat," Colonel Tin Oo said to my escort and me, his hand gesturing towards two small chairs in front of him.

"Daw Tinsa, President Ne Win received your letter and thanks you for your interest in bringing your husband back home. The military attaché in Bangkok has been tracking Bo Yan Naing for quite some time now and we know his exact whereabouts." I gasped when I heard this, my husband's life confirmed. "President Ne Win, the government, your family, everyone would like to see Bo Yan Naing return to Burma once again. This is why we encourage you to go to Bangkok and speak with him. Only you can do this. Convince him to come home."

"I don't have any spare money for travel. I don't even have a passport. Even if I had these things, I'm not sure about going to Bangkok alone. It doesn't feel safe," I admitted, thinking of every bad scenario in a solo venture across the border.

"You are free to take one or two family members with you," he offered. I had never seen or heard Tin Oo's tone so accommodating and flexible. It was unnerving.

"Might my eldest daughter, Yema, accompany me? Her daughter, who is a few months old, would need to come with us. I would also like my daughter, Tinthi, to help look after the baby." Tinthi's presence would have a two-fold effect. It was true that Yema would need help minding her baby. Additionally, Tinthi, born in August 1964, was only an infant when Yan Naing went into exile. She did not remember her father and it would be her first time seeing him in her adult life. I did not want to waste this opportunity for her sake.

Tin Oo sat back in his chair, weighing his choices. "Your daughters and granddaughter can travel with you. The government will provide travel expenses, 2000 USD in cash, and your passports will be issued immediately. Daw Tinsa, you must do everything in your power to bring your husband home."

I nodded in comprehension and prepared for Bangkok.

* * * * *

The government and I came to an agreement for the first time in my life. I would be going to Bangkok with Yema, granddaughter Einsi and Tinthi. I gave 300 USD to Khin Myint, asking him to take care of the household while we were away. He held the crisp, new dollar bills, in awe of the amount of money in his hand. We had not had that much money at our disposal in a very long time, especially not dollars which were the unofficial currency of the government. Khin Myint kissed his wife and baby daughter and carried our bags to the porch.

A fleet of military vehicles awaited us, the men and cars indistinguishable from one another. When we emerged from the airport in Bangkok, an exact replica of our armed entourage in Rangoon greeted us and took us to our hotel in the Silom district. I could hardly contain my anxiety during the long drive, our path meandering through perfectly smooth concrete highways and buildings taller than I had ever seen in my life. A stoic officer sat quietly in the passenger seat, breaking his silence to greet us as our main liaison for the trip.

Tin Oo promised that the embassy had found Yan Naing and I felt fully confident that I would be reunited with my husband. "Have you made contact with my husband? When will we be seeing him?" I asked our liaison.

The officer looked back at me with curiosity, a blank stare. "Daw Tinsa, we have no idea of your husband's whereabouts. It is your responsibility to bring him to the embassy and accept the terms of the amnesty."

Pure shock. Contrary to what Tin Oo had told me, the officer was ignorant of where Yan Naing was, or if he was even alive. Panic shot through my body. *Was this a trap? Did they take me out of the country to distract me while they found Yan Naing and brought him back in handcuffs? Would I even be able to return home?*

"And how do you suppose that I will find him?" I asked tersely, crossing my arms. The officer did not answer me, looking ahead at the gray concrete expanse that stretched for miles. The car stopped at the Narai Hotel, at the time one of the best and oldest first-class hotels in Bangkok. Yema, baby Einsi and Tinthi looked up at the high-rise in wonder, never having seen such a modern and opulent building in their lives. The hotel staff took us to a large second-floor suite with wall-to-wall windows overlooking the Bangkok skyline. Einsi clapped and shrieked at her surroundings, clearly pleased with her view and five-star accommodations. While I thought the hotel room to be beautiful and extravagant, I was panicking. The search for my husband could take weeks, even months. We could not afford to stay at the Narai for more than a few days, though I did not let my children know of this. I would let them enjoy the luxury surroundings, at least for one night.

I called my brother Zali, who had long abandoned the jungle campaign to move to Bangkok. He married a Thai woman and was working as an international attorney in the city, unrecognizable in his tailored suits and meticulously groomed hair. "Tinsa?" Zali's voice was shaking. We had not spoken in years and I could not tell him ahead of time of my plans to come to Bangkok due to political sensitivity.

"Zali, it's good to hear your voice."

"When did you arrive? Why didn't you tell me earlier?"

"We arrived yesterday. Yema, her daughter Einsi and Tinthi are here with me." A hesitant pause. "I've come to bring Yan

Naing home."

He sighed on the other end of the line, the futility of my campaign. Zali did not say anything to discourage me, agreeing to help in whatever way he could. He called every last contact that he had in the jungle, chasing the ghosts of my husband's war.

We moved into a small apartment just around the block. Our new home was much smaller and lacking in furnishings, but the price ensured that we could stay in Bangkok for weeks, even months. After two weeks of following dead-end leads, we received word from the embassy that they had found Yan Naing. He and what remained of his army, a handful of emaciated, stubborn guerrillas, were entrenched in the lowlands of the Thai-Burma border. They lived in squalor, on the brink of starvation and far from any semblance of civilization,.

"He's ready to come back. Are you ready to take him?" Zali asked me one last time.

"Zali, I've been waiting for this for fifteen years." My brother sent the final message to an emissary waiting on the border, whose sole duty was to find Yan Naing and to bring him to Bangkok through Victoria Point.

* * * * *

The man who had left fifteen years earlier materialized as a ghastly apparition of his former self. My husband had lost over one half of his body weight, bones protruding from beneath yellowed, jaundiced skin. His eyes were cloudy, covered with thin red rings, worms infecting his vision. The lips that had once been so full were permanently etched into a frown, thinned considerably from thirst. Baby Einsi screamed in the background, waking Yan Naing from his decade and a half-long slumber. His eyes lit up at the sight of his granddaughter, who instinctively knew her grandfather and reached out to him, unafraid of his haggard appearance. He took her in his arms, her chubby palms enclosed in his skeletal hands. "This is your granddaughter," were the first words I said to him.

"And this is Tinthi," I turned to let our daughter face him for the first time. She was only a toddler when he left, having no recollection of her father. Tinthi had grown to become a beautiful teenager with long silky black hair, a slender figure, and a beaming smile that won her many friends. Yan Naing was in awe of how much Tinthi had grown, remembering her as a rambunctious little baby crawling on bamboo mats.

He did not say anything, the shock of seeing us too much for him to grasp. I prepared coffee and snacks but he stared at the food in front of him, overwhelmed by the feast. "Forgive me for my rudeness. After years of living in the jungle, I'm not used to seeing such rich food."

Yan Naing finally spoke of his decision to return. "Tinsa, you would not believe how desperate we were in the jungle. We ran out of food and weapons years ago, living off the land and whatever we could beg off of villagers. My men were on the brink of mutiny until we heard of the amnesty on the radio." He searched my eyes for understanding. "You realize that I could not come back immediately, right? When I heard Ne Win's voice on the radio, he seemed to be calling out to me. What if it had been a trap, a setup to ambush and kill us for good?"

I had not considered my husband's fears of an ambush, a plausible explanation for his delay in contacting the embassy. He continued, "We lost the war but I had to make sure that I could trust Ne Win's words. We sent some men to the embassy for assurance, which we received verbally. You see, I needed time to figure out what was really going on. Then, the last time my men came to Bangkok, the embassy told them that you were here looking for me."

He paused, his voice drifting. "Then I knew it must have been true. The moment I found out that you were here, I disbanded my men, those loyal until the abject end, and called the ambassador." His eyes drifted into his sockets during the last part of his confession, fainting from extreme fatigue and hunger. He was conscious but in need of greater medical attention than he was letting on. Zali ran to the phone to call a doctor, punching the keys with furious desperation.

Please let him live. Let him live. Fifteen years, isn't that enough?

CHAPTER TWENTY-TWO

On August 15, 1980, we boarded a flight to Rangoon as a family. Yan Naing's trepidation was palpable in his silence. Over a dozen guerrilla fighters who had been with him on the borderlands had also accepted the amnesty and joined us on our flight, dog-tired and clinging to their last chance to see Burma again.

Yan Naing collapsed from exhaustion the first few days that he was home. I did not know it at the time but he must have been suffering from post-traumatic stress after years of living on the brink of death, starvation, disease and war. Our everyday routines, the monotony of our lives and surroundings in Rangoon were an extreme for him, a man so used to living in chaos. He spent several weeks monitored by Ne Win's personal physicians. The other patients and hospital staff stared at him in awe, the man who had eluded an entire regime for fifteen years. His name and reputation preceded him, a myth in the eyes of many people since his days as a student at Rangoon University, a legacy spanning half a century.

The day that he went to see General Ne Win in person, the sky was white sapphire blue, the sun casting a warm glow over the city. He sauntered to his old comrade's new presidential quarters, a golden, palatial fortress in the center of Rangoon rising above the steam and smoke. "How are you, old friend?" General Ne Win asked, as if the years had not passed between them.

"I've seen better days, brother," Yan Naing smiled.

They spoke of everything and nothing for half an hour, avoiding the difficult subjects that separated them since the split of the Comrades. General Ne Win inquired about our family, particularly our children who had remained friends with his children. Finally, he broke the silence that had divided them for years. "I am sorry about what happened to your sons, Yan Myo and Yan Lin. If I could have changed anything, I would have."

Yan Naing sat there like a statue, holding back the rage that consumed him in the jungle and still vexed him. Every time that he looked at his family, there was always a missing piece: our sons. They had given up everything to be by his side, always believing in duty and their father's words. His comrade was wrong, he had the power to change everything if he had wanted to at the time. Yan Naing replied, "You know, with whatever happened in the past, I never once hated you as a person. I just did not agree with your politics, and I still don't." Yan Naing left with those parting words, the last time that they would see each other alone again.

Soon afterwards, an official motorcade arrived at our house, ten officers in white uniforms lined across our lawn. They gave a full honorary salute reserved for the most honored occasions, for the greatest military heroes. The head officer held a scroll in his hand, announcing that Bo Yan Naing was to be awarded the highest honor in the country, the *Naing Ngan Gone-Kyi* title, celebrating heroes who fought for Burma's independence. Yan Naing was to be feted with a new pension as well as a new title – a directorship of a state-owned timber company under the Ministry of Construction.

My husband refused to step foot inside his new office in central Rangoon, a stone's throw from the Secretariat, his staff curious as to the whereabouts of their mysterious new boss. "Why don't you just go for a day?" I suggested to him, concerned with him staying in the house with nothing to do, wallowing in memories. Our family would receive his pension checks regardless, but my husband's state of mind was a bigger priority. I was well aware of the dangers of his restless spirit, a soldier's anxiety.

"I don't need anyone's pity," Yan Naing spat with venom. Amnesty to him meant that he would return to Burma and cease armed operations, not that he would be a willing participant in political games. He refused to touch his pension money, blood money in his eyes, so week after week I went to collect it at the government office, making sure that he did not see the stack of kyats accumulating in my drawer. One can judge me for taking the money but my family no longer went hungry. There was no more rationing of rice, meat and much-needed fresh vegetables. My grandchildren were multiplying and in my heart, a mother and grandmother's heart, there was no greater joy than to see them happily gulp a full bottle of formula, their round faces content and nourished. This was something that I could not give my own children in their childhood and I vowed that this would not repeat in the next generation, even if it was paid in blood money.

Out of the blue, Yan Naing announced that he would be going to his office. He offered no explanation as to why he changed his mind all of a sudden, appearing at breakfast in a traditional jacket one morning, eating a bowl of fish noodle soup, then driving the car downtown. He went to work every day after that. Part of his new position required going deep into the forests and jungles to oversee timber operations. Concerned that he was falling back to his old ways, I confronted him in our bedroom after one of his trips. "You're not doing anything stupid, are you?" I pointed a finger at him.

"Tinsa, when a soldier lays his arms down for good, he means it." The only assurance that I needed. He became calmer knowing that he could slip in and out of city life periodically and disappear into the thick forests of his birth, his glory years, and where he finally laid his armed resistance to rest. The jungle would never leave Yan Naing.

There was peace at University Avenue when I came to terms with that fact. We fit the role of happy grandparents quite well, Yan Naing doting on our grandchildren running amok in our verdant garden. I cleared a small space for him in the corner of the garden where he cultivated rare orchids acquired on his trips. The makeshift greenhouse bloomed in thousands of shades of orange, pink, red, yellow, purple. One day, I found him cradling his most prized orchid in his hands, the flower surviving one week in the Rangoon climate.

"This breed can only be found in the deepest parts of the Thai-Burma border. It's so rare because it needs to breathe its native air, to be in its own soil. I was foolish to think that it would survive here, but I couldn't help myself."

He paused. "Some things just shouldn't be taken from where they belong."

Bo Yan Naing and Tinsa after his return from exile

CHAPTER TWENTY-THREE

The house on University Avenue finally became a home. Yan Naing was the self-appointed social coordinator of his friends, inviting the remaining Comrades to a monthly picnic where they would discuss the old days over bottles of whiskey and brandy smuggled from across the murky Ayeyarwaddy. My children gathered around the old boys in a semi-circle, listening to stories about jungle warfare, women they loved and lost, anything and everything they remembered from standing at the front lines of history.

Yan Naing's insurgency stories brought the audience to their feet. The children's eyes went wide hearing about the massive jungle cats he encountered, paws as big as his head. He told tales of spirits and ghosts that inhabited the borderlands, such as one spirit that appeared in the form of someone you knew from your past, following you until you went mad in the desolation of the forest. There was another spirit that came in the form of the biggest snake any of them had ever seen, thick as a tree trunk and the length of ten men. The snake was believed to be a guardian spirit, trailing the troops wherever they went, creating a protective barrier between them and the edges of civilization. The stories were meant to be lighthearted, a respite from the country's bleak situation. Yan Naing never spoke of the darker elements of his insurgency, the mutinies, starvation, fatigue, death and failure. How he was so sure of his backers' support before he left and how he had crossed the border to find nothing on the other side. How his war, a bloodshed for democracy, disintegrated against an ever-powerful adversary. Yan Naing and his troops waited for any glimmer of justice, any hope for their cause at all. None came.

With grandchildren
Back row: Mu Mu, Kalya, Yan Naing, Tinsa, Thondra, Mayda
Front row: Einsi, Mi San, Yan Paing, Yin Mon

My husband spoke little about Yan Myo and Yan Lin, their loss the greatest of all. He could not talk about them, his voice crumbling to ashes as soon as he tried to utter their names. How our once-hopeful sons, enduring a treacherous journey through Southeast Asia's most unforgiving terrain to be with their father, found not a mythical battlefield but a decrepit rebel camp reeking with desperation and cynicism. Yan Myo, the more introverted of the two, grew despondent as their losses widened, government forces obliterating what little supplies and friends he had. Many of the soldiers turned to cheap heroin and liquor to combat their demons, trapped in limbo between a losing battle and a home that they could not return to. Malaria was his official cause of death, and what we keep telling ourselves to this day. As for Yan Lin, we discovered that an assassin masquerading as a trusted comrade shot him in the back as he walked away from an argument, the most cowardly deed of all. Their tales are lost now, to be remembered as characters in stories, blurred faces in photographs.

"I know that my efforts were a failure, Tinsa. We lost a war, we lost so many young men. Sometimes I wonder how I can sit here as an old man, with my family and friends around me, with a full belly, when so many others didn't make it," my husband reflected after the last and final Comrade meeting. Yan Naing, the fearless one, was confronted by his own mortality at last, surrounded by the ghosts of martyrs. Aung San assassinated. Bo Let Ya, who was like a brother to us and joined him on the border, was killed by the KNU on November 29, 1978 after returning to Burma. Bo Setkya died in the rebel camp waiting for U Nu to arrive. Thakin Than Tun, Bo Yan Aung and Bo Zeya, killed in action in 1967 and 1968. The people who understood him best had left him, an entire generation gone. Those were stories that he kept private, locked away in the most hidden part of himself.

I finally pitted the question that had been on my mind for fifteen years. "Do you regret what happened to us?"

He cried indignantly, "Of course I regret what happened to you and this family. It was the most selfish thing I had ever done. I cannot change what is in the past, I can only say that I did what I thought was best for this country and I didn't think that things would go that far. I saw hell during the independence war and I thought that I had seen it all, but how could I have predicted that innocent people, my own wife and children who had nothing to with this business, would be punished in such a way? How could I be sure that if I returned, that we would all be safe? That you and I and the kids wouldn't have been killed instantly? We were all half-mad with hunger and disease, yet the government's greatest advantage was to always keep us guessing. How could I know anything for sure, except to keep on fighting?"

Yan Naing furrowed his eyebrows, frozen with anger until he collected his thoughts. "There is no way to say *I'm sorry* in Burmese, either."

* * * * *

On November 9, 1981, General Ne Win resigned from the Presidency, handing the office to his close confidante and advisor, San Yu, and announcing that he would focus on the chairmanship of the Burma Socialist Program Party (BSPP). It was too late for changes. Burma's main exports of rice, timber, oil and minerals sharply decreased in the 1980s as neighboring countries recovered from civil wars and occupation, modernizing their economies while ours retreated. Crippled by foreign loans, lack of hard currency, another currency devaluation in 1985 and no policies to counteract Burma's decreasing competitiveness, the United Nations designated Burma as a Least Developed Country (LDC), another nail in our coffin. The government issued a final devastating currency devaluation on September 5, 1987, awakening a brewing storm.

Anyone who lived through the 1980s in Burma knew that something big, explosive, was ripening. Food, clean water, medicine and foreign currency were virtually inaccessible to anyone except for the elite. Lack of foreign exchange forced even the strongest national enterprises to cease operations. Black markets appeared on every corner and I had to fight my way through long lines every morning just to get my hands on some bread and baby formula.

People who could no longer afford basic food and shelter poured into the streets, a new class of urban poor, factory workers and hardworking people now homeless and destitute. Thousands resorted to begging, prostitution, theft and petty crimes to stay alive. Then, one by one, they began dying. They dropped dead in the middle of the streets. Rangoon was initially shocked by what was happening but was becoming immune to seeing the bodies in the gutters, desensitized by our own hunger.

Watching our country crash and burn yet again was too much for Yan Naing's failing health. Nearly seventy years old, his health had caught up with him. He was coughing up blood, became fatigued by the slightest tasks, his organs slowing by the day. That did not prevent him from taking his trips to the jungles, spending most of his time listening to villagers and observing the rapid decline of their livelihoods. He would come back a little wearier each time, the enormity of the country's problems too demanding for his weakened physical state.

In January 1988, we accepted an invitation to visit Japan on behalf of the Japan-Burma Economic Development Study Association. It had been nearly half a century since my husband visited Japan when he accompanied my father on a state mission. It was my first visit and I was thrilled to see old friends again, including the Nemotos who had been our neighbors and close friends when we first moved to University Avenue. The bright lights of Tokyo, Yokohama, Kamakura, Kyoto and Nara flashed before us as we made a hectic two-week jaunt through the country. I was astounded by the tall skyscrapers and bustling development in the country, a world away from Burma. They had built all of this in just four decades after Japan was completely leveled during the war. Our main stops were training facilities, companies and factories. Yan Naing was impressed by the workers' conditions combined with the Japanese's unparalleled production capabilities.

We had a private meeting with Deputy Prime Minister Miyazawa in Tokyo, who listened earnestly to my husband's briefing on Burma's economic crisis. Miyazawa was concerned by the troubles in our country, Japan's longstanding trading partner and regional neighbor. His eyes were fixed on Yan Naing as he described the mass starvation and suffering, unable to comprehend how quickly the situation had deteriorated in the span of a few short months. "It will continue to get worse, Deputy Prime Minister," my husband said bluntly.

Miyazawa sighed, acknowledging the hopelessness of our country's situation. He said the only thing he could have said as a gentleman. "If your government wants to seriously save the economy, we will do our best to lend our immediate support."

The floodgates opened in March 1988, the moment we feared. On March 12, a fight broke out between students at a local teashop, growing into a mass demonstration. The police shot and killed a student in a disproportionate use of force, prompting students at Rangoon University to protest the military. Thousands of students and soldiers met at *Da-Da-Phyu* (the White Bridge) on March 18. The concrete ground shook beneath the weight of thousands of energized young people who felt that they were changing the world at that very moment. Without warning or provocation, the soldiers opened fire, blood spattering on concrete, the streets painted pink.

Their final cries, pleas for help, last words of nationalism rang through the skies, reaching us at our home a few miles away. We barricaded ourselves, forbidding the children, grandchildren and household help to step outside. I tried to call my daughter, Nanda, who worked at UNICEF and lived across the street from the university, to check on her, her husband and two small children. The phones were out of service, thousands doing exactly what I was doing and jamming the lines.

Each gunshot ate away at Yan Naing, who no longer had the strength to fight even his own battles. "I was them once, you know," he said quietly. "It was a different time. At least it was easy to fight the British; they were foreign to us. But this," he paused to reflect, "this is our own people slaughtering each other." He shook his head, disbelief at the magnitude of the massacre.

This was not the end, but only the beginning. Millions of ordinary citizens, empathizing with the students and moved by the *Da-Da-Phyu Massacre*, mobilized and staged large-scale demonstrations in every city and village. The demonstrations became larger and louder until the regime could no longer control the situation. General Ne Win called an emergency meeting of the BSPP in late July, announcing his resignation as Chairman and offering San Yu's resignation on July 23. On July 27, the BSPP announced that Sein Lwin, nicknamed the *Butcher of Rangoon*, would be the new Party Chairman and President of Burma. General Ne Win's last official words to the country in a radio address were menacing. "When the army shoots, it shoots to kill."

Sein Lwin's brief tenure was devastating. Students launched a general strike on August 8, millions occupying Rangoon University and other high-profile landmarks all over the country. The Butcher ordered a nationwide curfew, mobilized the army and slaughtered protesters on University Avenue, Inya Road, Prome Road and all of the major arteries of the movement, gunning down thousands in Rangoon's despair. The crackdown was so violent, so brutal that it became known as the inspiration for Tiananmen Square. With the body count rising, the demonstrators persevered and outlasted Sein Lwin, who resigned after eighteen days in office.

U Maung Maung, an academic and historian, ascended to the Presidency and took several measures to curb the protests. He repealed the curfew, sent his people to negotiate with student leaders and attempted to curtail the army to no avail. People were no longer afraid, with nothing more to lose. *Democracy! Human rights! Free market! Elections!* People chanted in the streets, desperate for any change.

Student leaders and protest organizers knocked on the doors of their childhood heroes, seeking advice on staging a movement. Yan Naing and the Comrades formed the Patriotic Old Comrades League, a group of retired and neutral army leaders giving politics one last shot. Few knew that my husband was dying but he still made time to see the hopeful young faces whose tenacity invigorated him. His body racking with coughs and fatigue, he continued to see protesters at his deathbed. Yan Naing told them stories of his own struggle, his lesson the same time and time again. "Remember that protesting is the beginning and not the end goal. You need to mobilize, study other movements, train your forces and have good leaders. Look at your strategy carefully, analyze it and reorganize if need be. Don't be afraid to start over if it makes you stronger in the end."

The protesters went across the street to Daw Khin Kyi's home where she was also on her deathbed. Her daughter with Aung San, Aung San Suu Kyi, had returned from many years abroad to care for her mother in her final days. In between looking after Yan Naing and managing hordes of activists in our living room, I had not yet had the chance to pay my respects to their family. I had not seen Suu Kyi since she was a young teenager at Methodist High School, classmates and friends with Yema. What I remembered to be a skinny, bookish girl was now a striking woman with a family of her own.

On December 28, 1988, Daw Khin Kyi passed away. Yan Naing and I crossed University Avenue to her lakeside home, elbowing our way through the crowd gathering at the gate. After politely telling one of the house girls that Bo Yan Naing and Daw Tinsa Maw-Naing wanted to pay their respects to Daw Khin Kyi, we sat in the living room with Yan Naing having a coughing fit, waiting for nearly two hours. Tired, we got up to leave and I glanced at an ornate flower arrangement standing alone by an umbrella stand, red and yellow rose petals circling the hardwood floor beneath the whirring fan. It had been a long time since I had seen roses, their sickly sweet fragrance and fragile petals reminding me of my childhood when every house had a wild garden and lush rose vines used to crawl over all of the brick buildings in Rangoon. "Condolences from the government," a bystander informed me with one eyebrow raised at the flowers.

Before and after her mother's death, Suu Kyi welcomed the various students and protesters who came to her for advice. Stirred by their cries to help the country as the daughter of an independence hero, she became entrenched in internal politics. Two defected senior members of the military, former Minister of Defense U Tin Oo and former Brigadier General Aung Gyi, had broken away from the army to form a new political party, the National League for Democracy, with her at the helm. On August 26, Suu Kyi made her first formal speech at the Shwedagon Pagoda, thousands waiting to hear what Aung San's daughter had to say. Those expecting a breathy heiress were proven wrong. Her words were electrifying that day, her persona one with the people. Yan Naing and I listened to her speech on the radio, reaching masses of people. "Do you think she has the same spirit as her father?" spectators would ask Yan Naing and me. Questions like this would continue to dog her throughout her campaign and until today, people curious to see if she lived up to her famous name. The smear campaign was her first test. *Foreigner. Anglophile. Half-blood children. Elitist. Faker. Where was she for the past three decades? How can she possibly understand the rules of her forgotten homeland? Does she really live up to her name, or is it an act?*

I remembered the same insults hurled at my father, husband and family, far too easy to plunge someone's name in mud for the sake of politics. "She's learning the ways of Burmese politics," Yan Naing remarked. "I think she can take care of herself, as we all had to learn our way through these murky waters. Remember, her father and I were only in our twenties when we were going through this!"

* * * * *

Yan Naing was in excruciating pain. His breath was shortening and he was unable to walk in his final weeks. On January 6, I turned to look at my husband in the middle of the night. His pillow was doused in blood, leaking through the thin foam mattress and seeping into the cracks of the teak floor. I alerted Yema and Khin Myint, panicking when we realized that we could not leave our home during the curfew, even for emergencies. Blood poured from his lips, a wonder that he had any left in his body. Every second that passed was one less moment that we had with him.

The sun rose and we rushed him to Rangoon General

Hospital, a dilapidated colonial-era building that served the general public on four hours of power per day. The waiting area smelled of iron and urine, overflowing with the terminally ill, elderly and common drunkards. Yema called a doctor friend who took one look at Yan Naing and immediately referred him to Rangoon National Hospital, which had modern facilities thanks to development aid from Japan. At Rangoon National Hospital, doctors and nurses floated in and out of his room, unsure of how to treat someone during the last stages of stomach cancer. Strapped to two IVs and a heart monitor, Yan Naing's conditioned stabilized but he had fallen into a deep sleep, unaware of his surroundings. Delirium possessed him and he was unable to stir awake when the Japanese Ambassador Hiroshi Otaka came to his bedside.

"Thank you for coming, Ambassador," I said to him. He looked forlornly at Yan Naing's state, acknowledging that this would be the last time they would meet.

"Mrs. Maw-Naing, it is my pleasure and duty to be here. When I heard what happened, I wanted to pay my well wishes in person. It did not seem right to send a note or an emissary."

I offered a cup of coffee to the ambassador, sitting down for a brief chat. "Will your family be safe here?" he inquired politely, aware of our family's history and perhaps the fact that Yan Naing had been speaking with prominent protesters before his downturn, cause for further detention.

"I hope so. I believe so."

He gave a small smile. "As always, Mrs. Maw-Naing, if you need anything, please do not hesitate to contact me or the embassy."

Yan Naing emerged from his comatose state after an unsuccessful surgery, searching the room for my face and our children's faces. His lips were as blue as the sky, fingers and toes ashen white. The heart monitor shot up, lines dancing on the screen. "I'm sleepy," he uttered, his last words. At 9:00 AM on January 28, 1989, my husband, Bo Yan Naing, passed away.

CHAPTER TWENTY-FOUR

True to form, my husband left this world in an epic fashion. Government regulations forbade bodies to be taken from the hospital without being cremated first, but we thought it wrong not to have him lie in state at University Avenue so that his many family and friends could see him one last time. My children were thinking the same thing that I was: we needed to find a way to move him from the hospital without alerting the plainclothes officers lurking about the premises. We dressed Yan Naing in a fresh pair of clothes, placing him upright on a wheelchair appropriated from a locked supply closet. The whole family pretended that Yan Naing was well enough to go home, asleep as we wheeled him out of the front doors and into a waiting car. The hospital officials saw us but turned their heads away, shutting their eyes and ears in solidarity.

Just a couple of hours after placing the obituary notice, a messenger came to our house and dropped a warning from the authorities.

This is a reminder that the law forbids boisterous funerals, including large gatherings of people for extended periods of time. Any act challenging the law will be punished severely.

Thousands arrived at University Avenue to pay their respects. The young and old, poor and rich, from different religions and ethnicities spilled onto our property, the queue snaking from the front door to half a mile down the street. With his death and the revolution happening before us, people no longer feared the ramifications of defiance, immune to everyday terror and the banality of threats. In the custom of Burmese funerals, I placed some of Yan Naing's most treasured belongings in his casket to be taken with his spirit to the next life. His favorite shirt. Well-worn books. Cologne. A bottle of whiskey on behalf of the Comrades. I touched his cheek, cold as marble, one last time before we took him to the crematorium.

Student leaders and activists followed our car as we drove to the outskirts of the city where the crematorium was located. My family and I were accompanied by the families of the Thirty Comrades, several ambassadors, politicians old and new, and of course military intelligence. I had asked the activists and protesters to keep a low profile for their own safety and out of respect for Yan Naing's memory, to which they agreed but not without throwing side glances at our intelligence escorts, who were always watching from behind their blackened sedan windows. The brief impasse broke when a student protester broke rank and started shouting *Democracy! Let it be known that Bo Yan Naing stood and fought for democracy!* The military vehicle sounded its horn and chased the protesters from the procession, while all of the ambassadors jumped into their cars and drove off. Even in his final moments, Yan Naing had to attract some sort of political scuffle. It wouldn't have been his funeral without it.

In a final gesture of respect for their fallen brother, the Comrades and I knew of a monk from the legendary Mahagandayon Monastery in Mandalay who happened to be in Rangoon. We asked him to officiate the service and requested a special rite for Yan Naing. The monk was one of few still practicing an ancient funeral tradition, a privilege that cannot be bought or bullied into, reserved for the most pure and principled souls in the eyes of Buddhism. The octogenarian monk returned to Mandalay several days later with Yan Naing's urn in his creased palms. He mixed the ashes with red earth clay from Amarapura, molding them into a leaf-shaped tablet. Yan Naing's name, birthdate, date of death and a spiritual inscription guiding his soul to the next lifetime were inscribed with a centuries-old quill made from the bark of a Bodhi tree dating back to the time of Siddhartha. Yan Naing remains in that monastery to this day, impermeable to the tragedies of the outside world, finding peace at last.

*****

I'm afraid that this narrative stops here, not because my life ended when Yan Naing's did but because the next chapters ought to be written by a new generation. I need not delve into the events after the 8888 Revolution, the world seeing it with its own eyes. Another daughter of independence, Aung San Suu Kyi, imprisoned but not silenced. Student leaders taken away, never to be seen again. Another generation lost to the same evils that have haunted us for generations. Greed. Corruption. Power. Fear. My story is, of course, a view from the upper decks. For thousands of Burmese, there would be no VIP detention, no house arrest or chances to see their families again. Their stories must be heard, too.

I did the best thing that I could do for my children and grandchildren after the crackdown. I told them to leave, to think of a better future for their own children because I could not do the same for them. Nanda, her husband Thura, and their two young children Yan Paing and Yin Mon left for New York City, leaving with not much more than the clothes on their backs, to see if they could live the American Dream. And they did, a million times over. Kinsa took off for Canada with her husband and daughter Dali. Kethi became a medical volunteer with the United Nations Volunteers, meeting her husband Peter in the Comoros Islands, where he was working for the United States Embassy. Amaya moved to Bangkok with the World Health Organization, traversing Asia with her children in tow. Minshin remained in the United States and joined the army. Zarni, the youngest, studied engineering in Japan before returning to Rangoon. Yema and Tinthi, my eldest and youngest daughters, stayed in Rangoon.

Tinsa Maw-Naing

As for me, I returned to Burma (now called Myanmar) in 2011 after seeing the world as my sister Mala promised I would. Shortly after my husband's death and the rise of a new regime, I left Rangoon for the United States. I saw the towering skyline of New York City, the Empire State Building as beautiful as the Shwedagon. Quito beckoned, countless hours spent sifting through gem shops, rifling through bags of raw emeralds and amethysts from the deepest mines of Ecuador. I ate ceviche in Lima, felt the winter winds of Toronto, glimpsed the savannas of Gabon, roamed the slums of Port-au-Prince and much more. Yet, my mind and heart were always in Burma, in the ranch house that still stands at the corner of University Avenue.

I have learned to let go of things past, to forgive my jailers and those who turned their heads away. I used to hold so much anger in the pit of my stomach, a poison that consumed too many of my good years. It is the same anger that trails the Burmese's collective spirit, the feeling of having far too many opportunities taken away from us. Our monarchy and right to self-rule, no matter how imperfect it was. Occupation governments taking what little was left of Burma, leaving us to fight for scraps. Aung San's martyrdom and what could have been. The loss of half a century. It was too easy to believe that life owed me something, that the world was indebted to me, when it owed me nothing. When I realized the impermanence of life, that we enter this world with nothing and leave with nothing, it was the moment that I was finally set free.

My memories are not meant to invoke old wounds or to garner sympathy. This book is simply intended to record the things that I witnessed, for my children and grandchildren, because all of these things will die with me if I don't. It is perhaps not the life I would have chosen, but I consider myself blessed. I am not a hero in any form, but merely a passenger through history who saw incredible things and lived to tell about it, when so many did not.

GLOSSARY

U Abdul Razak — Cabinet minister in pre-independence interim government, assassinated on July 19 1947 (Martyrs' Day).

Amaya Maw-Naing — Tinsa's daughter, born in 1952.

Anashin Adipadi — Dr. Ba Maw's title from 1943 to 1945, also the Pali term for *Chief* and the title of a university rector.

Archibald Cochrane — Governor-General of Burma from 1936 until 1941.

Aung San — Thakin Party member, War Minister under Dr. Ba Maw, co-founded the Anti-Fascist People's Freedom League (AFPFL), assassinated with his cabinet on July 19 1947 (Martyrs' Day).

Azad Hind Government — Indian nationalist government supported by Japan. Netaji Subhas Chandra Bose was its leader.

Ba Han — Brother of Dr. Ba Maw; legal scholar and lexicographer.

Ba Hein — Student leader; member of Thakin Party.

[Dr.] Ba Maw — Tinsa's father; Prime Minister of Burma 1937 to 1939, Head of State under the Japanese 1943 to 1945. Born February 8 1893 and died May 29 1977.

Bandoola U Sein — Cabinet Minister in the wartime government.

Binnya Maw — Tinsa's brother, born in 1937.

Bo La Yaung — A member of the Thirty Comrades.

Bo Let Ya — A member of the Thirty Comrades, Commander in Chief of the Burma Defence Army (BDA) under Gen. Aung San in 1944, Deputy Prime Minister under U Nu until 1952, joined Yan Naing and U Nu in their insurgency in 1969, killed by the Karen National Union (KNU) on November 29 1978.

Bo Mo — A member of the Thirty Comrades.

Bo Setkya	A member of the Thirty Comrades, went underground after 1962 coup, joined Yan Naing in his insurgency and died before U Nu's arrival.
Bo Yan Aung	A member of the Thirty Comrades, leader in the Communist Party, participated in the 1963 peace parley, killed during Communist Party purge on December 26 1967.
Bo Yan Naing	Tinsa's husband. A member of the Thirty Comrades, student leader, hero of the Battle of Shwedaung in 1942, formed insurgent group from 1965 until 1980, returned to Rangoon after the 1980 amnesty.
Bo Ye Htut	A member of the Thirty Comrades, student leader, Communist leader of the 1948 Army rebellion, arrested after 88 Revolution
Bo Zeya	A member of the Thirty Comrades, Communist Party leader, returned from China for the 1963 peace parley, killed in action on April 16 1968.
Bose, Netaji Subhas Chandra	Leader of the Indian National Army and Azad Hind Government..
Captain Kyaw Zwa Myint	Former personal assistant to General Ne Win, resigned and formed an underground resistance group after the 1962 coup.
Colonel Hiraoka	Japanese liaison officer assigned to protect Maw family during occupation.
Colonel Tin Oo	Director of Military Intelligence 1972 to 1978, later to become Brigadier General. [Not to be confused with Tin Oo, former Commander-in-Chief of the Tatmadaw (Armed Forces) and co-founder of the National League for Democracy].
Daw Khin	Tinsa's paternal great-great-grandmother from Maubin.
Daw Kinmama Maw	Tinsa's mother; wife of Dr. Ba Maw.
Daw Kinmimi Maw	Tinsa's aunt; sister of Daw Kinmama Maw.
Daw Kyi Kyi	Wife of Thakin Zin; Tinsa's barrack mate at

	Ye Kyi Aing.
Daw Sein	Tinsa's maternal grandmother and renowned jewelry broker.
Daw Thein Tin	Tinsa's paternal grandmother, from Maubin.
Edward Law-Yone	Founded *The Nation* in 1948, Burma's most influential English language newspaper. Chief Editor until 1962 coup. Joined Yan Naing's insurgency in late 1960s.
Lieutenant Colonel Figges	
	Sitting officer for the British Commonwealth Occupation Force in Tokyo.
Freedom Bloc	*Bama Htwet Yat Gaing*, an alliance of the Thakin Party, All Burma Students' Union and Sinyetha Party.
General Council of Burmese Associations (GCBA)	
	Founded by radical, nationalist members of the YMBA in 1920 after a split within the Young Men's Buddhist Association.
Henzada U Mya	Member of the House of Parliament.
Hubert Rance	The last Governor-General of Burma from 1946 to 1948.
Insein Prison	Political prison with notable detainees including Dr. Ba Maw and Daw Aung San Suu Kyi.
Isamura, Major General	
	Japanese military head of Burmese-Japanese Relations.
Kalya Maw-Naing	Tinsa's daughter, born in 1947, died in 1952.
Kethi Maw-Naing	Tinsa's daughter, born in 1955.
Kinwun Mingyi	Chief Minister (Prime Minister) during the reigns of King Mindon (Mindon Min) and King Thibaw (Thibaw Min).
Kinsa Maw-Naing	Tinsa's daughter, born in 1953.
Kyi May Thein	Wife of Captain Kyaw Zwa Myint; imprisoned at Ye Kyi Aing.
Mahn Ba Khaing	Ethnic Karen; Minister of Industry in the pre-independence government AFPFL.
Mala Maw	Tinsa's sister, born in 1929, died in 2012.

Mandalay Conference	The last meeting of the Sinyetha Party in June 1940 and the site of Dr. Ba Maw's makes Mandalay Speech.
(King) Mindon Min	The penultimate king of Burma from 1853 to 1878, one of the most popular and revered kings in Burmese history.
Minshin Maw-Naing	Tinsa's son, born in 1959.
Myochit Party	Political party founded by U Saw in 1938.
Nanda Maw-Naing	Tinsa's daughter, born in 1957.
(General; Bo) Ne Win	A member of the Thirty Comrades, Commander in Chief of the Armed Forces in 1949, Prime Minister under caretaker government from 1958 to 1960, staged a coup in 1962 and became leader of Burma, died on 5 December 2002.
Neta Maw	Tinsa's brother, born in 1947.
Nyo Mya	Literary figure, writer, intellectual.
Onma Maw	Tinsa's sister, born in 1934.
Pyaw-bwe U Mya	Agriculture and acting home member.
Reginald Dorman-Smith	Penultimate Governor-General of Burma from May 1941 to August 1946.
Sao Sarm Htun	Chief of Mongpawng in Shan State, Minister of Hill Regions in Myanmar's pre-independence government. Assassinated July 19 1947.
Sao Shwe Taik	First president of the Union of Burma and the last Saopha of Yawnghwe in Shan State. Presumably died November 1962 after military coup.
Sinyetha Party	*Poor Man's Party*; founded in 1936 by Dr. Ba Maw.
Thakin Party	Formally known as the *Dobama Asiayone* Party; formed amidst the anti-Indian riots of the early 1930s.
Thakin Chit Maung	Helped established the Red Socialists in 1950. Member of Parliament representing the National United Front.

Thakin Mya	Minister of Home Affairs in Myanmar's pre-independence government. Assassinated July 19 1947.
Thakin Soe	Founding member of the Communist Party, formed in 1939. Minister of Land and Agriculture in Ba Maw government. Went underground in 1946 and assassinated on September 24 1968.
Thakin Than Tun	Founding member of the Communist Party, formed in 1939.
Thakin Zin	Became leader of the Communist Party after Thakin Than Tun's death in 1968.
Theda Maw	Tinsa's sister, born in 1931.
Thein Maung, Dr.	Burmese Ambassador to Japan.
(King) Thibaw Min	The last king of Burma. His reign ended when British Forces in the Third Anglo-Burmese War defeated Burma on November 29 1885.
Thirty Comrades	Founding fathers of the modern Burmese military.
Tinthi Maw-Naing	Tinsa's daughter, born in 1964.
U Ba Cho	Minister of Information 1946 to 1947.
U Ba Swe	Second Premier of Burma from 1956 to 1957.
U Ba Win	Minister of Trade in pre-independence government, Aung San's brother, assassinated July 19 1947.
U Boon Swan	One of the leaders of the Wunthanu Party and barrister.
U Chit Hlaing	Head of GCBA faction with U Soe Thein.
U Hla Pe	News broadcaster, translator and commentator for the BBC Burmese from 1942 to 1946. Linguist and contributor to the Burmese–English Dictionary.
U Kyaw Nyein	Deputy Prime Minister under the AFPFL.
U Maung Maung	Paternal great-great-grandfather, from Maubin.
U Nu	Member of the Thakin Party; Foreign Minister under Ba Maw government, first Prime Minister of the Union of Burma from January 1948 to June 1956, again from

	February 1957 to October 1958 and April 1960 to March 1962.
U Ohn Maung	Deputy Minister of Transport in pre-independence government, assassinated July 19 1947.
U Pe Khin	Architect of the Panglong treaty, later to become ambassador to various countries;
U Saw	Founder of the Myochit Party, third and final Prime Minister under British rule, convicted of Aung San's assassination and hanged 1948.
U Thein Pe Myint	General Secretary of Communist Party of Burma, journalist.
Yan Lin Maw-Naing	Tinsa's son nicknamed Ho Chi, Yan Myo's twin, born in 1951, killed in combat January 1976.
Yan Myo Maw-Naing	Tinsa's son nicknamed Mosie, Yan Lin's twin, born in 1951, died on Thai-Burma border on January 24 1972.
Ye Kyi Aing Prison	Interrogation center and prison run by the military. Location of Tinsa's incarceration 1966 to 1968 and 1974 to 1976.
Yema Maw-Naing	Tinsa's daughter, born in 1945.
Zali Maw	Tinsa's brother, born in 1928.
Zarni Maw-Naing	Tinsa's son, born in 1966.

ABOUT THE AUTHORS

Tinsa Maw-Naing was born in Rangoon (Yangon) in 1927. The eldest daughter of Daw Kinmama Maw and Dr. Ba Maw, the former Prime Minister, she married Bo Yan Naing of the famed Thirty Comrades in 1944. She was a lecturer at the University of Medicine in Rangoon before she was imprisoned from 1966 to 1968 and again from 1974 to 1976. Tinsa passed away in 2014 before the publication of this book.

Y.M.V. Han is the granddaughter of Tinsa Maw-Naing and Bo Yan Naing, and great-granddaughter of Dr. Ba Maw.

www.ingramcontent.com/pod-product-compliance
Lightning Source LLC
LaVergne TN
LVHW041539070426
835507LV00011B/822